THE
TALMUD
FOR
TODAY

THE TALMUD FOR TODAY

Selections Translated and
Edited by

RABBI ALEXANDER FEINSILVER

ST. MARTIN'S PRESS•NEW YORK

Library of Congress Cataloging in Publication Data
Main entry under title:
The Talmud for today.
1. Aggada—Translations into English.
I. Feinsilver, Alexander, 1910- II. Title.
BM516.T29 1980   296.1'27605   79-27398
ISBN 0-312-78479-1
ISBN 0-312-78480-5 de luxe.

To Lillian

AGGADAH VERSUS HALACHAH

RABBI ABBAHU and Rabbi Hiyya bar Abba once came to the same town. R. Hiyya b. Abba was to lecture on Halachah (law), while R. Abbahu was to speak on Aggadah (lore). Many prospective listeners deserted R. Hiyya in order to hear the Aggadah of R. Abbahu, and R. Hiyya was greatly upset. On being told what had happened, R. Abbahu said, "Let me give you a parable suitable to this situation. Two men came into a town, one selling precious stones and jewels, the other selling trinkets. To whom did the people flock in great numbers? To the man who sold the trinkets!"

Sotah, 40a

RABBI AMMI and Rabbi Assi sat with Rabbi Isaac Nappaha. One asked R. Nappaha to speak on Halachah and the other wanted him to talk on Aggadah. When he started to discuss Halachah, he was interrupted by the one who wanted Aggadah, and when he began to speak on Aggadah, he was interrupted by the one who wanted Halachah. He then said, "I shall give you a parable for my quandary. My plight is like that of a man with two wives, one young and one old. The young one pulls out all his gray hairs to make him look younger, and the old one pulls out all his black hairs to make him look older. The result is that he becomes bald."

Baba Kamma, 60b

CONTENTS

INTRODUCTION

THE aphorism ascribed to Socrates, that "the unexamined life is not worth living," comes close to expressing the spirit of Jewish thought through the ages. The vast literature of the Jews—the Bible, Talmud, Midrash and more—supports the observation of the Greek philosopher. However, the Jewish emphasis goes beyond an examination of life. It more typically dwells on the discipline of life, insisting that it is the *undisciplined* life that is not worth living.

While the rabbis of the Talmud, whose words are quoted here, at times engaged in abstract discussion, they were not essentially philosophers. They did not ask, "What is truth?" or "What is justice?" The pursuit of truth and justice was commanded by Scripture, and they were less concerned with the meaning of those concepts than with their implementation in the day-to-day life of the individual.

These men, who lived in the first five centuries of the Christian era, the period of time involved in the evolution of the Talmud, were assiduous students of the Bible. Each verse and every word of Scripture served as the basis for wide-ranging discussions in the academies they frequented. These deliberations of the rabbis were later recorded and preserved in the Talmud, which is, in effect, a compendium of commentary on the Bible.

In their study of Scripture, the rabbis paid special attention to the Torah, or Five Books of Moses. They built upon the numerous commands and prohibitions of the Torah a religio-ethical code of Jewish observance and individual conduct known as the *Halachah.* This distinctively Jewish design for living was to maintain the cohesiveness and uniqueness of the Jews as "a people apart" for centuries to come.

As an elucidation and extension of the "written Law" of the Torah, the Halachah was designated as the "oral Law." But just as the word *Torah* is derived from the Hebrew root "to teach" and may be rendered "the Teaching" rather than "the Law," so is the term *Halachah*

1

derived from the root "to walk," signifying the "path" to be pursued, or the "way" to be followed.

While there were those who rejected rabbinic efforts to elaborate upon the "written Law," deeming such attempts akin to heresy, the creation of the Halachah by the rabbis of the Talmud was farsighted indeed. The "way" of the Halachah was to become a way of life—and a way *to* life—for the Jewish people following the destruction of the second Temple in the year 70 and their dispersion among the nations, supplanting both their lost autonomy and their central sanctuary.

Practices prescribed in the Torah for a people living on its own soil and worshipping at a national shrine, as well as other practices no longer feasible, were sometimes modified by the Talmudic Halachah through reinterpretation of the Torah text. Innovative procedures and religious observances were introduced to suit the realities of Jewish life in the diaspora. Far from discrediting the Torah, the Halachah served ultimately to strengthen its authority. It did not replace the written Law but rather complemented it, providing a portable program for Jewish living under a variety of life situations.

The Halachah was destined to achieve a sanctity second only to that of the Torah. While the Torah was considered the God-given Constitution for the Jews, in dispersion the Halachah represented its bylaws. The Halachah discussed in great detail the observance of the dietary laws, the Sabbath, festivals and Holy Days, private prayer and public worship. Like the Torah itself, the Halachah also dealt with such matters as marriage and divorce, crime and punishment, property and damages—concerns which today are largely the province of secular law.

The rabbis displayed considerable dialectic skill in their exposition of the Halachah. But just as they were not really philosophers, neither were they simply legalists intent only on codifying Jewish practice. The rabbis were primarily teachers, as is implied in their title (*rabbi:* "my teacher"). Yet they were not teachers in any limited or academic sense of the term. They were also moralists or preachers. Heirs of both the priestly and prophetic traditions, the rabbis were concerned with ethical behavior, so consistently stressed in Scripture. Moreover, they were sensitive to the perplexities men confront, the pains they endure and the passions which drive them—the whole range of human experience.

Thus in the process of developing the Halachah the rabbis of the Talmud almost inadvertently produced an extensive body of secondary material, known as the Aggadah. Embracing all of the non-ritualistic and non-legalistic text of the Talmud, the Aggadic material is interwoven with the more dominant and more authoritative Halachah, usually in comment upon or in illustration of a point being made, but sometimes simply as an aside. It is to the Talmudic Aggadah that we direct our attention here, as the exclusive focus of this anthology.

The term *Aggadah* is sometimes translated as "legend," but has a broader meaning. The word is derived from the Hebrew root meaning "narrative" or "something told" and may be rendered as "lore." The Aggadah deals with such disparate subjects as animals and dreams, education and family life, health and justice, as well as the requirements for righteous living. It has always held a strong attraction for students of the Talmud as a pleasant diversion from more serious scholastic studies.

The Aggadah is essentially pietistic and moralistic in character. Perhaps paradoxically, it is in the Talmudic Aggadah rather than in the Halachah that we find the earliest attempts to clarify such theological concepts as the Jewish view of God, the Messiah and immortality. However, the rabbis recognized no insuperable barriers between one level of discourse and another, and often resorted to analogies and allegories, parables and proverbs, even in dealing with matters of theology, and at times allowed their imaginations free play.

In the Aggadah, the rabbis of the Talmud come alive for us. Some display remarkable humility; others, a certain measure of pride. Some are more demanding, while others are more tolerant of human failings, and a few display a sparkling sense of humor. At times they show a remarkable insight into what we today would call neurotic behavior. More importantly, it is in the Talmudic Aggadah, more appealing in style and diction than the strictures of the Halachah, that they express their views on individual integrity and family harmony, the achievement of justice and the pursuit of peace—concerns which are closely related to our own.

The reader should not object to rabbinic references to God as "King of the Universe" in an age when kings are few and often exercise only limited power. He or she should not resent allusions to God as "Our Father in heaven," alienated by the fact that the father image is often fraught with Freudian significance and that the very heavens have been penetrated by rockets to the moon without discovering Him there. Nor should the reader find unacceptable the description of God as a "jealous" God. The rabbis speak in the vocabulary employed by Scripture itself. Theirs is not the exact language of science, nor is it the speculative speech of philosophers; it is the intuitive language of faith.

Indeed, the rabbis make little effort to prove God's existence. The rabbis posit a primal, single Force at work in nature. They are convinced that all of creation is governed by a universal plan, and that all of human history represents an unfoldment of that plan. For them, God is not an "absentee landlord." They believe not only that God exists but also that He cares; that He is not only omnipotent, omniscient and omnipresent, but also deeply involved in the human enterprise. He is our Father, He is our King, and He is the Judge of all humankind. And we are to love Him *with all your heart, with all your soul, and with all your might* (Deut. 6:5)

Starting with the love of God, the rabbis move on to the love of humanity, persuaded that whoever loves God must love his fellowmen and whoever hates his fellowmen hates God. Indeed, they declare that God would rather have us ignore Him, by abstaining from prayer and worship, than ignore our obligation to feed the hungry and clothe the naked. They stress the need for compassion for the widow and the orphan, and insist that one must not only be sensitive to the physical discomfort of others, but must also be considerate of their feelings, never embarrassing anyone or putting another to shame.

The rabbis do not regard man as a helpless pawn of fate, but rather as a "partner of God" in the unfinished work of creation. While they recognize that some of life's experiences are beyond man's control, they declare that in the realm of moral choice this is not the case; that man is endowed with freedom of will, can choose between good and evil and master his own impulses, and is therefore responsible for his conduct.

This note of personal responsibility is one of the major keynotes of the rabbinic view of life. Charity, for example, is not regarded simply as giving alms to the poor. It is considered an act of justice, an attempt to right the economic injustice suffered by the needy. The performance of a good deed is not seen merely as an act of kindness but, like charity, the response to a divine command. Even the poor are expected to contribute to charity, as their means permit, and it is incumbent on all, rich or poor, to practise loving-kindness by visiting the sick and comforting the bereaved.

The rabbis deal not only with responsible behavior towards friends and neighbors, but also such behavior in the marketplace and in the pursuit of a livelihood. They are concerned about honesty in doing business, and provide for the appointment of commissioners of weights and measures to assure fair trade (but not to fix prices, which the rabbis oppose). They warn against deceiving anyone, whether Jew or Gentile, by misrepresenting articles for sale, and establish the principle of "Let the seller beware" to supplant the caveat "Let the buyer beware" in all business transactions.

The proper relationship between an employer and his employee also receives their attention. The workman is expected to give his employer his best efforts in return for the wages he receives. If employed by the day, for example, he must not waste time in idle chatter while at work. Similar demands are made upon the employer. He is cautioned not to pay his workman less than the prevailing scale of wages, and he is admonished to pay him promptly upon completion of his daily task, not withholding payment even overnight.

The rabbis have a good deal to say about marriage and the family, indicating the importance of appropriate speech and conduct between husbands and wives, and of a warm and loving atmosphere in the home. They warn against punishing children too severely or showing favoritism among them because of the unhappy consequences of such behavior. The possibility of an unsuccessful marriage is acknowledged, and they concede that a divorce may sometimes be necessary, stipulating the conditions under which it may be justified.

The practice of polygamy was accepted in their day, but the rabbis themselves are not known to have had more than one wife. Equality of the sexes, not fully achieved even now, was probably inconceivable in the world of the rabbis, yet rabbinic efforts to achieve greater rights for women are to be noted, such as the right to share in a father's estate. It is also of interest that the rabbis approve of women working outside the home, within certain limitations.

A few of the rabbis may have been misogynists, taking a dim view of women, yet others express great tenderness and even a high regard for them. The wives of Rabbi Meir and Rabbi Akiba are praised for their wisdom and for their loyalty to their husbands. While sons were generally preferred to daughters, one of the rabbis actually declares that he would rather have daughters!

In reading these selections from the Talmudic Aggadah, there are several things that one must bear in mind. First, we must take into account the fact that this material emerged from a time much earlier than our own and that the conceptual frame of reference of the Talmudic era was in many ways different from ours. We today have access to information which was not then available, and are the beneficiaries of a great deal of scientific progress. Thus a statement made by a third-century rabbi may not always seem sound to a twentieth-century reader with a wider knowledge of geology or astronomy.

Moreover, we must remember that these words were spoken over a period of about five centuries, during which many significant changes took place. In that interval the Temple was destroyed, the Jews were dispersed, and Babylonia became the new creative center of Jewish life. Social and political conditions differed from one area of settlement to another and from one generation to the next, with a profound impact on the circumstances under which the Jews lived and on rabbinic thought.

It is not surprising that an observation by a first-century rabbi may not agree with a statement made by a fifth-century rabbi living in a rather different social milieu. One finds, for example, disagreement on so significant a matter as the concept of the Messiah, due at least in part to the different life situations of the rabbis quoted. Some eagerly await the Messiah's imminent advent while others go so far as to deny his coming. And Hillel II, living in the fourth century, declares that the Messiah has already appeared, a full millennium earlier, in the person of Hezekiah, King of Judah.

It should also be noted that the rabbis do not speak collectively in the Aggadah, as spokesmen for the Jewish community. The views expressed here are not decisions arrived at in the academy or the courtroom after due deliberation, nor are they majority opinions; they are instead impromptu comments, expressions of individual feelings and predilections, which may of course differ even among men living in the same generation and subject to the same influences.

It is interesting, in this connection, that the rabbis, exercising scrupulous integrity, are quite careful to identify any colleague whose words they are quoting. We frequently encounter such passages as "Rabbi Johanan said in the name of Rabbi Simeon ben Johai" and "Rabbi Cahana declared in the name of Rabbi Jose" preceding a rabbinic remark in an attempt on the part of the speaker to assure proper attribution of the cited opinion.

In addition, it must be pointed out that these men often speak in exaggerated terms. This may at times be puzzling to the reader, or make the rabbis appear to be naive. Yet Rabbi Ammi states that even

"The Torah, the Prophets, and the Sages speak in hyperbolic language" (Hullin, 90b), and if it is true that Scripture itself sometimes resorts to hyperbole, due allowance must be made for this rabbinic tendency.

Finally, the reader must be alerted to the fact that the rabbis of the Talmud speak with great economy of language, expressing themselves very concisely, so that some effort may occasionally be required to get the gist of what they are trying to say. But the study of the Talmud has always been a challenging pursuit, and it is hoped that any such effort will not diminish but enhance its enjoyment.

When we take a total view of the Talmudic Aggadah, we find a striking consistency and continuity of thought in the statements made by so many men over so long a period of time and under such widely divergent conditions. In the sphere of basic theology there is little disagreement. There is instead an unwavering belief in the unity of God, in His immanence and transcendence, and in His compassionate concern with the destiny of the individual and the fate of humanity.

This theological consensus also perceives the Jewish people as a people uniquely covenanted with God through its possession of the Torah. As a "chosen" people, the Jews are believed to bear special responsibilities, guided by the principle of *noblesse oblige.* So too the "promised land" of Israel is regarded by the rabbis as different from all others—a "land of promise," in which the good society is to be established as an inspiration and example to the nations of the world.

In addition, the rabbis display an unfaltering belief in personal immortality, a doctrine not explicitly set forth in the Torah but for which they seek Scriptural support. While rabbinic notions of the world hereafter vary considerably and are often couched in hyperbole, the concept of a future life is nonetheless consistently affirmed. And in keeping with the rabbinic conviction that God is a God of justice, the rabbis envision a coming Day of Judgment when the wicked will be punished and the righteous rewarded.

In the realm of morality and ethics, as in the area of theology, the pattern of unity in diversity is again discernible. There is in the Talmudic Aggadah a persistent emphasis on the cultivation of the mind through study, the need for benevolence and the demands of justice. There is also an unrelenting insistence on truthful speech and righteous conduct, on personal responsibility and the spirit of compassion. These characteristic themes represent the universal aspects of rabbinic Judaism, as distinct from the more parochial concerns of the Halachah.

* * *

The terms *Halachah* and *Aggadah,* defined above, designate the two types of literary material found in the Talmud: the legalistic (or ritualistic) and the narrative (or moralistic). These are closely interwoven in the Talmudic text and separable only with considerable effort. It should be added here that on a structural level, there are two separate strata of text in the Talmud, clearly identified as such: the Mishnah and the Gemara. These were produced in two successive periods of Jewish history, the Mishnah stemming from an earlier time than the Gemara. The rabbis of the Mishnaic period are known as *Tannaim* (singular: *Tanna*), a word meaning "teachers" and related to the term *Mishnah.*

The Mishnah—a word which means "study" or "repetition"—consists of sixty-three books or tractates, and is a record of rabbinic deliberations in the Palestinian academies during the first two centuries of the Christian era. It is a commentary on the Torah, exploring and interpreting the statutes and ordinances of that sacred text. The Mishnah is sometimes published by itself, usually in six volumes which correspond to the six divisions or "orders" of its contents. The compilation of the Mishnah is credited to Judah HaNasi (c. 135–200).

The Mishnah constitutes the structural core of the Talmud and appears at the center of the Talmudic page. It is followed by additional text, known as the *Gemara,* a word meaning "learning" or "completion." Teachers quoted in this additional text are called *Amoraim* (singular: *Amora*), "completers" of the Talmud. The Gemara is a commentary on the Mishnah (a commentary upon a commentary), usually greater in bulk than the Mishnaic material on which it is based. Further comments by Rashi, an eleventh-century French rabbi, and by others occupy the margins of the page.

The Gemara is in Aramaic rather than the Hebrew of the Mishnah, and was compiled by Ashi, a Babylonian scholar (c. 354–427). It is the matrix in which most of the Aggadic material of the Talmud is imbedded, and from which the selections here presented have been drawn, with only occasional citations, labeled as such, from the Mishnaic text.

There are two somewhat different versions of the Talmud: the so-called Jerusalem Talmud *(Talmud Jerushalmi),* which is a product of the Palestinian academies, and the Babylonian Talmud *(Talmud Bavli).* In the latter, the Gemara is far more comprehensive, reflecting the decline of the schools in Palestine after the completion of the Mishnah. Reference to the Talmud without qualification in this anthology is intended to signify the Babylonian Talmud.

A term frequently encountered in these excerpts from the Talmudic Aggadah is the word *baraitha* (plural: *baraithoth*). A *baraitha* is a remembered rabbinic statement or tradition that is not a part of the received text of the Mishnah. These further observations of the Tannaim are often introduced in the Gemara in order to shed more light on the subject being discussed.

Unfamiliar Hebrew and Aramaic words are here defined or clarified by resort to bracketed text following the term or through the use of footnotes. The letter *b.* is used throughout as an abbreviation of *ben* or *bar,* the Hebrew and Aramaic words for "son" or "son of." The abbreviation *R.* is employed for Rabbi, the title generally accorded to the teachers of the Talmud. The title Rab is accorded only to Abba Aricha, a great Babylonian Amora. The designation Mar (Master) is applied in the Talmud to several individuals, notably Mar Samuel. Where it is used without the name of the rabbi, signifying simply "a Master," and it is unclear who is referred to, the honorific itself or its English equivalent is used in this translation.

Other honorifics that appear in the text of the Talmud, such as Raba, Rabbah, Rabban and Rabbi (the last written fully and not followed by the man's name, meaning Rabbi *par excellence* and applied only to Judah HaNasi), are variant appellations for specific individuals held in high esteem. The use of such titles differed between the academies of Palestine and those of Babylonia, and depended to some extent on the period in which these men lived. Hillel (the Elder), one of the greatest among them, who lived in the first century before the Christian era, before the title Rabbi had come into common use, is generally referred to without any title.

The presentation of these samplings of the Aggadic material of the Talmud would have been an awesome task were it not for the fact that several centuries ago Rabbi Jacob ibn Habib had already extracted from the massive text of the Talmud all of its non-ritualistic and non-legalistic portions. His compilation of the Talmudic Aggadah, produced in Salonica in 1515 and known as the *En Jacob (The Well of Jacob),* served as the source of this anthology.

A Hebrew-English edition of the *En Jacob* by Samuel Glick, called *Legends of the Talmud,* 5 vols. (New York: Rosenberg Press, 1916–22), was helpful in clarifying some of the more obscure passages. Use was also made of the Soncino translation of the Talmud in English, 18 vols. (London: Soncino Press, 1936–52) for comparative renditions of the Talmudic text.

It is common practice in anthologies to offer quotations detached from their context, as bare bones stripped of all contiguous flesh. Here, however, the immediate context of the individual selections and the supportive Biblical references cited by the rabbis generally have been retained to provide the reader with a more authentic exposure to these passages and a greater appreciation of the rabbinic mind and method. The reader should be forewarned that the Biblical citations presented by the rabbis to bolster their stated opinions are at times not completely convincing. Yet these Biblical "proof-texts" do serve to link the teachings of the rabbis to the spirit, if not always the letter, of Scripture, which is the rabbinic intent.

This compilation represents perhaps one-fifth of the text of the *En Jacob,* which in turn may comprise a similar portion of the Talmud. The number of extracts for inclusion here was necessarily limited and the choice of quotations inevitably arbitrary, but guided by two considerations: the selections were to exemplify rabbinic thought and values and also be of some interest to the contemporary reader.

While some of these passages deal with more than a single theme, I have tried in each case to single out what appeared to be the dominant motif in placing them under appropriate chapter headings, using cross-references wherever these might be helpful. The reader will find an introduction at the start of each chapter for orientation to the passages which follow. Captions precede the quotations to provide a measure of continuity and progression in the sequence of these excerpts, and the individual items are numbered consecutively for easy reference.

The source of each passage, by tractate and page of the Talmud, is indicated at its close. The two sides of a Talmudic page, in keeping with customary practice, are designated as *a* and *b.* With this information, the more serious reader may examine these quotations in their broader context, for a fuller understanding of the passages cited, by referring to the Soncino translation or to the original Talmudic text.

In the transliteration of the names of the rabbis and of Hebrew and Aramaic terms, I have generally followed the usage employed by the *Universal Jewish Encyclopedia,* 10 vols. (New York: Universal Jewish Encyclopedia, 1939). While this differs from the system of transliteration used in the Soncino Talmud, it is likely to be more familiar to the reader. The translation of Biblical verses is in most cases taken from *The Holy Scriptures,* first published by the Jewish Publication Society of America in 1917 and frequently reprinted. The Society's newer translation of the Bible (1962 ff.) is more readable and usually more accurate, reflecting recent research. However, it is only occasionally used here because, in addition to being less familiar, it is incomplete at the time of writing. Most importantly, it often eliminates the ambiguous or problematic wording upon which many of the rabbinic observations are based.

The reader is now invited to drink from the *Well of Jacob.*

A. F.

1

GOD AND HIS WAY

JUDAISM has been characterized as "ethical monotheism," a definition which is probably as correct as it is concise. For just as revolutionary in the Jewish faith as monotheism was the attribution of morality to the Deity.

Some of the gods of antiquity were nature gods: gods of the river, the forest, the mountain. Others were man-made gods, carved out of stone or wood or baked out of clay. There were domestic deities enshrined in the home and tribal deities entrusted with the protection of the clan. But, at best, they were perceived as amoral, largely governed by impulse and unhampered by moral constraints.

The gods were simply expected to serve the needs of their worshippers, without ethical considerations, in a *quid pro quo* fashion, as their devotees served them. But this was not so in Judaism. Central to the Jewish faith was the belief in a single, invisible and universal God, sympathetic to man's highest aspirations—a God conceived in moral terms. And there was a striking corollary to that belief: the concept of *imitatio dei,* coupling a more exalted view of God with greater expectations of man, created in His image.

The theology of the rabbis, as will be seen, is not formal or systematic. It is extrapolated from the various books of the Scriptures, and like Scripture itself, does not manifest a rigid doctrinal creed. Theology is wedded to morality, and logic is overlaid with imagery. Divergency is inevitable, and paradox possible, but only within the framework of an unshakeable faith in one God, Creator and Sustainer of man and his world.

A. THE NATURE OF GOD

God is supreme above all of creation

1. Resh Lakish asked, "What does the verse (Exod. 15:1) *I will sing unto the Lord, for He is highly exalted* intend? This [use of the word 'highly'] is intended to teach us that God is exalted above all other exalted ones. For a Master has said that the king among the beasts is the lion, the king among the domestic animals is the ox, and the king of the birds is the eagle. Man is exalted over all of these, and the Holy One is exalted above man, as well as above the entire universe."

Hagigah, 13b

He is omnipresent

2. The Caesar [*kesar*] said to Rabban Gamaliel, "You state that wherever ten Israelites are assembled, the *Shechinah* [Divine Presence] is found.[1] How many *Shechinahs* are there then?" Rabban Gamaliel summoned the ruler's servant, struck him on the neck, and asked, "Why did you permit the sun to enter the house of your master?" Thereupon the ruler replied, "The sun shines over all the earth." Rabban Gamaliel then said, "If the sun, which is only one of the hundred million servants of the Lord, can shine over all the earth, how much more would this be true for the *Shechinah*[2] of the Lord Himself?" *Sanhedrin, 39a*

None can behold Him

3. The ruler said to R. Joshua b. Hananiah, "I wish to see your God." He replied, "You cannot see Him." "But I must see Him," said the ruler. R. Joshua then placed him facing the sun during the summer solstice and said to him, "Look up at the sun." "I cannot," he replied. Then R. Joshua said, "If you cannot look at the sun, which is but one of the many servants of God, how can you expect to look upon the *Shechinah*?" *Hullin, 59b*

---

[1] Some editions of the Talmud use *kofer,* meaning "infidel" or non-believer, in place of *kesar;* the Hebrew spelling is somewhat similar. The Caesar's question refers to the fact that a quorum of ten Jews is required for public worship.

[2] *Shechinah* is a non-Biblical term which emerged after the close of the Biblical canon, and expresses the immanence and omnipresence of God. It is derived from the Hebrew word *shachan,* meaning "to dwell," and is used as a periphrasis for God dwelling among the children of Israel. The rabbis of the Talmud regarded the *Shechinah* only in a figurative sense. The Cabalists and mystics extended this view, regarding the *Shechinah* as a real entity. See *Universal Jewish Encyclopedia,* (hereafter cited as *U.J.E.*) s.v. "Schechinah".

The rabbis proclaim the unity of God

4. R. Johanan said, "Wherever the Sadducees [*Zaddokim*][1] give a faulty interpretation of Scripture [i.e., where God is spoken of in the plural], its refutation is to be found. They claim that (Gen. 1:26) *And God said: Let us make man in our own image* signifies that there are many gods.[2] However, the text continues: (Gen. 1:27) *And God created man in His own image* [singular]. They point to (Gen. 11:7) *Come, let us go down,* but the text states: (Gen. 11:5) *And the Lord* [singular] *came down.* Similarly, Scripture states: (Deut. 4:7) *For what great nation is there, that hath gods*[3] *so nigh unto it, . . .* but continues: *as is the Lord our God whenever we call upon Him?* Why then are all these references to God in the plural? It is because God does nothing without consulting the heavenly host."[4] *Sanhedrin, 38b*

A dualistic view of God is untenable

5. The Caesar said to Rabban Gamaliel, "He who created the mountains did not create the winds, and He who created the winds did not create the mountains; for Scripture states: (Amos 4:13) *He that formed the mountains, and* [another who] *created the winds.*"[5] Rabban Gamaliel replied, "If that is so, then the words (Gen. 1:27) *And God created,* followed by (Gen. 2:7) *And the Lord God formed,* should mean that He who formed man did not create him!"

R. Gamaliel added, "There is in the human body an area of one span [handbreadth] in which two openings are to be found [containing an eye and an ear]. Would you say that He who created one of them did not create the other? Indeed, Scripture declares: (Ps. 94:9) *He that hath planted the ear, shall He not hear? Or He that formed the eye,*

---

[1] The Sadducees consisted of the priestly class and members of the "establishment" during the period of the second Temple. They opposed Pharisaic (rabbinic) interpretation of the Torah text and rejected the oral tradition. The term is sometimes used in the Talmud for Jewish Christians. This is probably intended here. There were no Sadducees after the destruction of the second Temple in 70 C.E. See *U.J.E.,* s.v. "Sadducees," "Pharisees."

[2] The verse begins *Vayomer Elohim,* "And God said." The verb is singular, but the term *Elohim,* translated as "God," is a plural form, requiring the usage "Let us." The Bible also employs the Tetragrammaton JHVH, which is read as *Adonoi* and translated as "the Lord." In Scripture the two names are sometimes combined as *Adonoi Elohim* and translated "the Lord God." See *U.J.E.,* s.v. "God, Names of." See also n. 11 to item 771.

[3] The 1962 J.P.S. Bible here renders *Elohim* as "a god," but this would undermine Johanan's final comment.

[4] Johanan himself here seeks to explain the plural form of *Elohim,* generally regarded as a plural of majesty or extension.

[5] Two different verbs are used, taken to signify two creators.

shall He not see? Are two different gods involved here?" "Yes," replied the ruler. Then R. Gamaliel responded, "When death comes, must both creators agree [to end the life of the individual]?"

A magian [Zoroastrian] once said to Rabban Gamaliel, "The upper half of your body belongs to Ormuzd, and the lower half to Ahriman."[1] "If that is so," replied Rabban Gamaliel, "why does Ahriman allow water that enters the mouth to pass through his domain [as urine] to the ground?" *Sanhedrin, 39a*

Judaism renounces idolatry

6. R. Johanan said, "Whoever repudiates the worship of idols is considered a Jew [*Jehudi*]; for Scripture states: (Dan. 3:12) *There are certain Jews* [literally, 'Judean men'] . . . *who do not serve thy gods.*"[2]

Megillah, 13a

Idols cannot bring healing

7. Zunim once said to R. Akiba, "I know that the idols are without power. However, I would like to ask how it is that so many afflicted ones are cured by the idols in their temples." R. Akiba replied, "I will answer you with a parable. There once lived a very pious man, who enjoyed the unlimited confidence of his townsmen. They would all, from time to time, deposit money with him, without the presence of witnesses. But there was one man who insisted that witnesses be present.

"It once happened, however, that this man left something of value with the pious man and did not ask for witnesses. Thereupon the wife of the pious man said to her husband, 'Now we can take advantage of his previous distrust of us.' But her husband replied, 'Because this man has his shortcomings, shall I risk my own good name and reputation?'

"So too with infirmities, disease and the pains which beset us. They are often limited to a certain amount of time. It is further ordained by what person or medication the disease is to be eliminated. When

---

[1] In the Zoroastrian religion of the Persians, there are two gods: Ormuzd, the god of light, and Ahriman, the god of darkness. Founded by Zoroaster long before the Christian era, this faith teaches that the principles of good and evil are engaged in a struggle for the mastery of the universe.

[2] The Aramaic *guvrin Jehudain* is a reference to Daniel and his companions, addressed to the ruler. The implication is that they are called Jews because they do not worship idols, and that anyone refusing to do so could similarly be called a Jew.

the time of healing comes, the afflicted individual may go to the temple, hoping for a cure. The illness [may want to stay with him and] may protest, saying, 'Because this man has taken recourse to an idol, I ought not to leave him.' But instead it decides, 'Since I am committed to part from him now, why should I break that commitment [and delay my departure] simply because this man is a fool?' Thus the ailment leaves the afflicted man, and he is led to believe that this was the work of the idol."[1] *Abodah Zarah, 55a*

Why God is not jealous of the idols

8. Agrippa, the [Roman] general, said to Rabban Gamaliel, "It is written in your Torah: (Deut. 4:24) *thy God is a consuming fire, a jealous God.*[2] In our daily life, we find it to be the rule that a potentate is only jealous of his equal; a sage is only jealous of another sage, a hero of another hero, a rich man of another rich man. Now then, if God is jealous of an idol, the idol must have some power!" Rabban Gamaliel answered, "When a man who has a wife takes another wife, the first will not be jealous if the new wife is superior to herself; only if she is superior to the new wife will she be jealous."[3]

Abodah Zarah, 55a

Why God does not destroy the idols

9. A philosopher[4] once asked Rabban Gamaliel, "It is written in your Torah: (Deut. 4:24) *For the Lord thy God is a consuming fire, a jealous God.* Why does He express His jealousy against the worshipper, and not against the idol itself?" Rabban Gamaliel replied, "I will answer your question with a parable. This may be compared to the case of a king who had a son. The son had a dog, which he named after his father, the king. Whenever he swore an oath, he did so by the life of his dog. Would his father, on hearing of this, be angry with the dog or with his son? Surely he would be angry with his son!"

Said the philosopher, "You compare the idol to a dog, but this is not proper. Does not the idol possess certain powers?" "What are the

---

[1] This would today be called the "placebo effect."

[2] The 1962 J.P.S. Bible translates this as "an impassioned God," but that would weaken the analogy presented here and in the next item.

[3] The practice of polygamy was officially repudiated by Rabbi Gershom ben Judah, who lived in France and Germany from 960–1040, in his *Takkanoth de Rabbi Gershom.* He also decreed that a wife must give her consent to a divorce. See chapter 6.

[4] Hebrew: *philosoph.* A number of Greek and Latin terms are found in the Talmud.

powers it possesses?" asked Rabban Gamaliel. The philosopher replied, "Once there was a great fire which consumed our whole city, yet the temple of the idol remained intact." Then Rabban Gamaliel answered, "I shall use another parable. There was once a human king whose province revolted against him. Do you suppose he used his troops and weapons against the living or the dead? Surely he would have used them only against the living!" [Thus God destroyed the idolators without destroying the idol.]

Abodah Zarah, 54b

10. The philosophers once asked our elders in Rome, "If your God is displeased with idol worship, why does He not destroy the idols?" And they answered, "If the heathens worshipped only useless things, He would certainly destroy those things. But men worship the sun, moon, stars and planets. Shall He then destroy the whole universe because of these fools? Instead, the world is allowed to pursue its natural course. When someone steals wheat and sows it, should the seed be fruitless because it has been stolen? Similarly, an act of adultery is not without progeny simply because conception in that instance is due to an adulterous act. However, the culprit is not spared."[1]

Abodah Zarah, 54b

Magic is as powerless as the idols

11. (Deut. 4:35) *There is none besides Him.* R. Hanina [in comment on this verse] said, "Sorcery too is ineffective."[2] There once was a woman who tried to take some sod from under the feet of R. Hanina [for healing purposes, on the supposition that the ground on which he stood would have healing power]. He said to her, "Take it, but it will not help you a bit; for Scripture states: (ibid.) *There is none besides Him.*" *Hullin, 7b*

God's wisdom is greater than man's

12. The Caesar once said to Rabban Gamaliel, "Your God is a thief; for Scripture states: (Gen. 2:21) *And the Lord caused a deep sleep to fall upon the man and he slept; and He took one of his ribs.*" "Let me answer him," said Rabban Gamaliel's daughter. And she said to the

---

[1] A reference to the concept of reward and punishment. See chapter 13d.

[2] Lev. 20:6 forbade the use of sorcery or magic on pain of death. Saul attempted to drive the soothsayers and diviners out of the land of Israel (1 Sam. 28:3), but many remained. The same king at last went to consult one himself (1 Sam. 28:7,8, etc.).

ruler, "We were visited by thieves last night, and they stole from us a silver pitcher. However, they left for us a golden one instead." The Caesar said to her, "I would like to have such thieves visit me every night." And she replied, "Was it not better for Adam that one bone was taken from him and in its stead a woman was given to him as a helpmate?"

The Caesar said, "But why could He not have taken it from Adam while he was awake?" She then asked him to order a piece of raw meat and it was brought to her. She placed it under the ashes in a grate, and when it was roasted she took it out and offered it to him. "It is repulsive to me," he declared. Thereupon she responded, "Eve would have been repulsive to Adam if he had seen how she was made!"

The same ruler said to Rabban Gamaliel, "I am aware of where your God dwells and what He does." Rabban Gamaliel sighed deeply. When the ruler asked, "Why are you sighing?" he answered, "I have a son in one of the seaside cities, and I am anxious concerning him. Can you tell me of his whereabouts?" The Caesar said, "How should I know this?" Then Rabban Gamaliel responded, "If you do not even know about such things here on earth, how can you claim to know what is going on in heaven?"

On another occasion, the ruler said to Rabban Gamaliel, "Your Scriptures state that yours is a God (Ps. 147:4) *Who counted the number of stars,* etc. How remarkable is that? I too can do it." Rabban Gamaliel thereupon took a handful of grain, put it into a sieve, and asked him to count the individual grains while straining it. But the ruler objected saying, "Let the sieve stand still, and I will count them." To this Rabban Gamaliel replied, "But the stars are constantly moving!"

According to others, the ruler asked Rabban Gamaliel to count the stars, and Rabban Gamaliel replied, "Can you tell me how many teeth are in your mouth?" The ruler put his hand into his mouth and began to count them. Rabban Gamaliel then said to him, "If you do not know how many teeth are in your mouth, how can you pretend to know what goes on in heaven?"[1] *Sanhedrin, 39a*

---

[1] Confucius, when asked how many stars were in the sky, answered that he was more interested in things closer to him. When he was asked how many hairs were in his eyebrows, he replied that he neither knew nor cared. (R. W. Emerson, "Stonehenge," *Emerson's Works* [New York: Three Sirens Press, n.d.], vol. 2, p. 194.)

God is the greatest of all creative artists

13. (1 Sam. 2:2) *There is none besides Thee; Neither is there any rock like our God.* Do not read this as "any rock" [*en tzur*], but read it instead as "any sculptor" [*en tzayer*]. For a human being can produce a statue of stone, but can put into it neither entrails nor bowels, nor can he endow it with a soul; yet the Holy One creates not only the human body but also its internal organs, and puts into it also breath and spirit.

Megillah, 14a

Unlike man, God is imperishable

14. R. Judah b. Menassia said, "Do not read this [ibid.] as 'There is none besides Thee' [*en biltecha*], but read it rather as 'None can outlast Thee' [*en lebalatecha*]; for the handiwork of a man may survive him, but the Holy One outlasts His work."[1] *Megillah, 14a*

B. BETWEEN GOD AND MAN

God determines the destiny of man

15. R. Hanina said, "No one on earth bruises a finger unless it is decreed from above."[2] *Hullin, 7b*

16. God knows what is to happen in the future. *Sanhedrin, 90b*

17. R. Judah said in the name of Samuel, "Every day a *bath kol* [heavenly voice][3] declares, 'The daughter of so-and-so will marry the son of such-and-such.'" He also quoted Rab [Abba Aricha] as saying, "Forty days before a child is even born, a heavenly voice announces, 'The daughter of so-and-so will marry the son of such-and-such.'" [See also item 347.] *Moed Katan, 18b*

All that God does is done for good

18. R. Huna said in the name of Rab, who quoted R. Meir, "A man should always say, 'All that God does is done for good.' It once happened that R. Akiba was travelling through the countryside, and

---

[1] Judah retains the image of the rock (item 13). Rocks are long-lasting, yet God outlasts not only man but even the very rocks which He has created.

[2] Confronted by the problem of God's foreknowledge and man's freedom of will, the rabbis refused to deny either divine control of human affairs or man's freedom of choice. They believed that all events, good or evil, are ordained by God, and that all is done for a good purpose. However, they also held that in the realm of morality there is no determinism, thus affirming their faith in both God and man.

[3] Literally, "daughter of a voice," a voice descending from heaven to provide guidance in human affairs.

had with him an ass, a rooster and a lamp. At nightfall, he reached a village, where he sought lodging for the night, and it was refused. 'All that God does is done for good,' said he, and he proceeded toward the woods, where he planned to spend the night.

"Along came a lion and ate up his ass. Then came a cat, which devoured his rooster. Next, the wind extinguished his lamp. 'All that the Lord does is done for good,' said R. Akiba. Later that night a ravaging army ransacked the nearby village, taking its people into captivity. Then R. Akiba declared, 'Is not what I said true? All that the Lord does is indeed done for good.' " [The enemy also passed through the forest that night, and if the ass had brayed, if the rooster had crowed, or if the soldiers had seen his light, he would have been taken captive or put to death. See also the story of R. Nahum of Gamzu, item 834.] *Berachoth, 60b*

God is our protector

19. R. Hanina said, "How greatly God differs from mortal men! The custom among men is that while the king sits within [the palace] his servants guard him from without. But the way of God is not so. His servants sit within [their homes] and He watches over them from without. Indeed, Scripture states: (Ps. 121:5) *The Lord is thy keeper; the Lord is thy shade upon thy right hand* [i.e., near at hand, wherever one may be]." *Menahoth, 33b*

He is especially attentive to the righteous

20. R. Eleazar raised the following [seeming] contradiction: "Scripture states: (Ps. 145:9) *The Lord is good to all;* and it also declares: (Lam. 3:25) *The Lord is good* [only] *to those who hope in Him.* [How can these statements be reconciled?] This situation may be compared to one in which a person owns an orchard. When he waters it, he waters all of the trees, but when he covers the roots, he does so only to the best of them." [Similarly, the righteous receive God's special attention.] *Sanhedrin, 39b*

He attends to the needs of the lowly

21. R. Johanan said, "Wherever you find in the Scriptures a reference to the greatness of the Holy One, you will also find a description of His humility. This may be seen in the Torah, also in the Prophets, and in the Writings as well. In the Torah we read: (Deut. 10:17) *For the Lord your God is the God of gods and the Lord of lords;* and immediately

thereafter we read *Who executeth justice for the fatherless and the widow.*

"In the Prophets we read: (Isa. 57:15) *I dwell in the high and holy place*; then come the words *Yet also with the contrite and humble in spirit.* In the Writings we find: (Ps. 68:5) *Extol Him Who rideth upon the heavens, the Everlasting is His name;* there next follows *A father of the fatherless and the judge of widows."* *Megillah, 31a*

22. R. Avira (according to others, R. Eleazar) declared, "The Holy One differs from frail man. The custom among men is that a great man will take notice of another great man, but not of a lowly one. The custom of the Holy One is not so, for He is exalted yet takes notice of the humble; as Scripture states: (Ps. 138:6) *For though the Lord be exalted, yet regardeth He the lowly."* *Sotah, 5a*

God grieves for the wicked

23. R. Johanan said, "God does not rejoice in the downfall of the wicked." And R. Samuel b. Nahman said, in support of R. Johanan, "What does the passage (Exod. 14:20) *And the one came not near the other all night* mean? At the time of the crossing of the Red [Reed] Sea, the ministering angels wanted to sing their usual songs before the Holy One, but He said to them, 'My creatures [the Egyptians] are perishing in the waters of the sea, and you want to sing?' "

Sanhedrin, 39b

24. R. Meir said, "When a man suffers punishment, what does the *Shechinah* say? 'My head is heavy; I am deeply grieved.'[1] Now, if the Omnipotent grieves when the blood of the wicked is shed, how much more does He grieve over the blood of the righteous!"

Sanhedrin, 46a

He weeps for men's tribulations and failings

25. For the following three persons the Lord weeps daily: for him who has the opportunity to study the Torah but does not; for him whose circumstances do not permit him to study but nonetheless does; and for the chief officer of a congregation who conducts himself with unnecessary haughtiness.[2] *Hagigah, 5b*

---

[1] "My head is heavy" is obviously anthropomorphic. R. Meir here speaks in what the late Abraham Cronbach called "dramatistic" language.

[2] The word here translated as "chief officer" is *parnas*. It comes from the root "provide" or "sustain," designating an administrator or manager, and is sometimes applied to a manager of charity funds. The Talmud has several references to overbearing leaders, emphasizing the democratic note in Jewish life. See items 672 and 778. The word here translated as "congrega-

Despite God's greatness, He is accessible

26. R. Dustai b. Jannai said, "The Lord differs from mortal man. When a man brings a present to a king, it is uncertain whether it will be accepted or not. Even if it is accepted, it remains uncertain whether he will be permitted to see the king. But with the Lord it is not so. When a man gives a coin to one who is needy, he is rewarded by being permitted to greet the *Shechinah;* for Scripture states: (Ps. 17:15) *As for me, with tzedek* [righteousness, charity] *shall I behold Thy presence."*

Baba Bathra, 10a

God is not vengeful but merciful

27. R. Jose said, "The Lord acts differently from mortal man. When one person provokes another, the latter tries to embitter his life. But the Holy One does not do so. The serpent was cursed by Him [Gen. 3:14], yet it ascends to the roof and finds food, or descends to the ground and finds food there. Canaan was cursed [Gen. 9:25], yet the descendants of the Canaanites eat what others eat and drink what others drink. Woman was cursed [Gen. 3:16], yet men continue to run after her. Indeed, the earth itself was cursed [Gen. 3:17], yet the people of the whole world are constantly sustained by its produce."

Yoma, 75a

28. R. Cahana said in the name of R. Ishmael b. R. Jose, "The ways of man are unlike the ways of God. When a man is defeated [in discourse] by another, he sulks over it. But when God is overcome, so that He averts His wrath and is able to display His mercy, He is pleased; for Scripture states: (Ps. 106:23) *Therefore He said that He would destroy them, had not Moses His chosen stood before Him in the breach, to turn back His wrath, lest He should destroy them."*[1] *Pesahim, 119a*

29. R. Eleazar said, "Even when God is angry He remembers the quality of mercy; for Scripture states: (Hos. 1:6) *For I will not further have compassion upon the house of Israel* [i.e., even in His anger He speaks of compassion]."[2] *Pesahim, 87b*

---

tion" is *tzibbur,* from the root "gather" or "collect," and may be translated also as "community." Community organization is evidenced and responsible leadership stressed.

[1] Not only does God permit Himself to be appeased but Scripture even calls Moses His "chosen," indicating that God was pleased that Moses had intervened to plead for his people. The episode referred to is their worship of the golden calf (Exod. 32:7ff.).

[2] On God's special compassion for Israel, see items 621–625.

He seeks reconciliation with man

30. R. Isaac said that in the land of Israel they say in the name of Raba b. Mari, "The ways of the Lord differ from those of man. The custom of men is, that when someone is provoked by another, it is uncertain whether he will or will not accept an apology. And even if one is known to accept an apology, it is uncertain whether he will be appeased with mere words [and not a penalty or fine]. But the Holy One can be appeased even if a man commits a sin in secret;[1] for Scripture states: (Hos. 14:3) *Take* [bring] *with you words* [of apology], *and return unto the Lord; say unto Him: 'Forgive all iniquity'* [including secret sins]." *Yoma, 86b*

God is our Father

31. (Deut. 14:1) *Ye are children of the Lord your God.*[2] R. Judah said, "This means that when you [the Jewish people] conduct yourselves as dutiful children, you are indeed children of God. But when you do not, you are not considered children of God."

R. Meir differed. He said, "Scripture states: (Jer. 4:22) *They are sottish children,* and even speaks of the people as (Deut. 32:20) *children in whom there is no faith,* but regards them as God's children nonetheless." [See also item 124.] *Kiddushin, 36a*

32. R. Akiba used to pray, "Our Father, our King, we have sinned before Thee. Our Father, our King, we have no king besides Thee. Our Father, our King, have compassion upon us."[3] *Taanith, 25b*

The Lord loves justice and righteousness

33. R. Johanan said in the name of R. Simeon b. Johai, "What does the verse (Isa. 61:8) *For I, the Lord, love justice; I hate robbery with iniquity* mean? Its meaning may be found in the analogy of a mortal king who, passing through the customhouse, said to his attendants, 'Pay the duty to the officers.' His attendants thereupon said to him, 'O King, why should you have to pay duty? Do not all the revenues of the realm go to you?' The king answered, 'I do this because I want all travelers to

---

[1] A secret sin is more evil than an overt one. The sinner assumes that no one will know he has sinned, thereby insulting God, Who sees and knows all. See item 91.

[2] The concept of the fatherhood of God appears not only in the Torah (above), but also in the Prophets (Mal. 1:6) and in the Writings (Ps. 68:5). In the N.T., it appears in Matt. 6:9 and elsewhere.

[3] The prayer of R. Akiba is recited in the service for the Jewish High Holy Days. For the individual prayers of other rabbis, see items 507–510.

follow my example, and not try to escape their responsibilities.' That is why God declared, (ibid.) *I, the Lord, love justice; I hate robbery with iniquity*; that is, 'From Me shall My children learn, and thus will avoid robbery.' "[1] *Sukkah, 30a*

The seal of the Lord is Truth

34. R. Hanina said, "The inscription on the seal of the Lord is Truth [*Emeth*]."[2] *Yoma, 69b*

His secrets surpass our understanding

35. Four men entered into the heavenly garden [i.e., the divine mysteries]. They were Ben Azzai, Ben Zoma, Aher and R. Akiba. Ben Azzai gazed [at the *Shechinah*] and perished. To him may be applied the verse (Ps. 116:15) *Grievous in the sight of the Lord is the death of His righteous ones.*

Ben Zoma looked and went mad. To him may be applied the verse (Prov. 25:16) *Hast thou found honey? Eat* [only] *as much as may be enough for thee, lest thou eat too much and vomit it forth.* Aher,[3] upon penetrating the divine mysteries, severed the roots [of faith]. Only R. Akiba entered in peace and left in peace. *Hagigah, 14b*

God is best served through compassionate conduct

36. Scripture states: (Gen. 3:21) *And the Lord God made for Adam and his wife garments of skin and clothed them.* Just as God clothed the naked, so shall you clothe the naked. And just as God visits the sick, so shall you visit the sick; for Scripture states: (Gen. 18:1) *And the Lord appeared before him* [Abraham] *by the terebinths of Mamre* [after his circumcision].

---

[1] On God's involvement in the quest for justice, see items 544–547. On the matter of honesty, particularly in business transactions, see chapter 4b. See also items 68–70. A fuller treatment of the righteous life will be found in chapter 2. Concern with moral conduct appears throughout this volume.

[2] The word *Emeth* consists of the first, middle and last letters of the Hebrew alphabet: *aleph, mem* and *thav.* The implication here is that God is eternal and all-knowing. Cf. "I am *Alpha* and *Omega*" (N.T., Rev. 1:8).

   The alphabet served also for numerals, and the Cabalists drew many inferences not only from the arrangement of letters within a word but also from the numerical value of those letters in their interpretations of Scriptural passages. See fn. to item 117.

[3] Elisha b. Abuyah, of the Mishnaic period, was called Aher, meaning "another" or "one who is different," because he was lured by Gnostic teachings and left the Jewish faith. For an account of how this came about, see item 748 and its footnote. See also *U.J.E.,* s.v. "Gnosticism."

The Holy One also buries the dead; for Scripture states: (Deut. 34:6) *And He* [God] *buried him* [Moses] *in the valley.* So shall you bury the dead.[1] The Holy One consoles those who mourn; for Scripture states: (Gen. 25:11) *And it came to pass, after the death of Abraham, that God blessed Isaac his son.* So shall you as well comfort those who mourn.

Sotah, 14a

Loving God "with all thy heart"

37. (Deut. 6:4) *And thou shalt love the Lord thy God with all thy heart, with all thy soul, and with all thy might.* We are taught that R. Eliezer the Great said, "Since this passage states *with all thy soul*, why is it necessary to say *with all thy might?* And since it says *with all thy might*, why is it necessary to say *with all thy soul?*

"This is intended to teach us that if a man's soul is dearer to him than his money [*m'od*: "might"],[2] then the words *with all thy soul* [involving even greater sacrifice] apply to him. For him who values money more than his life are intended the words *and with all thy might.*"

R. Akiba declared that *with all thy soul* means that one should love God even if his life is taken from him. [See chapter 11 for the story of the martyrdom of R. Akiba.] *Berachoth, 61b; Pesahim, 25a*

C. ASPECTS OF GOD'S CREATION

The immensity of the universe

38. [God is declared to have said,] "Twelve constellations have I created in the firmament, and for each constellation I have created thirty hosts; for each host I have created thirty legions, and for each legion thirty files. For each file I have created thirty cohorts, and for each cohort thirty camps.[3] In each camp have I suspended three hundred and sixty-five thousands of myriads of stars, in accordance with the days of the solar year." *Berachoth, 32b*

---

[1] Concern for dignified treatment of the body of the dead was emphasized by the designation of a *hevrah kadishah* (burial society) whose function it was to wash the body, to prepare it for burial and to guard it overnight.

[2] The basic meaning of *m'od*, usually translated as "might," is "much" or as an adverb "very." The word may in this context be translated as "muchness," meaning wealth, as R. Eliezer translates it, without violence to the text.

[3] Roman military terms are used. The Roman army was a precise military machine. This implies care and precision as well as universal order.

On what does the earth rest?

39. The Sages [*hachamim*][1] declared that the earth rests upon twelve pillars; for Scripture states: (Deut. 32:8) *He set the borders of the peoples according to the number of the children of Israel.*[2] Others maintain that there are seven; for Scripture states: (Prov. 9:1) *Wisdom*[3] *hath builded her house, she hath hewn out her seven pillars.*

R. Eleazar b. Shammua said, "Upon one pillar only, whose name is The Righteous; for Scripture states: (Prov. 10:25) *But the righteous* [person] *is an everlasting foundation.*" [See also item 116.]

Hagigah, 12b

How the earth was formed

40. R. Isaac Nappaha ["the blacksmith"] said, "The Holy One cast a stone into the primeval sea, from which [as a center] the world was then formed;[4] for Scripture states: (Job 38:6) *Whereupon were the foundations thereof fastened, or who laid the corner-stone thereof?*"

But the Sages said that the world was created from Zion; for Scripture states: (Ps. 50:1) *A psalm of Asaph: God the Lord hath spoken, and called the earth* [into being]; then continues, (Ps. 50:2) *Out of Zion, the perfection of beauty.* This means that from Zion was the beauty of the world perfected.[5] *Yoma, 54b*

The oceans of the world

41. Abbaye said, ". . . the world is surrounded by ocean."

Erubin, 22b

42. R. Eliezer declared, "The whole world drinks from the ocean; for Scripture states: (Gen. 2:6) *There went up a mist from the earth, and watered the whole surface of the earth.*" To this R. Joshua replied, "But

---

[1] The term *hacham* was applied to a wise man, even if he was not a Jew (Megillah, 16a). It was used as an official title when the Hadrianic persecutions ceased and the Sanhedrin was reconstituted. R. Meir is referred to as a *hacham* (Horayoth, 13b).

[2] In this rather weak proof-text, the word "borders" is understood as "foundations," and "the number of" as referring to the number of tribes.

[3] In the Book of Proverbs, Wisdom is personified. Wisdom is identified with God as the Creator of the house, i.e., the earth.

[4] The legendary *eben shetiah* ("foundation stone") for the creation of the world. "It was believed to reach the bottom of the universal ocean and to form the stable point on which the earth was founded." (*U.J.E.,* s.v. "Shetiah.")

[5] Since the foundation stone of the world was regarded as the site where the Temple stood, the Temple mount, Jerusalem and the land of Israel occupied a central position in the creation of the world. See also item 594.

is not the water of the ocean salty?" And R. Eliezer answered, "It becomes sweetened in the clouds [then falls as rain]."[1] *Taanith, 9b*

Which came first, the heavens or the earth?

43. The school of Shammai[2] maintained that the heavens were created first, and that the earth was created afterward; for Scripture states: (Gen. 1:1) *In the beginning God created*[3] *the heaven and the earth* [mentioning heaven first]. But the school of Hillel held that both were created together; for Scripture states: (Gen. 2:4) *In the* [single] *day that the Lord God made earth and heaven.*[4]

The Sages also declared that both were created together; for Scripture states: (Isa. 48:13) *My hand also hath laid the foundation of the earth, and My right hand hath spanned out the heavens. I call unto them, and they stand forward together* [not separately]. *Hagigah, 12a*

How the moon's complaint was answered

44. R. Simeon b. Pazzi raised the following [seeming] contradiction: "First we read: (Gen. 1:16) *And God made the two great lights* [indicating no difference between them] but immediately thereafter we read *the greater light and the lesser light.* [Why the repetition, in modified form?]

"The answer is that at the time of creation [the sun and the moon were of equal size, so] the moon said to the Holy One, 'Sovereign of the Universe! Is it possible for two kings to wear the same crown [i.e., to occupy equal rank]?' Thereupon God replied, 'Go and make yourself smaller than the sun.'

" 'Sovereign of the Universe,' pleaded the moon, 'is it because I dared to question You that I am now asked to make myself smaller?' 'Go and shine by day and by night,' replied the Lord. But the moon pleaded further, 'Of what avail will my light be by day? Of what use is a lamp in broad daylight?' Then God said to the moon, 'Go, and be satisfied, for Israel will count the days of the month

---

[1] "Rain has its origin, for the most part, in the sea. Some four-fifths of the water that evaporates into the atmosphere each year comes from the ocean. And the ocean re-collects most of that again when it falls as rain or snow." (Robert E. Breeden, ed., *The Ocean Realm* [Washington, D.C.: The National Geographic Society, 1978], p. 23.) See also item 1001.

[2] The schools of Shammai and Hillel were in frequent disagreement, the former usually more conservative in interpreting the Halachah.

[3] The 1962 J.P.S. Bible translation is *When God began to create. . . .*

[4] This verse not only places the earth first, countering the claim of the school of Shammai, but also states specifically that both were created the same day.

after you, and also the years [by using the lunar calendar].' "

Hullin, 60b

How the second day of creation differed from the others

45. R. Bena'ah b. R. Ulla raised the question, "Why were the words *ki tov* ['that it was good'] not applied to the second day of creation [while they are spoken for the other days]?" His father [R. Ulla] answered him saying, "Because on the second day of creation, the fire of Gehinnom[1] was created [to which the term 'good' cannot be applied]." *Pesahim, 54a*

Why God created only one man when He could have created many

46. Our rabbis taught that only one man [Adam] was created in order to teach us that he who destroys one human being is considered by Scripture as one who has destroyed the whole world [since the whole world was created for the sake of one man]. So too does Scripture regard him who saves a single life as one who has saved the whole world.[2]

Only one man was created in order to preserve peace among men, so that none may say, "My grandfather was greater than yours," and also in order that a heretic should not be able to say that there are many creators in heaven. *Sanhedrin, 37a*

47. God created only one man in order to demonstrate His glory. A human monarch produces a great many coins, but stamps them all with the same image, so that they are all identical. But the King of Kings has stamped every man with the image of Adam, the first man, yet not one of them is exactly like another. Therefore every man may say, "The whole world was created for my sake [since I, like Adam, am unique]; and I must be upright and just [since, like Adam, I was created in the image of God]."

A single ancestor was created for all of mankind so that the righteous should not be able to boast, "We are the descendants of righteous men," and the wicked should not be able to say, "We are

---

[1] This designation for a place of punishment for sinners in the Hereafter was taken from the Valley of Hinnom, south of Jerusalem, where children were believed to have been sacrificed to Moloch. For an oblique Talmudic reference to this ancient pagan practice, see item 754.

[2] The democratic concept of the importance of the individual, a key principle in rabbinic thought, is illustrated here, as is the emphasis on the sacredness of life.

descended from wicked men [hence we are not to be blamed for our wickedness]." *Sanhedrin, 37a*

48. God created only one man in order to reduce the amount of dissension among men. If there is so much strife among men despite the fact that they have a common ancestor, how much more would this be the case if more than one man had been created![1]

Sanhedrin, 38a

All of God's creatures have their usefulness

49. R. Judah said in the name of Rab, "Among all of the things God created in His universe, He created nothing that is entirely useless." *Sabbath, 77b*

Further aspects of God's creation

50. R. Zutra b. Tubia said in the name of Rab, "With ten characteristics was the earth created: wisdom and understanding; knowledge and strength; rebuke and might; righteousness and justice; mercy and compassion."[2] *Hagigah, 12a*

---

[1] Other reasons given in rabbinic literature are: 1) that heretics might not say that men participated in the creation of the world; 2) to teach man humility, since the smallest gnat preceded him; 3) that man might be able immediately to enter upon the performance of a commandment, i.e., the observance of the Sabbath. See Bernard Bamberger, "Philo and the Aggadah," *Hebrew Union College Annual* 48 (1977): 160.

[2] The implication is that these powers have been made available to man to be used for constructive purposes.

2

THE RIGHTEOUS LIFE

MATTHEW Arnold defined religion as "morality tinged with emotion." For the rabbis of the Talmud, however, religion was righteousness steeped in faith. They did not disdain the pursuit of happiness; indeed, they admonished us not to forego any of life's legitimate pleasures. But, in their advocacy of righteous living, they deplored self-centered hedonism and indifference to the needs and sensibilities of others.

Goodness and virtue were not associated with a reclusive, cloistered existence, divorced from the demands life normally makes upon us. Nor were these seen by the rabbis as preordained personal qualities, imbedded in the germ plasm of the individual as part of his genetic endowment. Instead, they were regarded as facets of character to be constantly cultivated in the context of the family and the community.

In describing the righteous life, the rabbis extol humility as a great virtue, castigate the arrogant and scold those who recite their own merits or seek public prominence. They caution us against the sinful tongue, reminding us that the spoken word can result in much harm, and warn against words of anger and strife, lascivious language, lying, hypocrisy and slander. But they also encourage us to rebuke a friend when he has done wrong and to speak up in defense of justice.

The rabbis are persuaded that virtue begins with reverence for God; they urge the avoidance of evil because of its progressive hold upon us, and the constant performance of virtuous deeds so that these may become habitual. They commend the practice of patience and forbearance, stating that one should prefer to suffer abuse than to inflict it upon others. While fully aware that men are men and not angels, the rabbis are nonetheless convinced that by righteous living men can best fulfill their divine potential and express their love of God.

A. AVOIDING ARROGANCE

Humility is the greatest virtue

51. Humility is the greatest of all virtues; for Scripture states: (Isa. 61:1) *The spirit of the Lord is upon me, because the Lord hath appointed me to preach good tidings unto the meek.* The verse does not say "unto the saints" but rather *unto the meek*; hence we learn that humility is the supreme virtue [and not saintliness, which is not expected of us].

Abodah Zarah, 20b

God prefers the humble

52. R. Joseph said, "A person should always be humble, and take a lesson from the behavior of his Creator. The Holy One, in giving the Ten Commandments to the people of Israel, disregarded all the lofty mountains and caused His *Shechinah* to dwell on Mount Sinai [a relatively low mountain]. He also ignored all the stately trees and caused His *Shechinah* to abide in a bush." [This refers to the burning bush, Exod. 3:2.] *Sotah, 5a*

53. (Isa. 57:15) *Yet also with the contrite and humble of spirit do I dwell.* R. Huna and R. Hisda both commented on this verse. R. Huna said, "This means 'the humble are with me' [i.e., 'I exalt them']." R. Hisda said, "It means 'I am with the humble' [i.e., 'I lower Myself to them']."

R. Hisda's interpretation, "I am with the humble," is more acceptable; for we find that God caused His *Shechinah* to dwell on Mount Sinai [lowering Himself onto the mount] instead of elevating Mount Sinai [to Him]. *Sotah, 5a*

He laments over the haughty

54. R. Eleazar said, "One who is haughty causes the *Shechinah* to lament over him; for Scripture states: (Ps. 138:6) *For though the Lord be exalted, yet regardeth He the lowly, but the haughty He knoweth from afar.*"[1] *Sotah, 5a*

---

[1] The proof-text supplies rather weak support. Knowing the proud *from afar* implies keeping one's distance from them rather than lamenting their behavior. This may be seen as an example of putting something into a verse (eisegesis) rather than deriving something from it (exegesis). However, Eleazar may take this to mean that it is the proud who set themselves *from afar*, distancing themselves from God, yet God *knows* them, i.e., is concerned about them, nonetheless.

God cannot tolerate the arrogant

55. R. Hisda said in the name of Mar Ukba, "Of him who possesses an arrogant spirit the Holy One says, 'He and I cannot dwell in the world together'; for Scripture states: (Ps. 101:5) *Whoever is haughty of eye and proud of heart, him will I not suffer.*" *Sotah, 4b*

The arrogant are brought low

56. R. Avira said, at times in the name of R. Ammi and at other times in the name of R. Assi, "Whoever is proud of spirit will ultimately be brought low; for Scripture states: (Job 24:24) *They are exalted* [only] *for a little while.* Lest you assume that the arrogant will nonetheless endure in the world, the verse continues *they are no more* [i.e., they shall perish]."

R. Ashi said, and so also were we taught by the school of R. Ishmael, "This is comparable to a man going out into his field and plucking all the tallest produce. So too does the Lord pluck out the arrogant."

Sotah, 5a

57. (Exod. 1:6) *And Joseph died and all his brothers.* Why did Joseph die before his brothers? [Joseph is mentioned first.] Because he gave himself superior airs. *Berachoth, 55a*

On reciting one's own virtues

58. R. Simeon b. Johai said, "A man should recite his virtues in a whisper and his faults in a shout." *Sotah, 32b*

One should not seek personal prominence

59. Abaye said, "In any gathering where there are many [able] men, one should not try to make oneself prominent."

Berachoth, 63a

The advantage of anonymity

60. R. Eleazar said, "A man should always try to remain obscure [and not seek public notice] and he shall live [without the burdens involved]." *Sanhedrin, 92a*

Pride is unseemly in women

61. R. Nahman said, "Pride is unbecoming to women. Two women [of the Bible] were haughty, and both were given unlovely names. One was called Deborah [a bee or hornet] and the other Huldah [a

mole or weasel].[1] Of Deborah, Scripture states: (Jud. 4:6) *And she sent and called Barak,* instead of going to him [which would have shown greater humility]. And of Huldah, Scripture states that she commanded; (2 Kings 22:15) *Say unto the man who sent you to me* instead of saying [more humbly] 'Say unto the king.' "[2] *Megillah, 14b*

Arrogance is particularly unbecoming for a scholar

62. A person should always be as yielding as a reed and not unbending like a cedar tree. It once happened that R. Eleazar, the son of R. Simon, left the town of G'dor, where his teacher lived, to return home. As he rode along on an ass by the banks of a river, proud of the learning he had acquired from his master, he met a man who was terribly ugly.

"Peace unto you, my master," said the man to R. Eleazar. To this R. Eleazar replied, "Good for nothing! Are all the people of your town as homely as you are?" "That I do not know," the man answered, "but perhaps you should go to the Creator Who formed me and say to Him, 'How ugly is this vessel You have made.' "

Realizing that he had offended the man, R. Eleazar dismounted and prostrated himself before him saying, "I have sinned against you. Forgive me! But the man refused and said, "I shall not forgive you until you confront the Creator Who formed me and say to Him, 'How ugly is this vessel You have made.' "

R. Eleazar did not leave him, but followed him on foot until they reached the town where R. Eleazar lived. The people of his town [informed of R. Eleazar's arrival] all went out to greet him saying, "Peace unto you, our rabbi, our teacher!"[3] The ugly man, who preceded R. Eleazar, asked them whom they were addressing as "rabbi" and "teacher." And they replied, "The man who is following you."

The ugly man then said to them, "If he is a rabbi, then may there

---

[1] Some rabbis were inclined to misogyny. Deborah, the prophetess, was generally admired, and a Jewish women's philanthropic society is named after her. Huldah was a prophetess who lived in the reign of King Josiah (c. 638–608 B.C.E.). Josiah, best remembered for the Josianic reformation which removed all vestiges of foreign worship, sought counsel from Huldah.

[2] For a charming account of the association of names with character, see Noah Jacobs, *Naming Day in Eden* (New York: Macmillan, 1969).

[3] *Rabbi* and *Mori,* two different terms, are used here. While the terms are often used interchangeably, the latter is more specific in its application to the rabbi's role as teacher as distinct from his other functions.

not be many in Israel like him." "Why not?" they asked. And he replied, "Because of the way he treated me." When they heard his story they pleaded, "Forgive him, for he is a great Torah scholar." Then he said, "Only for your sakes will I forgive him, and only on the condition that he shall never do this again." Following this episode, R. Eleazar taught that one must be as humble as a reed and not unbending like a cedar tree. *Taanith, 20a*

B. GUARDING THE TONGUE

The power of the spoken word

63. R. Eleazar said, "Whence do we learn that speech is equivalent to action? Scripture states: (Ps. 33:6) *By the word of the Lord were the heavens made.*" [See Gen. 1:6f.] *Sabbath, 119b*

The evil potential of speech

64. R. Johanan said in the name of R. Simeon b. Johai, "Verbal wrongdoing is more evil than cheating in matters of money; for concerning the former, Scripture states: (Lev. 19:14) *but thou shalt fear thy God*, while this is not said of the latter."[1]

R. Eleazar said, "Harmful speech is more wicked because it affects the person [of the injured] while the latter affects only his money." And R. Samuel b. Nahmani declared, "Harmful speech is worse because money can be returned, but words once uttered cannot easily be recalled." *Baba Metzia, 58b*

The avoidance of words of anger and strife

65. R. Mani b. Patish said, "He who gives vent to anger will be deprived of greatness even if he has been predestined for it by heaven." *Pesahim, 66b*

66. Ulla said, "When two people quarrel, he who is the first to keep silent is the most praiseworthy." *Kiddushin, 71b*

67. (Prov. 17:14) *As one letteth loose* [a stream of] *water, so is the beginning of strife.* In comment on this verse R. Huna said, "Strife is compared to a burst of water because once it gets started it becomes increasingly strong." And Abaye the Elder [Abaye Kashisha] re-

---

[1] The passage reads *Thou shalt not curse the deaf, nor put a stumbling-block before the blind, but thou shalt fear,* etc. Involved here is odious speech or action which affects its victim more than the loss of money, in a very personal way. The comment by R. Eleazar expresses the same thought.

marked, "Strife is like the planks of a [wooden] bridge; the longer they lie in place the more firmly imbedded they become." [See also item 576.] *Sanhedrin, 7a*

Speaking honestly with others
68. Abaye said, "One should not speak differently with his mouth from what he thinks in his heart."[1] *Baba Metzia, 49a*

Lying is akin to idol worship
69. R. Eleazar said, "He who dissembles in his speech is like one who worships idols [a grievous sin]." *Sanhedrin, 92a*

We must not deceive a non-Jew
70. Samuel said, "We must not steal the mind of [i.e., deceive] a fellow-creature, whether he be Jew or Gentile." [See also item 224.]
Hullin, 94a

The making of vows is deplored
71. Do not get into the habit of making vows; for such a habit may, in the course of time, lead to a violation of your oath. [The more vows one makes, the greater the risk of violating one's oath.][2]
Nedarim, 20a

72. Samuel said, "Whoever makes a vow, even if he fulfills it, is considered to be wicked."[3] *Nedarim, 22a*

Hypocrisy is castigated
73. R. Eleazar said, "Any community where hypocrisy prevails will in the end be exiled; for Scripture states: (Job 15:34) *For the assembly of hypocrites shall be desolate.*"

R. Hisda said in the name of Jeremiah b. Abba, "Four types of

---

[1] This refers to a transaction in which a deposit is made, which may not be legally binding yet does have moral force. It applies equally, of course, to other matters.

[2] The subject of vows is a complex one. Vows are dealt with in Num. 6:1–21 and 30:2–17. The matter is treated at length in tractate Nedarim ("Vows") of the Talmud. See *U.J.E.*, s.v. "Vow."

[3] Jephthah, in Judg. 11, made only a single vow and felt constrained to slay his own daughter. He had vowed to offer as a sacrifice the first creature whom he would encounter if he were to successfully complete a military mission and his daughter was the first to greet him. Samuel contends that even if one fulfills his oath he has acted wrongfully by taking the risk of dire consequences since one does not know what the future holds in store. Cf. N.T., Matt. 5:34, "But I say unto you, Swear not at all."

people do not deserve to receive the *Shechinah*: scorners, liars, hypo-crites and talebearers." *Sotah, 41b, 42a*

The sin of slander

74. R. Shesheth said in the name of R. Eleazar b. Azariah, "Who-ever utters slander, or listens to slander, and whoever testifies falsely against another, deserves to be thrown to the dogs; for Scripture states: (Exod. 22:30) *Unto the dog shalt thou throw it* [him]¹ and this is followed by (Exod. 23:1) *Thou shalt not bear a false report."*

Pesahim, 118a

The consequence of calumny

75. R. Johanan said in the name of R. Meir, "Every statement in which there is no grain of truth weakens the credibility [of the speaker] in the end [i.e., when the truth is actually stated]."

Sotah, 35a

On calumniating a servant before his master

76. R. Johanan said in the name of R. Simeon b. Johai, "What does the verse (Prov. 30:10) *Slander not a servant unto his master, lest he curse thee and thou be found guilty* mean? Why does Scripture state [immedi-ately thereafter]: *There is a generation that curseth its father, and does not bless its mother?* Is it because that generation curses its father and does not bless its mother that you must not slander a servant? We must rather explain this [sequence] to mean that even in a [wicked] genera-tion that curses its father and does not bless its mother, a man must not slander a servant before his master [so grievous is this offense]."

Pesahim, 87b

Everyone is inclined to engage in indirect slander

77. R. Amram quoted Rab [Abba Aricha] as saying, "No one can escape from the following transgressions even for a single day: sinful fantasies, lack of true devotion in one's prayers, and slander." Are we then to believe that people slander each other constantly? This really refers to indirect slander.

---

¹ The Biblical text speaks against eating *any flesh that is torn of beasts in the field.* The word for *flesh* is the antecedent of the word for *it.* Since there is no neuter gender, and the word for *it* is here masculine, it can be read as "him." However, it is difficult to justify connecting this word to the following chapter, as Shesheth does, and concluding that the slanderer rather than the flesh must be thrown to the dogs. The exercise is purely homiletical. See also item 176.

R. Judah reported Rab [somewhat differently] as having said, "A majority of men are apt to steal [if given an opportunity], a minority are prone to lewdness, but all are inclined to slander," and said that Rab meant by this that all are inclined to engage in *indirect* [literally, "dust" or a "hint" of] slander. *Baba Bathra, 164b*

By avoiding flattery we may also avoid slander

78. R. Simeon once brought a folded divorce document to Rabbi [Judah HaNasi] his father, and Rabbi found fault with it saying, "There is no date on it." R. Simeon replied, "Perhaps it is written within the folds." Rabbi opened it and found the date. Then he turned and looked at his son with displeasure. Thereupon R. Simeon said, "It was not I who wrote it, but Judah the tailor." To this Rabbi replied, "Omit the slander."

On another occasion R. Simeon was sitting near his father, reading a chapter of Psalms. Rabbi commented, "How nicely it is written." To this R. Simeon replied, "I did not write it, but Judah the tailor." And his father once again said, "Omit the slander."

The reason why Rabbi told his son not to engage in slander in the first instance is clear, for Rabbi disliked the folding of documents and was therefore upset at the writer. But when his son said it was Judah the tailor who did the fine writing, why did Rabbi tell him to omit the slander? It was because R. Dimi, the brother of Safra, had taught that a man should not speak in flattering terms of another, lest he might be tempted to speak of his failings as well. *Baba Bathra, 164b*

One should not use lascivious language

79. R. Hanan b. Raba said, "Everyone knows why a bride enters the nuptial chamber; but if one speaks about it in indecent language, then even if a decree of seventy years of happiness had been sealed for him, the decree would be changed to evil against him."[1] *Sabbath, 33a*

80. Raba b. Shila said in the name of R. Hisda, "Whoever defiles his mouth [by lascivious talk] has Gehinnom made deeper for him;[2] for Scripture states: (Prov. 22:14) *A deep pit for the mouth that speaketh perversity.*"

---

[1] This refers to the concept of the Book of Life, in which one's destiny is recorded in heaven. The belief that the Book of Life is opened on Rosh Hashanah and sealed on Yom Kippur finds expression in the ritual for the Holy Days. See fn. to item 734.

[2] Varying degrees of future punishment are here implied. For the concept of Gehinnom, see chapter 13d.

R. Nahman b. Isaac declared, "Even he who only listens to such talk and remains silent will have the same punishment inflicted upon him."

Sabbath, 33a

Scripture too avoids indecent language

81. R. Joshua b. Levi said, "A person should never utter an unseemly word; for Scripture itself uses a circumlocution which adds eight [extra Hebrew] letters to the text in order to avoid an ugly word. Scripture states: (Gen. 4:2) *Of the clean beasts and of the beasts that are not clean* [avoiding the single word *tamei* for 'unclean']."

Pesahim, 3a

Why the fingers of the hand are tapered

82. Bar Kappara said, "If a person hears an unbecoming thing, he should put his finger in his ear." That is what R. Eleazar meant when he asked [rhetorically], "Why are a person's fingers tapered?" Was he asking why the fingers are separated from one another? [Not at all.] They are separated because each is needed for its own functions. We must infer that he was asking precisely why they are tapered. [And the answer is] so that if one hears an unpleasant word, he can put a finger in his ear.

In the school of Ishmael it was taught that the outer ear is rigid but the earlobe is soft so that when one hears an unsavory word he can place the earlobe over the ear to cover it. *Kethuboth, 5a*

Speaking softly and pacifying anger

83. Abaye used to say, "A person should always show reverence for God and consider in what manner he can serve Him best. He should reply to another softly, try to pacify anger, and speak peaceably with everyone, even with the heathen, so that he may be beloved in heaven and on earth and find favor in the sight of all."

It was said of R. Johanan b. Zakkai that he was never greeted first by anyone, even by a non-believer, for he always greeted others first.

Berachoth, 17a

Rebuking another for incorrect conduct

84. R. Eleazar said, "If one notices bad behavior on the part of a friend, it is one's duty to rebuke him."[1] *Berachoth, 31a*

---

[1] This does not contradict Abaye's statement (item 83). When one's actions can bring harm to himself or others, he can be set right by gentle language. See also item 974.

Speaking up against injustice

85. One who feels that his protest in the face of injustice may be effective and does not protest ought to be punished.

Abodah Zarah, 18a

86. He who has the power to protest [against wrongdoing] in his home and does not do so will be accountable for the sin of everyone in his household. In the community, when his protest could be effective, he will be held accountable for the transgressions of all its members. Outside the community, if his protest might do some good [and he does not speak out], he is responsible for the sinfulness of all.

R. Papa added, "And the princes of the exile [Exilarchs or leaders of the Jewish community] are held accountable for the transgressions of the whole household of Israel."[1] *Sabbath, 54b*

Abiding by one's spoken word

87. (Mishnah 5:6) Akabiah b. Mahalalel disagreed with his colleagues on four separate issues in interpreting the Halachah.[2] The Sages asked him to retract [i.e., to change his opinion in these matters], promising him the chair of Presiding Justice [*Ab Din*] if he would do so. Instead he replied, "I prefer to be called a fool among men rather than seem wicked in the sight of God. For people will say, 'He retracted his words for the sake of high office.' "

Eduyoth, 9b

Admitting one's ignorance

88. Teach your tongue to say, "I do not know," lest you be found mistaken [or led to falsehood]. *Berachoth, 4a*

---

1 Exilarch (Hebrew: *Rosh Golah;* Aramaic: *Resh Galutha*) was the title applied to the head of the Babylonian Jewish community, which was semiautonomous. The Jews regarded him as their ruler. He appointed judges and exercised police power as well as control over commerce, weights and measures. This power sometimes led to abuse, and was often contested by the heads of the Babylonian academies.

2 Of the first generation of Tannaim, Akabiah (c. 30 B.C.E.–10 C.E.) held opinions on certain laws of ritual purity and legal procedure (Niddah 2:6; Negaim 5:3) different from those of his colleagues. In the issues referred to here, the question of whether he was in accord with established majority opinion, as laid down by his predecessors, is involved. Akabiah maintained that his was actually the preexisting majority view. However, he instructed his son to abandon his own view and adopt the view of the new majority of scholars of his son's generation. See item 104; also item 651 and fn.

C. THE PATHS OF RIGHTEOUSNESS

Guarding the tongue is not enough

89. R. Alexandri called out, "Who wants to live? Who wants to live?" When a crowd gathered he quoted the words (Ps. 34:14) *Keep thy tongue from evil and thy lips from speaking guile.* But one may say, "Since I have kept my tongue from evil and my lips from speaking guile, I may spend my time sleeping." That is why the passage continues *Depart from evil and* [actively] *do good. Abodah Zarah, 19b*

Love of God is expressed in daily living

90. (Deut. 6:5) *Thou shalt love the Lord thy God.* This implies that one should study the Torah and wait upon scholars; that he should speak softly to others; that his purchases and presents should be suitable and his business transactions honest. *Yoma, 86a*

Righteousness is rooted in reverence for God

91. R. Johanan's disciples said to him, "Rabbi, bless us." And he replied, "May it be God's will that your awe [*yirah*][1] of Him will be as great as your fear of man." Then they asked, "Is that all, Rabbi?" And he answered, "When someone commits a transgression secretly he says to himself, 'I hope no one will see me,' yet he shows no awe of God, Who sees all." [See fn. to item 30.] *Berachoth, 28b*

Delighting in fulfilling God's commandments

92. (Ps. 112:1) *Happy is the man that feareth the Lord, and delighteth greatly in His commandments.* R. Eleazar pointed out that this verse speaks of one who delights in fulfilling God's commandments, regardless of any reward; and the Mishnah states, "Be not like servants who serve their master for the sake of reward, but like those who serve him without seeking reward." *Abodah Zarah, 19a*

Honor is earned by our own conduct

93. (Mishnah 5:7) "Father," said the son of Akabiah b. Mahalalel, "ask your friends to deem me honorable." But his father replied, "I

---

[1] The word *yirah* is here translated as "awe" of God and "fear" of man since the thought of fearing God may seem distasteful in English usage. In Hebrew the term suggests reverence or respect and is commonly so translated in passages dealing with a proper attitude toward parents (see item 416). The word "awe" best expresses the feeling for God and conveys the full meaning of *yirah.*

cannot ask this of them." "Why not?" asked his son. "Have you found any evil in me?" And Akabiah answered, "No, but only your own conduct will command respect for you, and only your own conduct will estrange you [from honor]." *Eduyoth, 9b*

One should be patient and forbearing

94. Those who are subjected to humiliation by others but do not themselves humiliate others; who hear themselves reproached but do not answer back; who perform their duty out of love for their duty, and are joyful in spite of their pains—it is of them that Scripture speaks when it states: (Judg. 5:31) *But those that love Him shall be like the rising of the sun in its might.* Gittin, *36b*

95. A person should always be as patient as Hillel, and not as intransigent as Shammai. It once happened that two men laid a wager with one another that whoever would succeed in rousing Hillel's temper would receive four hundred *zuzim.*

"I shall go and make him angry," said one of them. On a Friday afternoon, while Hillel was bathing [to prepare for the Sabbath], the man came to the door of his house and shouted, "Does Hillel live here?" Hillel wrapped his robe about him and went out to meet the man. "My son," he said to him, "What do you wish?" "I have a question to ask," he replied. "Ask, my son, ask," said Hillel. "Why are the heads of the Babylonians round?" he inquired.[1] And Hillel answered, "You have asked a good question, my son. It is because they have no trained midwives."

The visitor left, but he soon returned, calling out once again, "Does Hillel live here?" Hillel again wrapped his robe about him and greeted his questioner once more. "My son," said Hillel. "What do you wish?" "I have a question to ask," he replied. "Ask, my son, ask," said Hillel. "Why are the people of Tarmod [Palmyra] weak-eyed?" asked his visitor. And Hillel said, "You have asked a good question. It is because they live in a very sandy country [and their eyes are constantly irritated by the wind-blown sand]."

The man left, but returned once again, shouting, "Does Hillel live here?" Hillel greeted his questioner once more and said, "What do you wish, my son?" "I have a question to ask," said the man. "Ask, my son, ask," replied Hillel. "Why are the feet of the Ethiopians so broad?" asked his visitor. "You have asked a fine question," said

---

[1] Hillel was himself a Babylonian.

Hillel. "It is because they live in marshy land [and wide feet make walking easier]."

"I have many more questions," said the man, "but I am afraid that I will make you angry." Hillel then sat down and said, "All the questions you have to ask, please ask." Thereupon his questioner asked, "Are you Hillel, who is called the Prince of Israel?" "Yes," replied Hillel. "If that is so, then I pray that there may not be many more in Israel like you," said the man. And Hillel asked, "Why is that, my son?" To this he responded, "Because I have lost four hundred *zuzim* on account of you [on a wager that I could make you angry]."

Then Hillel said to him, "It is far better that you should lose four hundred *zuzim* than that Hillel should become angry and lose his patience." *Sabbath, 30b*

96. Fortunate is the person who hears himself abused and minds it not; he will escape a hundred evils. *Sanhedrin, 7a*

"Be of the persecuted, rather than the persecutors"

97. R. Abbahu said, "One should choose to be among the persecuted, rather than the persecutors.[1] There are no more persecuted birds than doves and pigeons; yet Scripture designates them [alone among the birds] as being suited for the [sacrificial] altar."

Baba Kamma, 93a

98. R. Judah said in the name of Rab, "There is a popular saying, 'Be the cursed and not the curser.' " *Sanhedrin, 49a*

How God measures our merits

99. Once a pestilence raged in Sura,[2] but in the neighborhood where Rab lived there was no sign of it. The people of the city thought that this was due to the special merits of Rab. However, they were informed in a dream that this would be too small a way [for God] to recognize Rab's merits, and that this happened rather because of a certain man [in Rab's neighborhood] who loaned his hoe and other digging tools for use in burials, without any compensation.

In Darograth there once was a great fire, but it did not reach the area where R. Huna lived. It was thought that this was due to the merits of R. Huna. But the people were told through a dream that this would be inadequate recognition of R. Huna's greatness, and that it

---

[1] Cf. N.T., Matt. 5:10, "Blessed are those who are persecuted for righteousness' sake."

[2] Sura was a major Babylonian community with a Jewish academy.

was rather in consideration of a certain woman who would heat her oven and place it at the disposal of those who wanted to bake bread, without accepting compensation.[1] *Taanith, 21b*

The merit of Abba the surgeon

100. Abba the surgeon used to be greeted daily by a *bath kol* [heavenly voice], while Abaye received such a greeting only on the eve of each Sabbath, and Raba would be greeted in this manner only on the eve of each Day of Atonement. Abaye felt unhappy about the greater distinction conferred upon Abba the surgeon. But he was told [by the heavenly voice], "The things Abba does, you cannot do."

What did Abba do that won him such esteem? First of all, when treating patients, he had a separate cubicle for men and another for women. He also had a special garment for women, which was split at various places so that he could insert his instruments at any point without embarrassing the woman. Also, he had a box outside his house, where his fee was to be deposited. Those who could afford it put money into it, while those without means would simply walk in and be seated, without the least cause for embarrassment. If a student came to him, he would accept no fee, but would give him money instead, saying, "Go and refresh yourself."

One day Abaye sent two of his disciples to Abba to observe his actions. Abba entertained them with meat and drink, and laid down mattresses for them on which they could spend the night. In the morning, the disciples picked up the mattresses and carried them to the market to sell them. There they encountered Abba, and they said to him, "Let our master estimate the worth of these." "They are worth so much and so much," he said to them. "Perhaps they are worth more," the students replied. But he answered, "I can buy them for that amount."

They then said to him, "These mattresses are yours. We took them from your house. Now, pray tell us, what did you suspect us of?" He replied, "I thought that perhaps some captives had to be ransomed, and you did not want to tell me last night what amount of money that would require, so you took the mattresses [to be sold] for that purpose."[2] They then said to him, "Now let our master take them back."

---

[1] The point here and in the preceding paragraph is that God sets great value on even the smallest meritorious deed. For various observations on dreams, see chapter 17b.

[2] Jews were sometimes taken captive and held for ransom. Payment for their ransom was regarded as one of the noblest forms of charity. See items 153 and 154. On judging others in a favorable light, see items 110 and 578.

But he answered, "No, for I had previously decided to use them [or their value] for charitable purposes, hence I cannot take them back."

Raba, in turn, felt disheartened by the greater distinction conferred upon Abaye, who heard the *bath kol* each Sabbath eve, while Raba heard it only on the Day of Atonement. But he was told in a dream, "It ought to suffice for you that your entire community is shielded from harm by virtue of your merits." *Taanith, 21b*

The merit of a humble teacher

101. Rab happened to come to a town where they had no rain, and he ordained a fast day, but no rain came. The public reader [of the prayers] went to the reading-desk [pulpit] and began to pray for rain. When he got to the sentence *He causeth the wind to blow,* a wind arose. And as soon as he recited *He causeth the rain to descend,* [1] the rain began to fall.

"What are your merits?" Rab asked him. And he replied, "I teach little children, and I treat the children of the poor just like the children of the rich. Those who cannot afford to pay I teach without remuneration. I also have fish ponds, and I entice those children who do not want to learn to do so by giving them fish to take home with them." *Taanith, 24a*

Those who win God's favor

102. R. Johanan said, "There are three persons for whose sake the Holy One sends out the crier every day [to proclaim their praise]: a bachelor who lives in a large city and does not sin [despite his anonymity and the prevailing temptations]; a poor man who restores to its owner a lost article that he has found; and a rich man who gives the tithes of his crop secretly." *Pesahim, 113a*

103. The Holy One favors the following three persons: the one who never gets angry; the one who is never drunk; and the person who never insists on revenge. *Pesahim, 113b*

---

[1] These words are from the *tefilath geshem* (prayer for rain) and are found in the Mishnah (Taanith 1:1). This formula is still recited by traditional Jews in the Amidah after the first benediction from Shemini Atzereth to Passover.

One should respect majority opinion

104. (Mishnah 5:7) On his deathbed Akabiah b. Mahalalel said to his son, "Reject the four rules I have taught you. I adhered to them because I received them from a [presumed] majority, and those who disagreed with me took their view from [what they perceived as] a majority. Both they and I have thus abided by our respective received traditions. However, you have been following the view of an individual [myself], and not of a majority. Now you should abandon my approach and embrace that of the [new] majority."[1] [See item 87, also 651.] *Eduyoth, 9b*

How to curb the tendency toward pruriency

105. Scripture states: (Isa. 33:15) [The righteous one is he that] *shutteth his eyes against looking upon evil.* R. Hiyya b. Abba said, "This refers to one who does not gaze upon women who are washing." How is this to be understood? If there is another way to pass and one does not take it, so that he may look at them, then he is wicked. But what if there is no other way, and he is compelled to pass them? R. Hiyya's statement holds true only if there is no other way to pass, and suggests that one must nonetheless manage not to look at them.[2] *Baba Bathra, 57b*

One is not to converse at length with women

106. R. Jose the Galilean was walking along the road when he met Beruriah [the wife of R. Meir], and he asked her, "Which way must I take to get to the city of Lud?" And she replied, "You Galilean fool![3] Did not our Sages teach that a man should not speak at length to a woman? You should have asked simply, 'Which is the way to Lud?'" *Erubin, 53b*

Avoiding the very appearance of evil

107. The Sages declared, "Avoid what is sinful, and even the very appearance of sinfulness."[4] *Hullin, 44b*

---

[1] The controversy between Akabiah and the Sages was as to what had been the opinion of the majority of the Sages before them.

[2] Cf. N.T., Matt. 5:28, "Whoever looketh on a woman to lust after her hath committed adultery with her already in his heart."

[3] Galileans were reputed to be inexact in their speech.

[4] This principle is known as *maras ayin* or "what the eye perceives," and applies as well in matters other than the suspicion of lewdness. The principle is that all of one's actions, at all times, should be above suspicion.

The virtue of modesty

108. It once happened that a man married a woman with a stumped hand, and he did not discover it until she died. Rabbi said, "How modest that woman must have been if even her husband did not discover the defect in her until she died." But R. Hiyya countered, "That is nothing. It is natural for a woman [to conceal such a thing]. See rather how modest her husband must have been if he did not discover it until her death!" *Sabbath, 53b*

Modesty can be carried to an extreme

109. R. Joshua used the expression, "A foolish saint." What did he mean by this? He referred to someone who sees a woman drowning but makes no effort to save her because she is not dressed.

Sotah, 21b

Judging others in a favorable light

110. He who judges others in a favorable light [and gives them the benefit of the doubt in questionable circumstances] will himself be judged favorably. It once happened that a man from upper Galilee hired himself out to an employer in the south for a period of three years. On the eve of the Day of Atonement, when his term of service was to expire, the workman said to his master, "Give me my earnings so that I may return to my wife and children."

His employer replied, "I have no money available right now." "Then give me my earnings in fruit," said the man. But his employer answered, "I have none." The hired man pleaded, "Then give me my salary in land." "I have none," said his employer. "Give it to me in cattle," the workman requested. But his employer again refused, saying, "I have none." "Pay me then with furniture," the man implored him. "I have none," was again the reply. The workman then put his bundle on his back and sadly left for home.

After the Holy Days, the employer took the hired man's wages and, in addition, three boxes—one laden with foodstuffs, another with liquors, and the third with spices—and went to his workman's home in Galilee. After they ate and drank together, the employer paid him his wages, gave him the gifts, and said to him, "When I told you that I did not have the money to pay your wages, what did you suspect?" The man said, "I thought you came across a bargain, and paid out all of your ready cash for it." "And when I said that I had no cattle, what did you think?" asked his employer. "I thought perhaps you had leased it to others, and therefore could not touch it," the workman replied.

"When I said I had no fruit, what did you suspect?" the employer continued. "I thought that you had not yet set aside the tithes," the man answered.[1] "And when I said I had no furniture, of what did you suspect me?" asked the employer. "I thought you might have pledged all of your possessions to the Temple treasury," the workman replied. Then said the employer, "I assure you that the things you have surmised come very close to the truth. I had made a pledge to give away all of my possessions because my son Hyrcanus did not want to engage in Torah study. Later on, I came to my associates in the South, and they released me from that pledge. And now, since you judged me with favor, so may God judge you with favor."[2]

Sabbath, 127b

The relativity of righteousness

111. (Gen. 6:9) *And Noah was in his generation a man righteous and whole-hearted.* According to R. Johanan, this means only in his generation, but not in others which were more righteous. According to Resh Lakish, however, if one is righteous when living among those who are wicked, he would be even more so in a more perfect generation.

Said R. Hanina, "R. Johanan's view would compare Noah to a barrel of wine placed among barrels of vinegar. The fragrance of the wine is noticed, which would not be the case if it were placed among other barrels of wine."

R. Oshia said, "Resh Lakish's view would compare Noah with a vial of perfume put in a dirty place. If its fragrance is noticed there, how much more would it be noticed if it were put in a clean place."

Sanhedrin, 108a

God is present in the virtuous deed

112. The *Shechinah* does not dwell in the midst of idleness, sadness, jocularity, levity or idle chatter, but rather in the joy derived from a virtuous deed.[3] [See also item 126.] *Pesahim, 117a*

---

[1] Untithed fruit could not be used to pay debts. On tithing, see item 131.

[2] On absolution from vows, see item 291. On judging others favorably, see items 100 and 578.

[3] For Spinoza, too, true joy lies in virtue. Associating happiness with blessedness, he declares, "Blessedness . . . is virtue itself." See Joseph Ratner, *The Philosophy of Spinoza* (New York: Modern Library, 1927), p. 375.

The virtue of influencing another to do good

113. R. Abbahu said, "He who causes another to perform a meritorious act is considered by Scripture as if he himself had done it.
Scripture states: (Exod. 17:5) *And take in thy hand thy staff, wherewith
thou smotest the river, and go.* [God speaks these words to Moses.] Did
Moses smite the river? Did not Aaron do this? This serves to teach
us that whoever causes another to do a meritorious deed is considered
by Scripture as if he himself had done it." [See also item 157.]

Sanhedrin, 99b

The worth of one truly righteous man

114. Rabbah b. bar Hana said, "The life of a single righteous person
is equal in value to the whole world." *Sanhedrin, 103b*

The righteous succeed one another

115. Mar [a Master] said, "At the death of Akiba, Rabbi was born;
at the death of Rabbi, R. Judah was born;[1] at the death of R. Judah,
Raba was born; and at the death of Raba, R. Ammi was born. This
teaches us that a righteous man does not leave the world until another
like him is born; for Scripture states: (Eccles. 1:5) *The sun also riseth,
and the sun goes down."* *Kiddushin, 72b*

The world survives because of the righteous

116. R. Hiyya b. Abba said in the name of R. Johanan, "The Holy
One saw that the righteous were few, so He placed them in every
generation; as Scripture states: (1 Sam. 2:8) *For the pillars of the earth
are the Lord's* [champions; i.e., the righteous]; *and He hath set the world
upon them."*

R. Hiyya b. Abba also said in the name of R. Johanan, "Through
the merit of one righteous man the world survives; for Scripture states
(Prov. 10:25) *But the righteous* [person] *is an everlasting foundation."*
[See also item 39.] *Yoma, 38b*

The secret thirty-six saints

117. Abaye declared, "There are [at all times] no fewer than
thirty-six righteous persons in the world who [are privileged to] greet

---

[1] Judah Nesiah was of the first generation of Palestinian Amoraim, and is not to be confused
with his grandfather, Judah HaNasi, known as Rabbi. See Gershom Bader, *The Jewish Spiritual
Heroes,* 3 vols. (New York: Pardes, 1940), 2:37.

the *Shechinah* daily; for Scripture states: (Isa. 30:18) *Happy are they who wait for Him.* [Notice that] *for Him* is expressed by the word *lo,* and the numerical value of that word is thirty-six."[1] *Sukkah, 45b; Sanhedrin, 97b*

---

[1] As noted in fn. to item 34, Hebrew letters also serve as numbers. The letters in *lo* ("for Him") are *lamed* and *vav*, representing the numerals 30 and 6. Saintly persons are to this day designated as *lamed-vavniks* ("thirty-sixers"). This concept was used as the theme of a novel by André Schwarz-Bart, *The Last of the Just*, trans. Stephen Becker (New York: Atheneum, 1960).

3

LOVE OF FELLOW MAN

IN rabbinic teaching there can be no love of God without a corresponding concern for one's fellowman. This entails extending hospitality to the wayfarer and stranger, contributing to charity, and feeling an all-embracing compassion for others.

Jews have welcomed strangers into their homes ever since Abraham, the first Jew, greeted the angels in the guise of men with food and drink (Gen. 18:1–9). The lonely were invited to join them, particularly on the Sabbath and on the eve of Passover. Indeed, the ritual for the Seder supper includes the words, "Let all who are hungry come and eat."

Contributing to charity, like extending hospitality, is commanded in Scripture. Through the centuries every Jewish community maintained a community fund (*kuppah*). This was used to feed the hungry and clothe the naked, assist transients, enable orphans to receive an education, provide dowries for brides, and assure burial plots for the dead.

In rabbinic thought, as in Scripture, concern for one's fellowman goes well beyond monetary aid. This sentiment is expressed in such words as *hesed* ("kindness"), *gemiluth hesed* ("acts of kindness") and, most strikingly, in the terms *rahamim* and *rahmanuth* ("mercy" and "compassion"), derived from the word *rehem* ("the womb") and relating all men to each other as members of one human family.

Indeed, the principle of compassion is extended to include animals as well, demonstrating the rabbinic conviction that "When we lose respect for any form of life, we diminish all life" (Albert Schweitzer).

A. HOSPITALITY

The importance of hospitality

118. R. Johanan said, "Hospitality is as great [a virtue] as attendance at a place of learning; for the Mishnah uses the words 'For hospitality and for attendance at a house of study,' putting the two on an equal plane." R. Dimi of Nehardea[1] pointed out that hospitality is even greater, for the Mishnah mentions hospitality first. *Sabbath, 127a*

119. R. Judah said in the name of Rab that hospitality is considered even greater than receiving the glory of the *Shechinah.*

Sabbath, 127a

120. R. Johanan said in the name of R. Jose b. Kisma, "A little refreshment often plays an important role, for the denial of food and drink served to alienate two peoples from the people of Israel. Scripture states: (Deut. 23:5) *An Ammonite or a Moabite shall not enter into the congregation of the Lord . . . because they met you not with bread and water on the way, when you came forth out of Egypt."*

R. Judah said in the name of Rab, "Had Jonathan supplied David with some loaves of bread, the priests of the city of Nob would not have been slain, Doeg the Edomite would not have done evil, and Saul and his three sons would not have been killed." [Jonathan had not denied food to David, but had neglected to offer it. See 1 Sam. 20–22.][2] *Sanhedrin, 103b*

Welcoming the wayfarer into our homes

121. Raphram b. Papa said, "When R. Huna used to sit down to a meal, he opened the door and exclaimed, 'Let whoever is in need enter and eat.' " *Taanith, 20b*

122. He who prolongs his stay at the table prolongs his life; perhaps a poor man will come along, and he will give him some food [thereby atoning for his sins and prolonging his life].[3]

R. Johanan and R. Eleazar both declared, "So long as the Temple was in existence, its altar used to atone for Israel [through sacrifice]. But now a man's table atones for him [when he has the needy as his guests]." *Berachoth, 55a*

---

[1] Nehardea was the site of a Babylonian Jewish academy.

[2] Judah's remark attempts to show that even an oversight may have serious results.

[3] The opening statement may also mean that eating slowly is conducive to good health. Here it is suggested that one will earn merit by doing so.

The propriety of waiting upon others

123. It once happened that R. Eliezer, R. Joshua and R. Zadok attended the wedding feast for the son of Rabban Gamaliel, and Rabban Gamaliel [a *Nasi*, head of the Sanhedrin] waited upon them. When he offered a cup of wine to R. Eliezer, the latter refused to accept it; but when he gave it to R. Joshua, he did accept it. R. Eliezer then said to R. Joshua, "Why should we be seated and have Rabban Gamaliel serve us?"

R. Joshua answered, "We find that even a greater man than he served others. Abraham was the greatest man in his generation, yet of him it is written (Gen. 18:8) *And he stood by them under the trees* [to serve them]. One might counter by saying that Abraham's visitors appeared before him as angels, but the fact is that they appeared before him as ordinary desert travelers. Why should not therefore Rabban Gamaliel Berabbi[1] wait upon us?" *Kiddushin, 32b*

B. CHARITY

Why God does not help the poor

124. We are taught in a *baraitha* that R. Meir said, "When a person asks, 'If your God loves the poor, why does He not provide for their need?' you are to answer him by saying, 'For the purpose of saving us [through our charitable deeds] from the punishment of Gehinnom.' "

Turnus Rufus [the governor of Judea] once asked R. Akiba this question, and R. Akiba answered him in that fashion. To this Turnus Rufus replied, "On the contrary; for this you deserve to be punished. I will give you a parable to show you why. Once a human king became angry with his servant, cast him into prison, and announced his desire that no one should give him either food or drink. In spite of this, someone provided for his needs. When the king became aware of it, would he not have become angry at that person? And you Israelites are called 'servants' of God [who carry out His commands]. Your Scriptures state: (Lev. 25:55) *For unto Me are the children of Israel servants.*"

R. Akiba answered, "I will offer a different parable to indicate that I am right about this. A king once became angry with his son and cast him into prison, ordering that no one should give him either food or

---

[1] A contraction of *Be Rabbi*, meaning "Distinguished Rabbi."

drink. Despite his command, someone fed him and gave him drink. When the king became aware of this, would he not have been grateful to this man [who provided for his child]? Similarly, we Israelites are called God's children; for Scripture states: (Deut. 14:1) *Ye are children of the Lord.* [Should not God then be grateful if we provide for His children?]" [See also item 31.]

The Roman governor then said to him, "You Israelites are called both 'children' and 'servants' of the Lord. When you carry out God's will you are called 'servants' of the Lord. However, [by assisting the poor] you are not carrying out God's will [for He has decreed that they shall be poor]."

Thereupon R. Akiba replied, "Scripture states: (Isa. 58:7) *Is it not* [incumbent upon you] *to deal thy bread to the hungry and bring the poor that are cast out* [of their homes by the tax collectors] *into thy house? When is it that you should bring the poor that are cast out into thy house?* [Immediately!] And this very same passage states also: *Is it not to deal thy bread to the hungry?* [Therefore, just as the poor must be given shelter in their time of need, so should they be provided with sustenance when they suffer hunger.]" *Baba Bathra, 10a*

Charity is greater than sacrifice

125. R. Eleazar said, "Giving charity is greater than offering sacrifices; for Scripture states: (Prov. 21:3) *To do righteousness* [*tzedakah:* "charity"][1] *and justice* [*mishpat*] *is more acceptable to the Lord than sacrifice."* Sukkah, 49b

Through charity we invoke God's presence

126. (Ps. 17:15) *As for me, I shall behold Thy face in righteousness* [*b'tzedek*]. R. Eleazar used to give a coin to a poor man before starting to say his prayers, quoting this verse as he did so. [See also item 112.]
Baba Bathra, 10a

The commandment to give charity outweighs all others

127. R. Assi said, "One must not fail to give at least a third part of a *shekel* each year to charity; for Scripture states: (Neh. 10:33) *And we*

---

[1] The word *tzedakah*, here translated as "righteousness," is commonly employed for "charity." The variant form *"tzedek,"* used in item 126 and similarly rendered as "righteousness," also conveys the meaning of "charity." The latter, however, is generally translated as "justice," as in Deut. 17:20.

established for ourselves commandments, to impose on ourselves the third part of a shekel every year [for charity]. Moreover, giving to charity is considered as important as fulfilling all of the other commandments combined; for Scripture states: (ibid.) *And we established for ourselves commandments, to impose on ourselves,* etc. This verse does not speak of [charity as] *a commandment,* but [refers to it] in the plural; [thus the commandment regarding charity outweighs all others]."

Baba Bathra, 9a

Even the poor are expected to contribute

128. If a man sees that his earnings are low, he should nonetheless use a part of that money for charity; and one should give more when his earnings are high. This follows from Mar Zutra's statement that even a person who receives his support from charity should give to charity. *Gittin, 7a,b*

More important than the amount is the intent

129. It matters not whether one gives much or little, as long as his heart is directed toward his heavenly Father. [See item 169.]

Shebuoth, 15a

Every little bit helps

130. (Isa. 59:17) *He put on righteousness* [*tzedakah*] *as a coat of mail.* [1] This teaches us that just as in a coat of mail one link is added to another, so in the case of charity is one coin added to another to realize a larger sum. *Baba Bathra, 9b*

The principle of tithing

131. R. Johanan said to a pupil of Resh Lakish, "Tell me the verse you studied today." And the child replied, *"Asser t'asser* [*'Thou shalt surely tithe'*],"[2] then asked, "But what does *asser t'asser* mean?" R. Johanan answered, "Give tithes, and you will become rich."[3]

The lad then asked, "How do you know this is so?" And R. Johanan said, "Go and try it [and see if it is not so]." "But is it permitted to test God?" the boy asked; "for Scripture states: (Deut. 6:16) *Ye*

---

[1] See fn. to item 125 on *tzedakah.*

[2] *Thou shalt surely tithe all the increase of thy seed* (Deut. 14:22). For a discussion of tithing, see *U.J.E.,* s.v. "Tithe."

[3] *Asser* ("to tithe") and *ashar* ("to become rich") are spelled alike.

shall not tempt [test] *the Lord thy God.*" Then R. Johanan replied, "R.
Hosea said that in all other things one is not permitted to test God,
except in the matter of tithing; for Scripture states: (Mal. 3:10)
*Bring ye all the tithes into the storehouse, that there may be provision in
My house, and probe Me but therewith, if I will not open for you the win-
dows of heaven, and pour out for you a blessing, until it be more than
enough.*"

When the lad heard this he said, "Had I come to that verse [in
my study of the Bible], I would not have needed your help, nor
would I have needed [the aid of] R. Hosea, your teacher!"

Taanith, 9a

The limits of charity

132. Mar Ukba gave away half of his wealth. How could he do this?
Did not Ilai say that in Usha it was ordained that one should not give
more than one-fifth of his money to charity? This applies only during
one's lifetime. At the approach of death there is no limit.

Kethuboth, 67b

Giving charity in secret is especially virtuous

133. R. Eleazar said, "He who gives charity in secret is greater than
Moses our Teacher;[1] for concerning Moses Scripture states: (Deut.
9:19) *For I was afraid of the anger and the indignation wherewith the Lord
was wroth.* But regarding him who gives charity secretly Scripture
states: (Prov. 21:14) *A gift in secret pacifieth anger.*" [One who gives a
gift in secret need not fear the wrath of God.] *Baba Bathra, 9b*

134. R. Hiyya b. Abba said in the name of R. Johanan, "One should
give a donation without knowing who receives it and without the
recipient knowing who gave it." How then is one to contribute to
charity? Through the charity collector. *Baba Bathra, 10b*

The noble example of King Monobaz

135. In a period of famine King Monobaz[2] distributed all of his
wealth and all that he had inherited from his parents. His brothers and
other members of his family protested, saying, "Your ancestors saved,
and they increased the wealth of their ancestors, while you are giving
away not only your own money but also the money which you have

---

[1] *Moshe Rabbenu,* a title affectionately bestowed upon Moses the Lawgiver.
[2] Monobaz, King of Adiabene, embraced Judaism in the first century C.E.

inherited." To this he replied, "My ancestors stored up treasure here below, but I store up treasure in heaven;[1] for it is written: (Ps. 85:12) *Truth will grow up out of the earth, and righteousness* [charity] *will look down from heaven.*

"My ancestors stored up treasure in a place which could be reached by human hands, but I have stored it in a place that no human hand can reach; as it is written: (Ps. 89:15) *Righteousness* [charity] *and justice are the props of Thy throne.* My ancestors stored away treasure which yielded them no interest, but I have stored away treasure which does yield interest; for it is written: (Isa. 3:10) *Say unto the righteous* [charitable] *that they have done well; for the fruit* [increment] *of their doing shall they eat.* My ancestors stored away money in their treasury, but I have stored away saved souls [lives] in my treasury; as it is written: (Prov. 11:30) *The fruit of the righteous is a tree of* [sustains] *life and the wise draweth souls unto himself* [to testify in his behalf].

"My ancestors stored up treasure for their descendants, but I have saved treasure for myself; for Scripture states: (Deut. 24:13) *And unto thee it shall be* [credited] *as righteousness before the Lord thy God* [in the heavenly accounts]. My ancestors stored up treasure for this world, but I have stored it up for the world to come; for Scripture states: (Isa. 58:8) *And before thee* [into the future world] *shall go thy righteousness* [to intercede for thee]." *Baba Bathra, 11a*

The case of R. Eleazar

136. The charity collectors used to hide when they saw Eleazar, the man of Birtha,[2] because he would give away everything he had. One day he went out to the market to buy a wedding outfit for his daughter's marriage. The charity collectors saw him, and hid themselves. However, he had seen them, so he followed them and said, "Tell me for what purpose you are collecting funds today."

They answered, "To supply wedding outfits for two orphans who are about to be married." "They have priority over my own daughter," said Eleazar, and he gave them all that he had, leaving for himself only one *zuz.* For this he bought some wheat, which he deposited in his shed. Later, his wife asked their daughter, "What did father bring you?" The daughter replied, "Whatever it was, he placed it in the

---

[1] The concept of "treasure in heaven" appears frequently in the N.T., as in Matt. 19:21 "Go and sell all that thou hast, and give to the poor, and thou shalt have treasure in heaven."

[2] Birtha is sometimes identified as Beiruth.

shed." The mother then went out to the shed, and tried to open the door, but the wheat was piled so high and the shed was so full that she could not open it.

When her husband returned from the academy, she said to him, "Come and see what your Creator did for you." When Eleazar saw what had happened he said, "All this wheat shall be given to the poor, and we shall have only a share in it equal to that of the poor."

Taanith, 24a

God reimburses the river

137. R. Joshua said, "Whoever makes it his business to give charity will be blessed with sons having wisdom and wealth." And R. Isaac added, "Whoever seeks out opportunities to engage in charity is provided by God with the means to do it." *Baba Bathra, 9b*

One's own family may be saved from want

138. R. Hiyya advised his wife, "When a poor man comes to the door, give him food so that the same may be done for your children." She exclaimed, "You are cursing them [by suggesting that they may become beggars]!" But R. Hiyya replied, "There is a wheel which revolves in this world [i.e., the wheel of fortune turns, so that the rich may become poor and vice versa]." *Sabbath, 151b*

Charity delivers us from death

139. R. Judah said, "Charity is great, for it brings the redemption nearer; for Scripture states: (Isa. 56:1) *Keep ye justice and do righteousness [tzedakah], for near is My salvation to come and My favor to be revealed* [if this is done]."

He also used to say, "Rock is hard, but iron cuts it; iron is hard, but fire softens it; fire is powerful, but water extinguishes it; water is heavy, yet the clouds carry it; the clouds are strong, but the wind scatters them; the wind is strong, yet the body endures it; the body is strong, yet fear shatters it;[1] fear is strong, but wine dispels it; wine is strong, yet sleep conquers it; death is stronger than all of these, yet righteousness [tzedakah] delivers from death; as it is written: (Prov. 10:2) *But righteousness delivers from death.*" *Baba Bathra, 10a*

140. It was said about Benjamin the Righteous, who was a treasurer of charity funds, that at one time, during a year of famine, a woman

---

[1] Psychosomatic illness is here perceived. See also items 320 and 321.

appeared before him asking for help. He told her there was nothing left in the fund. "But rabbi," she replied, "if you will not provide me with food, you will be responsible for the death of a woman and her seven children." He then aided her out of his own money.

Some time later, he became sick and was near death, when the ministering angels pleaded before God, saying, "Sovereign of the Universe, You have declared that he who saves one life is considered as one who has saved the whole world! Should then Benjamin the Righteous, who has saved the lives of a woman and her seven children, die in his prime?" And the decree was immediately revoked. It is further taught in a *baraitha* that twenty-two years were added to his life. *Baba Bathra, 11a*

Charity may deliver us from Gehinnom

141. In the academy of R. Ishmael it was taught that whoever sets aside part of his wealth and devotes it to charity is delivered from the penalty of Gehinnom. This is comparable to the case of two lambs crossing a stream, one of which is shorn and the other unshorn. The lamb which was shorn passes safely across, but the unshorn lamb does not.[1] *Gittin, 7a*

But one should not give with impure motives

142. R. Simon b. Eleazar said, "Greater is he who performs the commandments [*mitzvoth*] from love than he who is motivated by fear." *Sotah, 31a*

143. R. Johanan b. Zakkai once saw in a dream that his nephews would lose seven hundred *denars* in the current year, and he told them to give that amount to him, for distribution to charity. After doing so, they still had seventeen *denars* left. And on the eve of the Day of Atonement the tax collectors came and took these away from them.

R. Johanan said to them, "Seventeen *denars* were left for yourselves, and they were taken from you." "How do you know this?" they asked. "I saw it in my dream," came the reply. "Then why did you not tell us, so that we could have distributed the whole amount to the poor?" they asked. "Because," he replied, "I wanted you to give to charity purely for the sake of doing God's will [and not to defraud the government]." *Baba Bathra, 10a*

---

[1] Its wet wool weighs it down so that it perishes. Cf. the difficulty of the rich in entering the kingdom of God (N.T., Matt. 19:24).

Indifference to charity is equivalent to idolatry

144. R. Joshua b. Karcha said, "He who closes his eyes to [a request for] charity is considered as one who worships idols [for he worships money]." *Baba Bathra, 10a*

Public promise versus actual performance

145. R. Johanan said, "Rain is withheld because of those who publicly promise to give charity and then do not fulfill their promise; for Scripture states: (Prov. 25:14) *Like clouds and wind without rain, so is he that boasteth himself of a false gift.*"[1] *Taanith, 8b*

Accepting contributions from women

146. Charity collectors may accept contributions from women without their husbands' consent, but not in large amounts. Rabina, who was a collector of charity, was once in the city of Mehuza[2] and the women gave him golden chains and rings, which he accepted. When Rabba Tospha said to Rabina, "Are we not taught in a *baraitha* that charity collectors may not accept large gifts from women?" the latter replied, "For the people of Mehuza [who have substantial means], these are considered small contributions." *Baba Kamma, 119a*

Investigating the needs of an applicant for aid

147. R. Huna said, "If one comes to ask for food, he may be investigated [as to whether or not he is in need]; but no investigation should be made of him who asks for clothing." R. Judah, however, maintained that the contrary should be the case: no investigation may be made of an applicant for food, only of an applicant for clothing. We are taught in a *baraitha,* in support of R. Judah's opinion, "If one says, 'Clothe me,' he should be interrogated; but if one says, 'Give me food,' it must be done at once, without investigating." [The degree of human pain is the determining factor. One suffers more from hunger.] *Baba Bathra, 9a*

When one begs from door to door

148. There was a poor man who begged from door to door, and R. Papa paid no attention to him. R. Samma, the son of R. Yiba, said

---

[1] The scriptural analogy of clouds and wind without rain is extended by Johanan to mean that an unfulfilled public pledge causes heaven itself to withhold the blessing of rain.

[2] A city of trade on the Tigris River.

to R. Papa, "If you pay no attention to him, then no one will, and he may starve to death." But is there not a *baraitha* which tells us that if a man begs from door to door, the community has nothing to do with him? The *baraitha* is simply trying to tell us that he should not be given a large amount, but a small contribution should be made.

Baba Bathra, 9a

When one has means yet starves himself

149. Our rabbis taught that if one has means yet refuses to supply himself [preferring hunger], he is to be given aid as a gift, but afterwards it is to be collected from him. However, if we collect from him, may he not refuse to accept assistance again? R. Papa answered, "This rule applies only to the time after his death."

R. Simeon said, "If one has the means but refuses to support himself we are not obliged to help him." *Kethuboth, 67b*

When one has no means yet refuses charity

150. Our rabbis taught that if one has no means yet refuses to be supported by charity, he is to be given a loan, which is afterward regarded as a gift, in order that his feelings may not be hurt. So says R. Meir. Others, however, maintain that it is to be given him as a gift, and thereafter it is to be considered a loan. *Kethuboth, 67b*

Showing consideration for the life-style of the poor

151. There was a poor man in the neighborhood of Mar Ukba, to whom he used to send four hundred *zuzim* on the eve of each Day of Atonement. Once he sent it with his son, who returned with the money, saying, "He does not need it." When his father asked why he thought so, he replied, "I saw him indulging himself in costly old wine." "If he is accustomed to such things," said his father, "then he surely needs more." He thereupon doubled the amount and sent it to him. *Kethuboth, 67b*

152. A poor man once came to Raba[1] seeking aid. Raba asked him, "What do you usually eat?" "Stuffed fowl and aged wine," came the reply. "What!" said Raba, "Are you not concerned about being a burden on the community?" But the poor man answered, "I ask nothing of others, only that which the All-Merciful provides for all. This we know from a *baraitha* on the verse (Ps. 145:15) *The eyes of*

---

[1] Raba b. Joseph b. Hama of Babylonia, 280–352 C.E.

all wait for Thee [and none else], *and Thou* [alone] *givest them their food in due season.* Moreover, the verse does not say 'in their [collective] season,' but says 'in his season' [*b'ito*].[1] Thus we may infer that the Holy One provides for each person in his own time of need."

While they were talking, Raba's sister, who had not seen him in thirteen years, came to visit him, bringing with her a gift of stuffed fowl and some old wine. "What is this!" exclaimed Raba in amazement, and he said to the poor man, "I beg your pardon, my friend. Rise and eat." *Kethuboth, 67b*

Ransoming captives is the most worthy form of charity

153. Aiphra Hurmiz, the mother of King Sabur,[2] once sent a purse of *denars* to R. Joseph, with the message that this was to be used for the greatest form of charity. He deliberated as to what he should do with it. Then Abaye said to him, "Since R. Samuel stated that orphans must not be taxed [for charity], even for the ransoming of captives, it is to be inferred that ransoming prisoners is considered the noblest form of charity." *Baba Bathra, 8a*

154. Raba said to Rabba b. Mari, "Whence do the rabbis infer that redeeming captives is the greatest charity?" He answered, "From the passage (Jer. 15:2) *Such as are destined for death, to death; for the sword, to the sword; for famine, to famine; for captivity, to captivity.* For R. Johanan has pointed out that each type of death mentioned in this verse is worse than the one preceding it; as, for instance, to be killed by the sword is more severe than to die a natural death.

"One may prove this by common sense or by a passage from Scripture. By common sense, one put to death by the sword is disfigured, while he who dies naturally is not. It can also be proved by the Scriptural passage (Ps. 116:15) *Precious in the eyes of the Lord is the* [natural] *death of His pious.* Again using common sense, one who dies of hunger suffers long anguish, while the other, who dies by the sword, does not. Also, we may quote the passage (Lam. 4:9) *Happier are they that are slain by the sword than those who are slain by hunger.*

"Captivity, however, is the worst form of death, for in it all [the aforementioned sufferings] are included [i.e., the captors can resort to any of these methods]." *Baba Bathra, 8b*

---

[1] The literal meaning of the Hebrew *b'ito,* translated above as *in due season,* is "in its (or his) season (or time)." This may be construed as "in his time of need."

[2] Sabur II, King of Persia, 310–379 C.E.

Who has priority for ransom?

155. If someone is held for ransom, together with his teacher and his father, and he is able to redeem only one of them, he himself has priority over his teacher, and his teacher has priority over his father. His mother, however, would have priority over all.

A Sage has priority [to be ransomed if captured] over a king of Israel; for if a Sage dies, he is irreplaceable, but if a king of Israel dies, any son of Israel is suited for the throne. *Horayoth, 13a*

156. A certain man had a purse of money deposited with him for the ransoming of captives. He was attacked by thieves, and handed the money over to them. He was then summoned before Raba, who declared him exempt [from any charge of wrongdoing]. Said Abaye to Raba, "Was not that man rescuing himself by means of money intended for another?" But Raba replied, "There could hardly be a case more urgent than his own." [See also item 190.]

Baba Kamma, 117b

Inducing others to contribute

157. R. Eleazar said, "The collector of charity funds is to be considered more virtuous than the contributor; for Scripture states: (Isa. 32:7) *and the work of charity* [i.e., getting others to give] *shall be* [bring] *peace."* [See also item 113.] *Baba Bathra, 9a*

Alternatives to charity

158. R. Abba said in the name of R. Simeon b. Lakish, "To lend money [to the needy] is more meritorious than to give charity; and investing money [with the poor in a business venture] is the highest form of philanthropy [since it helps the individual to help himself]."[1] *Sabbath, 63a*

C. DEEDS OF LOVING-KINDNESS

The greatness of loving-kindness

159. R. Simlai declared, "The Torah begins and ends with acts of loving-kindness [*gemiluth hasadim*]. Near the beginning we read: (Gen. 3:21) *And the Lord made for Adam and his wife coats of skin and*

---

[1] Cf. Maimonides' Eight Rungs on the Ladder of Charity, in *Yad Hahazakah, Mattenoth Aniyyim,* 10:7–13.

clothed them. Toward the end we read: (Deut. 34:6) *He* [God] *buried him* [Moses] *in the valley.* "[1] *Sotah, 14a*

Why loving-kindness is greater than charity

160. Our rabbis taught that deeds of loving-kindness are greater than contributions to charity in three respects. Charity entails only one's money, while deeds of loving-kindness involve the giving of one's self. Charity is extended only to the needy, while acts of loving-kindness may be performed for the rich and poor alike [as in visiting the sick or bereaved]. Charity is only for the living, while deeds of loving-kindness can be performed for the dead as well as the living [by preparing the dead for burial or assisting at a funeral].

Sukkah, 49b

Charity must be motivated by loving-kindness

161. Whenever R. Janai saw someone give a coin to a poor man publicly he would say to him, "It would have been better if you had not given him anything, rather than give him money in public view and cause him embarrassment." *Hagigah, 5a*

162. R. Eleazar said, "Charity is rewarded only in accordance with the kindness [*hesed*] by which it is motivated; for Scripture states: (Hos. 10:12) *Sow for yourselves according to righteousness* [*tzedakah*: "charity"], *that ye may reap the fruit* [reward] *of kindness.* "[2] [See item 732.] *Sukkah, 49b*

The compassionate attitude in charity

163. R. Isaac said, "He who gives a coin to a poor man is rewarded with six blessings. But he who encourages him with friendly words is rewarded with eleven." *Baba Bathra, 9b*

164. R. Eleazar said, "When a person engages in charity with the spirit of compassion, it is as if he filled the whole world with kindness [*hesed*]." *Sukkah, 49b*

---

[1] So reads the 1962 J.P.S. Bible. The 1917 version renders this as *And he was buried. . . .* The newer translation seems more suitable here.

[2] The 1917 J.P.S. Bible translates the verse as *Sow to yourselves according to righteousness, Reap according to mercy.* The various terms expressing compassion are often translated interchangeably. For a discussion of the term here translated as "kindness," see Nelson Glueck, *'Hesed' in the Bible* (New York: Ktav, 1975).

Showing compassion for all of God's creatures

165. A calf being led to slaughter ran away from its owner, put its head under the cloak of Rabbi, and bleated with fright.[1] "Go," said Rabbi to the calf, "since you were created for this purpose." It was then declared in heaven that because he had shown no compassion he would be visited with affliction.

One day, as his maid-servant was sweeping the house, she tried to sweep away some young weasels she saw there. Rabbi, noticing what she was trying to do, said to her, "Leave them alone; for Scripture states: (Ps. 145:9) *And His mercies are over all His works.*"[2] It was thereupon decreed in heaven that because he had shown compassion for God's creatures, he would receive compassionate treatment.

Baba Metzia, 85a

One must not eat before feeding his animals

166. R. Judah said in the name of Rab, "One must not eat before feeding his animals; for Scripture states: (Deut. 11:15) *And I will give grass in thy field for thy cattle,* and then continues, *and thou shalt eat and be satisfied.*" *Berachoth, 40a; Gittin, 62a*

Letting one's servants eat first

167. There were two pious men—according to some, R. Mari and R. Phineas, the sons of R. Hisda—one of whom would allow his servant to eat before he ate, and the other, only after he himself had eaten. Elijah [the prophet] used to speak to the one who permitted his servant to eat first; but Elijah did not speak to the one who ate first himself [because he subjected his servant to unnecessary hunger].

Kethuboth, 61a

A servant should eat what his master eats

168. (Deut. 15:16) *Because he* [your servant] *is well with thee.* This refers to food and drink. It signifies that you should not eat white bread while your servant eats dark bread; you should not drink old wine while he drinks new wine; and you should not sleep on cushions while he sleeps on straw.

---

[1] It has been said that animals led to slaughter do feel fear, that this adversely affects the animal's endocrine system and may affect the person who eats its flesh. See Juliette de Bairacli Levy, "The Blessings of Being a Vegetarian," *The Health Quarterly* 3, no. 4 (1978):10.

[2] Josephus says of the Jews, "Creatures which take refuge in our houses like suppliants we are forbidden to kill" (*Contra Apionem* 2:213).

Our rabbis observed that from the foregoing we may infer that whoever acquires a Hebrew servant [or slave][1] acquires a master over himself. *Kiddushin, 22a*

Regard for men of humble callings

169. The rabbis of Jabneh[2] used to say, "I am a human being, and so is my neighbor. My work is in the city, and his work is in the field. I rise early to do my work, and he rises early to do his. Shall I say that I advance the cause of learning more than he does? We are taught that it matters not whether one offers much or little, so long as one's heart is directed toward heaven." [See also item 129.] *Berachoth, 17a*

Raising an orphan in one's home

170. He who brings up an orphan is considered by Scripture as if he had brought the child into being. R. Hanina said, "This may be inferred from the passage (Ruth 4:17) *There hath been a son born unto Naomi* [Ruth's mother-in-law]. Did Naomi actually give birth to the child? Was it not Ruth who bore him? Therefore one must deduce that while Ruth bore him, he was brought up by Naomi, and was thus referred to as hers." *Sanhedrin, 19b*

Sparing the feelings of a female orphan

171. When both a male orphan and a female orphan ask for aid, the female should receive priority because it is easier for a man to go from door to door. This is unseemly for a woman.

When a male orphan and a female orphan both apply for assistance [from the charity fund] in getting married, we must give priority to the female orphan because the embarrassment of a woman is greater than that of a man. [See also item 402.] *Kethuboth, 67a*

We must never embarrass another person publicly

172. R. Judah b. Tubia said in the name of Rab, "It is better for a man to be thrown into a fiery furnace than to bring another to shame in public." [See also item 783.] *Kethuboth, 67b; Baba Metzia, 59a*

173. Abaye asked R. Dimi, "What is the one thing that is most

---

[1] A Hebrew slave was one who sold himself for food and lodging or was sold by a court as punishment for theft. Self-enslavement was considered abhorrent (Exod. 21:6).

[2] The Jewish academy at Jabneh was established by R. Johanan b. Zakkai at the fall of Jerusalem. See item 836.

strictly observed in the West [i.e., Palestine]?" And he answered, "Taking care not to make pale the face of another [by embarrassing him]." *Baba Metzia, 58b*

Exposing another to shame is worse than adultery

174. Rabba the son of b. Hana said in the name of R. Johanan, "A man should rather commit adultery[1] than expose his fellowman to shame in public." *Baba Metzia, 58b*

It is tantamount to shedding blood

175. A disciple said in the presence of R. Nahman b. Isaac, "He who shames [literally, 'makes pale the face of'] another in public is like one who sheds blood." "Your observation is correct," said R. Nahman, "for the blood of the individual who is publicly embarrassed is drained from his face, and he becomes pale." *Baba Metzia, 58b*

Regard for the feelings of penitents and proselytes

176. If a person has repented, you must not remind him of his previous deeds. If one is a descendant of proselytes [to Judaism], you must not say to him, "Remember the ways of your ancestors." If a prospective proselyte comes to you with the intention of studying Torah, you must not say to him, "The mouth that has eaten animal carcasses [*nebeloth terefoth*][2] wants to utter the words of the Torah, spoken by the mouth of the Almighty!"

R. Judah added, "One must not even inquire about the price of an article if he has no money to buy it [out of consideration for the feelings of the seller]." *Baba Metzia, 58b*

Consideration for another in his moment of anger

177. R. Johanan said in the name of R. Jose, "Whence do we learn that we must not try to appease a man at the moment of his anger? Scripture states: (Exod. 33:14) *My presence shall go before thee, and I shall give thee rest.* The Holy One [Who had been angry] said to Moses, 'Wait until My anger subsides, and I shall give thee rest!' " [God is depicted as asking Moses to be tolerant of His anger.] *Berachoth, 7a*

---

[1] Literally, cohabit with a woman whose prior divorce is of doubtful validity.

[2] The eating of animals that have died of themselves or have been torn by beasts is forbidden in Lev. 11:39, 40. See also item 74 and fn. For further comments on proselytes to Judaism, see chapter 17g.

Making allowance for what one says in his distress

178. (Job 24:35) *Job hath spoken without knowledge, and his words are without understanding.* Raba said, "From this it may be inferred that a man is not held accountable for what he says in his distress." [The passage says *without understanding* but not "with wickedness."]

Baba Bathra, 16b

Avoiding embarrassing a teacher

179. R. Hiyya said to Rab, "Did I not tell you that when Rabbi is engaged with one tractate, you must not ask him about a matter discussed in another tractate for he may not have the subject matter in mind? If Rabbi were not a great man, you could have caused him embarrassment for he could have given you an answer which might not be correct. In this instance, he gave you the correct answer [but this does not alter the principle]." *Sabbath, 3b*

180. A pupil of R. Janai who used to ask questions of the latter whenever he lectured would refrain from doing so on a Sabbath or on a holiday [because of the many strangers present, and his concern that he might embarrass R. Janai if his questions were difficult to answer]. *Moed Katan, 5a*

Shielding others from shame

181. It once happened that when Rabbi was lecturing, he detected the odor of garlic, and he said, "Whoever has eaten garlic, please leave." Thereupon R. Hiyya arose and left. Seeing R. Hiyya leave, everyone else did the same.

The next day, R. Simeon, the son of Rabbi, met R. Hiyya and asked him, "Was it really you who annoyed my father [by eating garlic] yesterday?" And he answered, "God forbid! Such a thing I would never do. [I merely walked out to ward off disgrace from someone else, and the others walked out to shield me]." *Sanhedrin, 11a*

That one shame not others nor be put to shame

182. When R. Simeon b. Halafta took leave of Rabbi, Rabbi said to his son, "Go along with him that he may give you his blessing." He did so, and R. Simeon pronounced upon him the blessing, "May it be God's will that you shall not cause shame to others, and that others may not cause you shame." When Rabbi's son returned home, his father asked him, "What did he say to you?" And he replied, "R. Simeon did not bless me, but merely counselled me."

When he told his father what R. Simeon had said, his father replied, "That is indeed a blessing. It is the blessing with which the Holy One blessed Israel twice over; for Scripture states: (Joel 2:26, 27) *And ye shall eat and be satisfied, and shall praise the name of the Lord your God. . . . And My people shall never be put to shame. And ye shall know that I am in the midst of Israel, and that I am the Lord your God, and there is none else; and My people shall never be put to shame.*" [The last eight words are said twice.] *Moed Katan, 9b*

Compassionate concern for the sick

183. R. Aha b. Hanina said, "Whoever visits a sick person removes one-sixtieth of his illness [or pain]." *Nedarim, 39b*

184. R. Dimi said, "Whoever visits a sick person helps him to recover; and whoever does not, hastens his death." *Nedarim, 40a*

185. R. Kahana said, "When one of R. Akiba's disciples was ill, none of the Sages went to visit him. But R. Akiba did visit him, and because he swept the room and sprinkled water on the floor the sick man said to him, 'You have restored me to life.' Thereafter R. Akiba preached, 'Whoever does not visit the sick is like one who sheds blood [by hastening his death].'" *Nedarim, 40a*

186. R. Judah said in the name of Samuel, "Whoever visits a sick person will be saved from the judgment of Gehinnom." *Nedarim, 40a*

When to visit the sick

187. R. Shesheth, the son of R. Idi, said, "One should not visit a sick person during the first three hours of the day nor during the last three hours of the day so that he may not stop praying for divine mercy. During the first three hours of the day, a sick person feels better [and the visitor may think that he is already well]; and during the last three hours of the day he always feels worse [so that prayer may seem to be futile]." *Nedarim, 40a*

God shows mercy to the merciful

188. Rabban Gamaliel the Great said, "What do the words (Deut. 13:18) *and* [He] *will show thee mercy* [*rahamim*], *and will have compassion upon thee* [*v'rihamhah*] mean?[1] These words mean that whoever

---

[1] The first clause reads *v'nathan l'chah rahamim* ("and will give thee mercy"). Gamaliel interprets the entire statement as "God will grant you [the capacity to exercise] mercy, and [if you are merciful] He will have mercy upon you."

shows mercy to others is shown mercy from heaven; and he who does not show compassion [*rahamim*] toward others is not shown compassion from heaven." *Sabbath, 151b*

Examples of truly compassionate conduct

189. Elijah the Prophet at times appeared before R. Beroka of Hazar when R. Beroka was in the marketplace of Be-Lepht.[1] One day he asked Elijah whether he saw anyone there who would have a share in eternal life, and Elijah answered, "No." But then along came a man wearing black shoes and on whose garments no show-fringes were attached.[2] "That man will have a share in the Hereafter," said Elijah.

R. Beroka called out to the man, but he refused to draw near. R. Beroka then went up to him and asked him his occupation. The man replied, "I have no time today. Come back tomorrow." The next day R. Beroka again asked him about his occupation, and the man answered, "I am the warden of a prison. I keep the men and women in separate quarters, with my own bed in between. I sleep alone, and take care that no unseemly acts are committed. If there is a daughter of Israel upon whom lustful eyes are cast, I do my best to save her, even at great personal risk."

R. Beroka then asked the man, "Why do you wear black shoes?" "Because I mourn over Jerusalem," he answered. "And why are your garments without fringes?" asked R. Beroka. "So that I will not be recognized as a Jew; for thus, if I hear of any plot against my coreligionists, I can inform the rabbis so that they may pray to God to avert the impending disaster," came the reply.

"And yesterday, when I asked what your occupation was, why did you tell me to come back today?" asked R. Beroka. "Because," answered the man, "I had heard talk about actions to be taken against the Jews, and I hastened to inform the rabbis so that they could pray to God for mercy to annul the evil decree."

Just then two other men passed by, and Elijah said to R. Beroka, "These two shall also have a share in the World to Come." R. Beroka then approached them and asked, "What is your occupation?" "Our occupation," they replied, "is to cheer and comfort all who are cast down, and when we see men quarreling, we try to restore peace between them." *Taanith, 22a*

---

[1] Hazar is Huzistan, a province of Persia (Iran). Be-Lepht is the capital of Huzistan.
[2] Jews were commanded to wear show-fringes (Num. 15:38).

How far should compassion for others be carried?

190. There is a *baraitha* concerning two persons who are on the road together, one of whom has a container of water sufficient to sustain only one person until he can reach an inhabited place. If both drink of it, both would die before reaching a village.[1]

B. Paturah said that in such a situation it is better that both should drink and die than that one should witness the death of the other. But R. Akiba disagreed. He maintained that the words (Lev. 25:7) *That thy brother may live with thee* [not by himself] mean that one's own life has preference over that of another. [*With thee* implies that your life comes first, and his right to life is assured only after yours. See also item 156.] *Baba Metzia, 62a*

---

[1] The problem presented here confronts only the possessor of the container of water. Since both must die if the water is shared between them, and since one life is not here said to be more valuable than the other, Akiba's contention that the possessor of the water should drink it would appear to be valid.

4

LIVELIHOOD AND SUSTENANCE

ALTHOUGH they were men of learning, the rabbis of the Talmudic period had not yet become an established professional class, supported by a community or congregation. That development was to come much later. Some of the rabbis of the Talmud were blacksmiths, carpenters or shoemakers by trade; others engaged in business. As rabbis, sensitive to moral issues, they were of course concerned with the ethics of the marketplace. But as heads of families, who themselves had to earn a living, their interest in the problems of livelihood and sustenance was more than merely academic, and rabbinic observations on these matters were often born of experience.

At times the rabbis link poverty with piety, but they do not regard poverty as a blessing, as has often been the case in more ascetic faiths. In Hebrew, the very term for poverty *(oni)* means also "misery" or "affliction," and the rabbis are well aware of the suffering engendered by poverty, stressing the importance of charity, as we have seen. While they indicate that undue anxiety about a livelihood reflects a lack of trust in God, Who provides for all His creatures, they extol work as a virtue, declaring that no form of work is degrading and that all work is honorable.

The rabbinic belief in the dignity of labor is far removed from the notion that work is a curse imposed upon Adam for his disobedience to God. Recognition of the worth of the individual, regardless of his occupation, is rather remarkable at a time when societies were so largely divided into masters and slaves. The rabbis' concern for the protection of the workman, their warnings against speculation in grain, their condemnation of usury, their insistence upon the practice of fair trade and protection of the consumer against fraud and deceit are of no less importance in our own time than they were in the time of the Talmud.

A. WORK AS A DUTY

Poverty is not praiseworthy

191. Phineas b. Hama said, "Poverty in a home is more painful than fifty lashes." *Baba Bathra, 116a*

Concern about a livelihood can be debilitating

192. Ulla said, "Anxiety about a livelihood [adversely] affects the memory, even with regard to the words of the Torah, and makes an individual forget what he has studied." Rabba added the comment, "If, however, one occupies himself with the study of the Torah for its own sake [i.e., out of love for the Torah], this is not so."[1]

Sanhedrin, 26b

It is sad when one must depend upon others

193. R. Nathan b. Abba said in the name of Rab, "If one is dependent on the table of his neighbor, the whole world is dark for him; as Scripture states: (Job 15:23) *He wandereth abroad for bread,* [asking] *'Where is it?' He knoweth that there is at hand the day of darkness."* To this R. Hisda added, "His very life is no life at all." *Betzah, 32b*

194. There are three types of persons whose lives are not worth living: the person who depends on his neighbor's table; the person who is dominated by his wife; and the man who is beset by constant bodily suffering. *Betzah, 32b*

God provides for all His creatures

195. R. Simeon b. Eleazar declared, "I have never since my earliest days seen a deer drying figs in the field, a lion carrying bundles, or a fox acting as a storekeeper. These creatures, who were only created to serve me, somehow manage to take care of their needs. And if they manage to sustain themselves without trouble, how much more should I be able to do so, since I was put on earth to serve my Creator!"[2] *Kiddushin, 82b*

---

[1] Since the motivation is stronger, the learning lasts longer. R. Eleazar b. Azariah goes even further than Ulla when he says, "If there is no food, there is no learning" (Mishnah Aboth 3:17).

[2] It is hard to see how the lion or fox serves man. What R. Simon is saying is that man is their master or superior, and if they can find ways to survive, so can he. The belief that all of creation was but prelude to the creation of man is of course Biblical, stemming from the opening chapters of Genesis. "Consider the ravens: for they neither sow nor reap" Cf. N.T., Luke 12:24.

He also provides for our special needs

196. R. Tahlipha, the brother of Rabanai of Huzanah,[1] taught that provision is made in heaven for all of the necessities of life [for a full year ahead] during the ten days between Rosh Hashanah and Yom Kippur, with the exception of one's expenditures for the proper observance of the Sabbath and for the education of one's children. For these two purposes, one who spends little is granted little, while one who spends much is granted a large allocation.[2]

Betzah, 15b

We must have faith in God's goodness

197. We are taught in a *baraitha* that R. Eliezer the Great[3] declared, "Whoever has bread in his basket [for today] and says, 'What shall I eat tomorrow?' is to be regarded as a person who is lacking in faith." *Sotah, 48b*

However, it is ordained that man must work

198. R. Joshua b. Levi said, "When the Holy One informed Adam (Gen. 3:18) *Thorns and thistles shall it* [the earth] *bring forth to thee,* Adam's eyes filled with tears, and Adam said to the Holy One, 'Sovereign of the Universe! Am I and my ass to feed in the same manger [i.e., eat the same food]?' However, when God added the words (Gen. 3:19) *By the sweat of thy brow shalt thou eat bread* [and not straw], Adam's mind was set at ease [since man's preeminence over the beast was thus confirmed]." *Pesahim, 118a*

We all benefit from the work of others

199. Ben Zoma said, "Think how much labor Adam, the first man, had to perform in order that he might have bread to eat! He was obliged to plough, sow, reap, bind [the wheat] into sheaves, thresh it, winnow it, grind it, sieve it, knead it and bake it. Only after all this labor was he able to eat. Yet I arise in the morning and find everything done for me.

"And how much more work did Adam have to do in order to have clothes to wear! He had to shear [the sheep], wash [the wool], comb

---

[1] Huzistan, in Persia (Iran).

[2] God does not fix in advance the sums we are to spend for these two purposes because He wants us to recognize their value and spend for these purposes freely without fear.

[3] Eliezer b. Hyrcanus, who lived in the latter part of the first century, was a pupil of Johanan b. Zakkai and teacher of Akiba.

it, spin it and weave it to be able to make a garment for himself. Yet I get up in the morning and find that this is already done for me. Moreover, all kinds of tradesmen come quite early to my door, so that when I wake up I find all of their wares provided for me!"[1]

Berachoth, 58a

It is good for a man to engage in work

200. R. Hiyya b. Ammi commented in the name of Ulla on the verse (Ps. 128:2) *When thou eatest* [the product of] *the labor of thy hands, happy shalt thou be, and it shall be well with thee.* He declared that *happy shalt thou be* refers to this world, while *and it shall be well with thee* refers to the World to Come. *Berachoth, 8a*

Labor is praiseworthy

201. R. Meir said, "How great is labor! If a man steals an ox, thereby preventing it from laboring, the thief pays a fivefold penalty. If he steals a sheep, which does not perform any work, he pays only a fourfold penalty."

R. Johanan b. Zakkai said, "How great a thing is human dignity! For stealing an ox, which walks by itself, the thief pays a fivefold penalty; but if he steals a sheep, for which he must humiliate himself by carrying it on his shoulders, he pays only a fourfold penalty." [See Exod. 21:37.] *Baba Kamma, 79b*

Work honors the workman

202. Whenever he went to the house of study, R. Judah would carry a pail[2] and say, "Work is great for it honors the workman."

Nedarim, 49b

One must do his work diligently

203. Our rabbis taught that four things are to be done with diligence: study of the Torah, good deeds, prayer and the performance of one's worldly occupation. [See also item 214.]

Berachoth, 32b

---

[1] Just as others' work enables us to live more comfortably, so must we work to enrich the lives of others. It is interesting that the Hebrew word for work *(avodah)* is the same as the word for worship. So too is the English word "service" or "services" used for both.

[2] It has been suggested that besides symbolizing work, the pail may have served as a seat at lectures.

All work is honorable

204. R. Zutra b. Tobiah said in the name of Rab, "What does the verse (Eccles. 3:11) *He hath made everything beautiful in its time* mean? This serves to teach us that the Holy One makes every occupation agreeable in the eyes of those who follow it." *Berachoth, 43b*

205. Rab said to Kahana, "Flay [dress] a carcass in the street [to earn a living] and say not, 'I am a noble priest [to whom work is unbecoming].'" *Baba Bathra, 110a; Pesahim, 113a*

All occupations are useful, but . . . .

206. We are taught in a *baraitha* that Rabbi [Judah HaNasi, compiler of the Mishnah] stated, "There is no occupation which does not have its usefulness. However, fortunate is he whose parents are engaged in a praiseworthy pursuit, and woe unto him whose parents are engaged in an unworthy occupation. The world requires both perfumers and tanners, but fortunate is he who works with perfumes, while this is not true for those who work in tanneries." *Kiddushin, 82b*

Observations on several vocations

207. (Mishnah) Abba Guryon of Tsadian said, "A man should not train his son to be a mule-driver, camel-driver, waggoner, sailor or storekeeper, for these occupations are associated with robbery [fraud]."

R. Judah quoted him [Abba Guryon] as saying, "Most mule-drivers are wicked, while camel-drivers are generally worthy men [for they travel through the desert and have time to meditate]. The majority of seamen are pious [because they are exposed to daily peril, which turns their thoughts to God]. As for doctors, even the best of them are destined for Gehinnom [because they experiment with their patients]."[1] *Kiddushin, 82a*

208. R. Kapara declared, "One should teach his son a vocation that is clean and easy." What sort of work is that? R. Judah said, "Needlework."[2] *Kiddushin, 82a*

209. R. Eleazar said, "There is no poorer occupation than farming." He once noticed a man ploughing a field in its width and

---

[1] Some of the rabbis were themselves physicians. This remark is obviously ironic, recognizing their limitations.

[2] Over the centuries, in periods when the safety of the Jews was not always assured, needlework served as a highly portable vocation. Farming (item 209) did not lend itself to easy mobility, and Jews were often forbidden to own land by governmental edict.

remarked, "Even if you were to plough the field lengthwise as well [i.e., over and over again], engaging in business would yield greater profit." *Yebamoth, 63a*

B. BUSINESS ETHICS

Usury is condemned

210. R. Simeon b. Eleazar declared, "Whoever has money and lends it to another without interest, of him Scripture states: (Ps. 15:5) *He that putteth not out his money to usury*[1] . . . *shall never be moved.* From this we learn that if a man lends his money to another on interest his possessions will be [re]moved." *Baba Metzia, 71a*

Storing up food for speculation is castigated

211. People who store up food [to sell later at higher prices], as well as usurers and those who give false measure, are those referred to as saying, (Amos 8:5) *When will the new moon be gone, that we may sell provisions, and that we may open the corn warehouses, making the ephah* [a measure] *small and increasing the shekel* [price], *and cheating with deceitful scales?* *Baba Bathra, 90b*

An employer must be considerate of his workmen

212. The porters engaged by Rabbah b. bar Hanah [negligently] broke a cask of wine belonging to him and as a penalty he took their coats from them. They thereupon complained to Rab, who ordered him to restore their garments. He asked, "Is that the law?" And Rab replied, "It is; for Scripture states: (Prov. 2:20) *That thou mayest walk in the way of good men.*"[2] Rabbah then returned their coats.

The laborers said to him, "We are poor, and have worked all day and are hungry. We are penniless." And Rab said to Rabbah, "Go and pay them their wages." He thereupon asked, "Is that the law?" and Rab answered, "Yes; for Scripture adds: (ibid.) *And keep the paths of the righteous.*" *Baba Metzia, 83a*

---

[1] In the Bible the term "usury" is understood to mean any interest on a loan, whether in money or in wheat or in any other commodity. Modern usage has redefined the term to mean an unlawful rate of interest. The Israelites were commanded in Exod. 22:24 to take no interest. Free loan associations have long been a part of Jewish communal life.

[2] Good men do not demand strict justice.

A workman's wages must be paid promptly

213. Our rabbis taught that whoever defers paying the wages of a hired laborer transgresses five commandments of the Torah: (Lev. 19:13) *Thou shalt not oppress thy neighbor, neither shalt thou rob him*; (Deut. 24:14) *Thou shalt not oppress a hired servant that is poor and needy*; (Lev. 19:13) *The wages of a hired servant shall not abide with thee all night until the morning*; (Deut. 24:15) *In his day shalt thou give him his hire*; and (ibid.) *Neither shall the sun go down upon it. Baba Metzia, 111a*

The workman must also be considerate of his employer

214. R. Meir said, "Whoever disregards the instructions of his employer is considered a robber." [See also item 203.]

Baba Metzia, 78a,b

On the practice of fair trade

215. (Mishnah) R. Judah said, "A shopkeeper must not give children dainties of parched corn or nuts, for he [thereby] entices them to buy [everything] at his place [which constitutes unfair competition]." The Sages, however, permit this. R. Judah also prohibits lowering prices for the above reason, but the Sages say that one who does so is to be remembered for good. *Baba Metzia, 60a*

216. (Mishnah) Abba Saul said, "A shopkeeper must not remove the shells of beans in order to raise the price above their cost in the shells." The Sages permit this, for the buyer usually knows why there is a difference in their price. But they agree that one must not remove the shells at the top of the measure only, for this deceives the eye [of the purchaser]. *Baba Metzia, 60a*

217. It is not permitted to embellish men [slaves], animals or vessels in order to sell them at a higher price. *Baba Metzia, 60a*

Using correct weights and measures

218. In the verse (Lev. 19:35) *Ye shall do no unrighteousness in judgment, in meteyard* [*midah,* a lineal measurement], *in weight, or in measure* [*mesurah,* a liquid measure], the word *meteyard* means real estate. One should not measure land with the same rope for two heirs, doing so for one in the summer and for the other in the winter [for the rope shrinks in the winter]. *In weight* means that one should not keep the weight in salt [which makes it heavier]. *Or in measure* means that one should not fill up a liquid measure in a manner producing foam.

Baba Metzia, 61b

219. R. Judah of Sura elaborated on (Deut. 25:14) *Thou shalt not have in thy house diverse measures*, and explained that this was in order to prevent the *use* of diverse measures. As to (Deut. 25:13) *Thou shalt not have in thy bag diverse weights*, this too was to avoid the use of diverse weights. And he added that if one follows the admonition (Deut. 25:15) *A perfect and just weight shalt thou have,* and also *a perfect and just measure shalt thou have*, he will be rewarded with prosperity.

Baba Bathra, 89a

220. Concerning the matter of weights and measures, Rabban Johanan b. Zakkai said, "It is painful for me to speak of this, and it is painful for me not to speak of it. It is painful to speak of the art of measuring, for this may serve as an aid to swindlers. It is [also] painful not to speak of it, for then swindlers would say that the rabbis know nothing about their [the swindlers'] profession [and would take unfair advantage of others]."

Did R. Johanan then speak of it or not? Samuel b. R. Isaac said, "He did, on the basis of the passage (Hos. 15:10) *For righteous are the ways of the Lord, and the just shall walk in them, but transgressors will stumble through them.*" [Swindlers will ultimately be caught in their own nets.]

Baba Bathra, 89a,b

Heaping or levelling a dry measure

221. Whence may it be deduced that one must not make the measure level where the custom is to heap it, nor heap the measure where the custom is to level it? From the passage (Deut. 25:15) *A perfect and just measure shalt thou have.*

Whence is it to be derived that where the custom is to heap the measure, if one says, "I will make it level and reduce the price," he must not be permitted to do so? From the verse (ibid.) *A perfect and just measure shalt thou have.* Baba Bathra, 89a

222. The levelling-stick must not be thick at one end and slender at the other, as this permits of cheating. Also, one must not level the measure with a single, rapid stroke, since this would be of advantage to the buyer and a disadvantage to the seller. Nor should one do the levelling slowly and repeatedly, for this constitutes a disadvantage to the buyer and a benefit for the seller. *Baba Bathra, 89b*

Appointing commissioners of weights and measures

223. Our rabbis taught (Deut. 25:13,14) *Thou shalt not have in thy bag diverse weights. . . . in thy house diverse measures* implies that weights-

and-measures commissioners should be appointed to supervise the markets. But this does not apply to fixing prices [since prices are not mentioned]. The Exilarchs once appointed commissioners for measures and prices. Thereupon Samuel said to Karna, "Go and issue instructions that commissioners are to be appointed only for weights and measures, but not for fixing prices."[1]

Karna, however, instructed that commissioners should be appointed not only to supervise weights and measures but also to fix prices. Samuel scolded him for this. But Karna did so in accordance with the view of Rami b. Hama, who said in the name of R. Isaac, "Supervisors should be appointed for weights and measures, and to fix prices, because of potential swindlers."

Baba Bathra, 89a

Further comment on dishonest business practice

224. R. Johanan said, "He who robs [cheats] his fellowman[2] of even that which is worth but a single coin is like one who has robbed him of his life; for Scripture states: (Prov. 1:19) *So are the ways of everyone who is greedy for gain; it takes away the life of the* [defrauded] *owners thereof.*"[3] *Baba Kamma, 119a*

225. We are taught in a *baraitha* that R. Eliezer b. Jacob said, "If one steals a measure of wheat, grinds it, kneads it, bakes it, and separates the dough, what blessing should he say over it?[4] He cannot recite a blessing over it or he blasphemes. Of such actions Scripture states: (Ps. 10:3) *And the covetous vaunteth himself though he contemn the Lord* [i.e., the robber who utters a blessing over ill-gotten gain despises God]." *Baba Kamma 94a*

226. R. Johanan said, "How grievous is the act of robbery! The generation of the flood committed many offenses, yet they were not doomed until they turned to robbery; for Scripture states: (Gen. 6:13) *the earth is filled with extortion* [*hamas*][5] *through them;* [therefore] *I will destroy them with the earth.*" *Sanhedrin, 108a*

---

[1] While Samuel defends the principle of free competition, the view of Rami b. Hama (see next paragraph) may apply to monopolies and public utilities in our day.

[2] This applies to non-Jews as well as Jews. See item 70.

[3] The word *life* is here understood as "livelihood."

[4] See Num. 15:21. When the Temple was destroyed, the custom survived of burning a piece of the dough and reciting a blessing. But a blessing over something stolen is an affront to God.

[5] The word *hamas* may mean "extortion" or "violence." The latter term appears in the J.P.S. 1917 Bible translation; the 1962 translation offers "lawlessness."

227. Raba said, "Jerusalem was destroyed because honest men ceased therein." [See also item 667.] *Sabbath, 119b*

Leadership as a source of personal profit

228. R. Nehilai b. Ide said in the name of Samuel, "After a man is appointed administrator of a community, he gets rich. When Saul first took a census of Israel, Scripture states: (1 Sam. 11:8) *And he counted them* with pebbles [*b'bezek*].[1] However, when he became king [and took a second census] we read: (1 Sam. 15:4) *And Saul summoned the people and numbered them in Telaim* ['with sheep']."[2] *Yoma, 22b*

Let the seller beware

229. We are taught in a *baraitha* that a man should not sell anyone shoes made from the hide of an animal that died by itself, representing them as being made of the hide of a slaughtered animal, for two reasons. First, because the seller thereby deceives the buyer [for the hide of a diseased animal may not be as durable as that of a slaughtered animal]. Second, there is an element of danger involved [for the animal may have died from a disease which could endanger the life of the one wearing shoes made from its hide]. *Hullin, 94a*

Human rights versus property rights

230. R. Giddel was negotiating for the purchase of a parcel of land when R. Abba went ahead and bought it. Thereupon R. Giddel lodged a complaint against him with R. Zera, who delegated it to R. Isaac Nappaha ["the smith"]. The latter said to R. Giddel, "Wait until R. Abba comes up [to Jerusalem] during the festival and we will discuss it with him." When R. Abba did come up, R. Isaac said to him, "If a poor man is considering the purchase of a cake, and someone else in the meanwhile comes along and buys it, what would be your judgment?" R. Abba replied, "I would call that man wicked."

"Why then did the Master [R. Abba] do such a thing to R. Giddel?" asked R. Isaac. "I did not know [about his intentions]," said R. Abba.

---

[1] The term *b'bezek*, rendered "in Bezek" in the J.P.S. 1917 Bible translation, may be read as "with pebbles" or "with shards." That would be required in this instance.

[2] The word *telaim* is not translated in the J.P.S. 1917 Bible but appears in capitalized form to denote a place. However, the word can be taken to mean "sheep," and should be so translated here. See item 893 where *telaim* can be rendered only as "sheep." See also item 614 regarding the restriction against counting the Jewish people.

"But now that you do know, let the Master turn the property over to him," R. Isaac replied. But R. Abba answered, "I cannot agree to sell it to him since this is the first such purchase [which I have ever made] and it would be inauspicious for my future transactions [if I do so without a profit]. However, if he will accept it as a gift, he may have it."

[The upshot of the matter was that] R. Giddel did not take possession of the property; for Scripture states: (Prov. 15:27) *But he that hateth gifts shall live.* [1] Nor did R. Abba take possession of it because R. Giddel had originally negotiated for it. Since neither took possession, the field became known as "the field of the rabbis."[2]

Kiddushin, 59a

C. MONEY MANAGEMENT

How to lose money quickly

231. R. Johanan said, "If one's father has bequeathed him a large sum of money and he is eager to lose it, he should dress in fine linen garments, use costly glass utensils and hire laborers without supervising them." "Dress in fine linens" refers to Roman linen garments [expensive and easily soiled]; "costly glass utensils" refers to cut glass; and "hire laborers without supervising them" refers to those who plough with oxen, capable of doing extensive damage.

Baba Metzia, 29b

Lending money without witnesses

232. R. Judah said in the name of Rab, "He who lends money to anyone without witnesses transgresses the Biblical commandment (Lev. 19:14) *Nor put a stumbling-block* [temptation] *before the* [morally] *blind.*" [The borrower may succumb to moral blindness and deny the loan, in which case the lender will be guilty of having caused him to transgress.] *Baba Metzia, 75b*

---

[1] The cited verse deals with accepting bribes.

[2] This narrative is somewhat parallel to one that is sometimes titled The Field of Brotherly Love. It deals with two brothers, one married and with a family, the other single and poor, who live some distance apart. On a moonlit night following the harvest, the married brother puts a sack of produce on his shoulder to carry to the house of the one who is single and poor. The latter, thinking of his brother with a large family to feed, does the same. They meet in an open field and embrace one another, and the field is subsequently referred to as "the field of brotherly love."

Those who get into financial difficulties

233. The following three persons cry for help but are not helped: he who lends money without witnesses; he who buys a master over himself; and he who is ruled by his wife. "He who buys a master over himself" refers to one who assigns his possessions to his children while he is still alive [for he becomes their servant].[1]

Others include among those whose cries for help are not heeded the person who suffers [from want] in one community and makes no effort to improve his lot by moving to another.

Baba Metzia, 75b

Why property deteriorates

234. Rabba said, "Three things cause one's property to deteriorate: not paying the wages of laborers on time; not paying laborers adequately; and casting off responsibility [for supervising them] from oneself and placing it upon others." *Gittin, 35a*

How money should be handled

235. R. Isaac said, "A man should always keep his money ready at hand; as Scripture states: (Deut. 14:25) *And bind up the money in thy hand.* This means that though the money is bound up it should nonetheless be at hand [to take advantage of a bargain]."

R. Isaac also said, "A man should always divide his money into three parts. He should invest one part in real estate and the second in business, and the third should always remain accessible."

Baba Metzia, 42a

Using one's money wisely

236. R. Avira said in the name of R. Ammi, and at other times in the name of R. Assi, "What does the verse (Ps. 112:5) *Well is it with the man who dealeth graciously, who ordereth his affairs rightfully* mean? This means that a man should spend for eating and drinking less than his means permit; should clothe himself according to his means; but should honor his wife and children beyond his means, for they depend upon him while he depends upon Him who spoke and the universe came into being." *Hullin, 84b*

---

[1] This is sometimes applied to one who acquires an indentured servant, who must be given excellent treatment. See items 167 and 168.

Living up to our means

237. Rab said to R. Hamnuna, "My son, if you have the means, then live in accordance with them [literally, 'do good to yourself']; for there is no enjoyment of them in *sheol* ['the grave'], and death does not linger [but may come suddenly]. Should you be tempted to reply, 'I shall leave the money for my children,' who will tell you [what becomes of it when you are] in the grave? Children are [as unpredictable] as the flowers of the field; some blossom while others fade."[1] *Erubin, 54a*

Contributing to scholarly endeavor

238. R. Johanan said, "Whoever puts the profits of business into the purse of a scholar [by contributing to his support] will be rewarded with the privilege of sitting in the Academy on High." *Pesahim, 53b*

Depending on the income of a wife

239. Our rabbis taught, "Whoever depends upon the earnings of his wife or upon the proceeds of a hand-mill will never perceive any sign of blessing." "The earnings of his wife" refers [only] to a woman who goes about with a pair of scales for hire. Regarding the hand-mill, this is only meant if one hires it out to others. If he is engaged in the use of the hand-mill himself, or if his wife is actually engaged in business, he [may depend on the earnings of the hand-mill and] may even be proud of his wife; for Scripture states: (Prov. 31:24) *Fine tunics she maketh, and selleth them.* [2] *Pesahim, 50b*

Defining wealth

240. Our rabbis asked, "Who is to be considered rich?" R. Meir answered, "Whoever enjoys his riches [whether great or small]."[3] R. Akiba said, "He who has a wife who is becoming in all her actions."[4] *Sabbath, 25b*

---

[1] Rab's words parallel observations found in the Book of Ben Sirah, an apocryphal book also called Ecclesiasticus. Cf. Ecclus. 14:11ff. See also introduction to chapter 16 and item 936.

[2] Prov. 31, an ode to "A woman of valour," lauds a woman who engages in business activities as a source of income. While a woman's going about with a pair of scales for hire may be embarrassing for a wife, the objection is no stronger than that against a man's hiring out a hand-mill to others. These were considered poor ways to earn money.

[3] Cf. (Pirke Aboth 4:1) "Who is rich? He who rejoices in his lot." Note that there is no real objection to wealth in either case. The emphasis is on the enjoyment of what we have. See also item 237.

[4] Rabbi Akiba had a very devoted wife, who made it possible for him to achieve greatness.

5

CARE OF THE BODY

RABBINIC Judaism does not glorify the human body by extoling martial arts and athletic contests. Nor does it advocate indulgence of the body's appetites. This may be due in part to the revulsion of the rabbis against the hedonistic practices of the Romans and other ancient cultures. But the rabbis also reject the opposite temptation: the denigration of the body and its demands upon us.

Like Scripture itself in its concern for the hungry, detailed dietary laws and standards of sexual behavior, the rabbis are not insensitive to man's physical nature and bodily welfare. They regard the human body as God-given and entrusted to our care, to be treated with respect and given proper attention. Thus, such matters as hygiene, diet and health are not beyond their purview, but elicit frequent comment.

The rabbis express the need for personal cleanliness, particularly for washing the hands upon waking and before and after meals. While the rabbis knew nothing about microbes and bacteria, it may well be that such precautions, whatever the rationale which prompted them, saved the lives of many Jews through succeeding centuries, especially during periods when bubonic plague was rampant.

Rabbinic comments on the nutritional or medicinal value of certain foods may not be altogether scientific, but there is still much uncertainty in this area. On the use of wine the rabbis differ, but moderation is recommended in matters of both food and drink. Of special interest is their recognition of the possibility of psychogenically induced illness, and their disparagement of reading Scriptural passages for purposes of healing.

A. HYGIENE

"Cleanliness is next to Godliness"

241. Our rabbis taught, "One should wash his face, hands and feet every day out of respect for his Maker; for Scripture states: (Prov. 16:4) *The Lord hath made all things for His own purpose* [and man is made in His image]." *Sabbath, 50b*

Physical cleanliness leads to spiritual purity

242. R. Phineas b. Jair said, "Study leads to precision, precision leads to zeal, zeal leads to cleanliness, cleanliness leads to restraint, restraint leads to purity, and purity leads to holiness."

Abodah Zarah, 20b

243. R. Johanan said, "Whoever wishes to receive upon himself the yoke of the kingdom of Heaven in perfection [during his morning prayers] should first have evacuation, then wash his hands, put on phylacteries,[1] and only then offer his prayers."

Berachoth, 15a

The importance of obeying nature's call

244. Raba said, "Whoever delays answering nature's call is guilty of transgressing the commandment (Lev. 20:25) *Ye shall not make yourselves abominable.*" *Makkoth, 16b*

245. R. Simeon b. Gamaliel said, "To hold back feces brings on dropsy; to hold back urine brings on jaundice." *Tamid, 27b*

Cleanliness is the best preventive of disease

246. Samuel said, "Better is cold water [on the eyes] in the morning, and washing of the hands and feet in the evening than all the eye salves in the world."[2] *Sabbath, 108b*

---

[1] The phylacteries are two small leather boxes containing the Torah passages Deut. 6:4–9; Deut. 11:13–21; Exod. 13:1–10; Exod. 13:11–16. These are strapped to the left arm and to the forehead, in literal fulfillment of the injunction, *And thou shalt bind them as a sign upon thy hand, and they shall be for frontlets between thine eyes* (Deut. 6:8).

[2] Head of the academy at Nehardea, Samuel (c. 180–257) was himself a physician as well as an astronomer and friend of King Sapur. He was a liberal in his interpretation of Sabbath regulations (Sab. 19b; 22a) and established the principle that "the law of the land is law" with regard to Jewish legal practice; i.e., that in the diaspora, Jewish law must operate within the framework of civil law.

Ill effects of uncleanliness

247. Samuel said, "Uncleanliness of the head may lead to blindness; uncleanliness of clothing may lead to insanity; uncleanliness of the body may lead to skin ailments." *Nedarim, 81a*

Special care is recommended for infants

248. Abaye said, "The proper care of a baby is to bathe it in warm water and rub it with oil."

Yoma, 78b

249. It was said of R. Hanina that at the age of eighty he could put on and take off his shoes while standing on one foot. R. Hanina himself remarked, "The warm baths and the oil with which my mother rubbed me down in my childhood have protected me in my old age."

Hullin, 24b

Three things that benefit the body

250. Three things benefit the body though they do not enter it: bathing, anointing with oil and regular motion [exercise].

Berachoth, 57b

When bathing, hot water should be followed by cold

251. Our rabbis taught, "If one bathed in hot water and did not follow it with cold water, it is as if iron is inserted in a furnace and not afterwards plunged into cold water." [As the iron would not be fully tempered, so the body will not derive the full benefit.] *Sabbath, 41a*

Washing the hands upon waking

252. R. Muna used to say that a hand that touches any part of the body [without being washed upon waking] deserves to be cut off. Such a hand makes the eye blind and the ear deaf, and it causes a polyp. [The hands remain in a dangerous condition until they are washed.][1] *Sabbath, 108b*

Washing the hands before eating

253. R. Avira said, at times in the name of R. Ammi and at times in the name of R. Assi, "Whoever eats bread without previously

---

[1] Many centuries later, Dr. Ignaz Semmelweis (1818–65) roused the ire of his colleagues by insisting that puerperal fever was transmitted to parturient mothers by physicians who had not washed their hands.

washing his hands is like one who has intercourse with a harlot."

Sotah, 4b

254. R. Zerika said in the name of R. Eleazar, "Whoever eats bread without washing his hands is like one who eats [ritually] unclean food." *Sotah, 4b*

The hands should also be washed after eating

255. R. Judah said in the name of Rab, in comment upon the words (Lev. 11:44) *Sanctify yourselves therefore and be ye holy*, "*Sanctify yourselves* means washing the hands before the meal, and *be ye holy* means washing them after the meal." *Berachoth, 53b*

How to wash the hands before and after eating

256. R. Hiyya b. Ashi said in the name of Rab, "When washing the hands before a meal, one should hold his hands up. But when washing the hands after a meal, one should keep his hands down." We are similarly taught in a *baraitha* that whoever washes his hands before a meal should lift them up so that the water should not flow back on his hands causing his hands to become unclean.[1] *Sotah, 4b*

B. DIET

Food must be chewed properly

257. It was taught in the name of R. Meir, "Chew well with your teeth and you will feel it in your heels [i.e., you will have more energy]." *Sabbath, 152a*

One should not overindulge in eating

258. R. Hiyya taught, "Withdraw your hand from the meal you are enjoying."[2] *Gittin, 70a*

259. R. Aha, the son of R. Huna, said in the name of R. Shesheth, "A full stomach is a bad thing; for Scripture states: (Hos. 13:6) *When they were fed, they became sated and their heart was exalted. Therefore they have forgotten Me.*" [See also item 616.] *Berachoth, 32a*

260. Elijah once said to R. Nathan, "Eat a third [of the stomach's capacity], drink a third and leave a third empty [literally, 'for when

---

[1] This matter is discussed at length in Jacob Neusner's *Invitation to the Talmud* (New York: Harper & Row, 1973). The procedure described here is followed by surgeons now.
[2] See Num. 11:31–34, where God condemns the lust for food.

you get angry']; otherwise, if you get angry you will burst." [This may refer to apoplexy.] *Gittin, 70a*

The practice of the Persians is praised

261. R. Gamaliel said, "For three things I admire the Persians: they are moderate in their eating habits, modest in the privy and modest in their marital relations." *Berachoth, 8b*

Eating an early breakfast

262. Rabbah said to Rabbah b. Mari, "Whence can we derive the statement, 'Rise up early and eat; in summer on account of the heat, and in winter on account of [to provide warmth during] the cold'? There is a proverb that says, 'Sixty[1] runners ran, but did not overtake the man who breakfasted early.'" *Baba Kamma, 92b*

The importance of salt

263. Salt sweetens meat. *Berachoth, 5a*

264. Bread with salt[2] in the morning and a jug of water will banish all illness. *Baba Kamma, 92b*

Water is also essential

265. Our rabbis taught, "He who has partaken of food without salt or drunk any beverage without drinking water will be troubled with a bad odor in his mouth during the day and with croup at night."
Berachoth, 40a

266. Our rabbis taught, "He who makes his food float in water [i.e., drinks much water with his food] will not suffer from indigestion." How much water should he drink? R. Hisda said, "A cupful to a loaf [of bread]." *Berachoth, 40a*

On eating meat

267. R. Eleazar b. Azariah said, "He who possesses a *maneh* [one hundred *zuzim*] should buy a measure of vegetables for his pot. If he has as much as ten *maneh* he should buy fish. If he has fifty *maneh* he may buy some meat. And if he has a hundred *maneh* he may have meat prepared for him daily." *Hullin, 84a*

268. Our rabbis taught that the passage (Deut. 12:20) *When the Lord*

---

[1] Sixty is a common hyperbolical term.
[2] The ordinary meal of the poor.

thy God shall enlarge thy border, as He hath promised thee, and thou shalt say, 'I will eat flesh' teaches us a rule of conduct: that a person should not eat meat unless he has a special craving for it. *Hullin,* 84a

Eating fish is particularly healthful

269. R. Hiyya b. Ashi said in the name of Rab, "One who eats small fish regularly will not suffer with his bowels. Moreover, the eating of fish stimulates sexual activity and strengthens the whole body." *Berachoth,* 40a

Foods that prevent disease

270. R. Mari said in the name of R. Johanan, "If one takes lentils regularly once in thirty days he will keep croup away from his house.[1] He should not, however, take them daily." *Berachoth,* 40a

271. R. Mari also said in the name of R. Johanan, "If one takes mustard seed regularly once in thirty days, he keeps illness away from his house. He should not, however, take it every day. Why? Because it weakens the heart." *Berachoth,* 40a

Preventing heartburn

272. R. Hama b. Hanina said, "One who takes black cumin regularly will not suffer from heartburn." *Berachoth,* 40a

Avoiding stomach trouble

273. R. Hiyya taught, "If a man wants to avoid stomach trouble, he should take *tibbul*[2] regularly, both summer and winter."

Gittin, 70a

Garlic is highly rated

274. Our rabbis taught, "Five things are said of garlic: it satisfies the appetite, warms the body, makes the face glow, increases seminal fluid and also kills tapeworms." Some add that it promotes affection and drives away enmity [by the feeling of well-being it produces].[3]

Baba Kamma, 82a

---

[1] Rashi comments that eating lentils prevents indigestion, which he assumes to be the cause of croup.

[2] Literally, *tibbul* means "dippings": bread or other food dipped in wine or vinegar.

[3] The use of garlic has been attributed to David, Solomon, Deborah and Homer. See Nathan Ausubel, ed., *A Treasury of Jewish Humor* (New York: Doubleday, 1951), pp. 363–364. For another view of garlic, see items 181 and 686.

Dates are also recommended

275. A Master has said, "Dates fill and warm a person, promote digestion and strengthen one, without spoiling the taste for food."

Gittin, 70a

The value of eggs

276. R. Janai said in the name of Rab, "The egg is better than anything equal in size."

Rabin said, "A soft-boiled egg is better than six ounces of fine flour."

Dimi said, "A soft fried egg is better than six ounces of flour; a hard fried egg is better than four ounces." *Berachoth, 44b*

Foods of varying value

277. Our rabbis taught, "A milt is good for the teeth but not for the stomach; vetch is bad for the teeth but good for the stomach; . . . cabbage is a nourishing food; beetroot is good for medicinal use. But woe unto the house where turnip enters!" [Turnips cause flatulence.] *Berachoth, 44b*

One should be seated when eating or drinking

278. Three things enfeeble a man's body: to eat standing [hastily], to drink standing and to have marital intercourse standing.

Gittin, 70a

When travelling, food intake should be reduced

279. R. Judah said, "One who is on a journey should not eat more than the amount customary in years of famine because of the possibility of bowel disorder [i.e., unfamiliar foods and the tensions of travel may upset one's digestion]." *Taanith, 10b*

Less food is needed as one gets older

280. R. Judah said, "Up to the age of forty, eating is beneficial; after that age, drinking is beneficial." *Sabbath, 152a*

Eating on the street

281. Whoever eats while on the street is like a dog. According to some, he is disqualified from serving as a witness [since he lacks self-respect and is not trustworthy]. *Kiddushin, 40b*

Food is important to our mental outlook

282. R. Abdimi from Haifa said, "Before a man eats and drinks he has two hearts [minds].[1] After he eats and drinks he has but one heart." *Baba Bathra, 12b*

C. THE USE OF WINE

Drinking on Purim

283. Rabba said, "A man is obliged to drink enough [wine] on Purim so that he cannot distinguish between 'Cursed be Haman' and 'Blessed be Mordecai.' "[2] *Megillah, 7b*

In praise of wine

284. R. Hanan said, "Wine was created in order to comfort mourners and to compensate the wicked [for any good they may have done, since they have no reward in the next world]; for Scripture states: (Prov. 31:6) *Give strong drink to him who is about to perish* [i.e., the wicked], *and wine to the heavyhearted.*" *Sanhedrin, 70a*

285. R. Hanina b. Papa said, "A person in whose house wine is not poured like water has not attained the state of blessedness."

Erubin, 65a

286. Raba said, "Wine and spices have helped to make me wise."

Horayoth, 13b

287. At the head of all medicines is wine; only where there is no wine are drugs required.[3] *Baba Bathra, 58b*

How much wine should one drink?

288. R. Judah said in the name of R. Samuel, "He who drinks one-fourth of a cup of wine should not decide any legal question." "This tradition is not a good one," said R. Nahman, "for I know that unless I drink a quarter of a cup of wine my head is not clear."

Erubin, 64a

---

[1] The heart was associated with the mind, as we associate it with love. The passage means that one who is hungry may be indecisive and confused.

[2] This refers to the villain and hero of the Book of Esther, which is read on Purim. The letters of the two phrases have the same numerical value.

[3] A recent study of the unusual longevity of the Italian residents of Roseto, in eastern Pennsylvania, who customarily have wine with their meals, may serve to support this observation. See Stewart Wolf and John Bruhn, *The Roseto Story* (Norman, Okla.: University of Oklahoma Press, 1979).

The art of drinking

289. A man should not empty his goblet at one draught for he will be considered a drunkard. *Betzah, 25b*

290. R. Ishmael, the son of R. Jose, once visited the home of R. Simon, the son of R. Jose b. Lekunia. He was offered a cup of wine, which he eagerly accepted and drained at one draught. He was asked, "Does not the Master know that he who drinks a cup of wine at one draught is considered a drunkard?" To this he replied, "Yes, but this does not hold true for your small cup, your delicious wine and my capacious stomach." [R. Ishmael was quite stout.]

Pesahim, 86b

The disadvantages of drinking

291. When Rabban Gamaliel arrived at Chezib, a man came to him and asked him to nullify a vow. Thereupon R. Gamaliel asked his companions, "Have we drunk a fourth of a cup of Italian wine?" They answered, "Yes, we have." "If so," said R. Gamaliel, "then let him follow us until the effect of the wine shall have worn off." The man followed them for three miles, until they reached a mountain.[1] When they arrived at the mountainside, Rabban Gamaliel dismounted from his ass, wrapped himself in his cloak, sat down and nullified the man's vow.

From these actions we learn several things: one-fourth of a cup of wine intoxicates a man; when a man is intoxicated, he must not decide any legal questions; walking on the road reduces the effect of wine; and a vow may not be nullified while riding, walking or standing, but only when seated. *Erubin, 64b*

292. The letters of the word *yayin* ["wine"] have the numerical value of seventy. The word *sod* ["secret"] also has the numerical value of seventy. Thus we learn that as soon as wine enters the mouth, all secrets escape.

R. Hiyya added, "Whoever remains clearheaded while drinking has the qualities of seventy sages." *Erubin, 65a*

Wine brings sorrow to mankind

293. R. Meir said, "The forbidden tree of whose fruit Adam partook was a vine, for there is nothing which brings more sorrow to man

---

[1] The Soncino translation of the Talmud identifies this mountain as Scala Tyriorum, a promontory south of Tyre.

than wine."[1] [Adam's act brought him sorrow.] *Sanhedrin, 70a*

294. Rabba said that the verse (Prov. 23:31) *Look not upon the vine when it is red because its end is bloodshed* means that wine leads to bloodshed.[2] *Sanhedrin, 70a*

Women in particular are cautioned against wine

295. A Tanna taught, "One cup of wine is good for a woman; two are debilitating; three render her dissolute; and four cause her to lose all sense of self-respect and shame." *Kethuboth, 65a*

Moderation in the use of wine is recommended

296. Elijah, the brother of R. Sala Hasida, said to R. Judah, "Do not become intoxicated and you will not sin [i.e., one who exercises self-control will avoid transgression]." *Berachoth, 29b*

One need not abstain from wine completely

297. Eleazar HaKappar BeRabbi asked, "Why is it stated: (Num. 6:11) *And make atonement for him* [the Nazirite][3] *for that he sinned against the soul* in the Scriptures? How has he sinned?" [And he replied,] "By withholding himself from drinking wine." We may thus argue that if a person who abstains from wine is called a sinner, how much greater a sinner is one who abstains from all [innocent] pleasures! *Taanith, 11a*

God wants us to enjoy life's pleasures

298. If one who abstains from wine is called a sinner [since the Nazirite must bring a sin-offering], how much more is he a sinner who habitually refrains from everything [good]! Thus he who engages in frequent fasting is also to be called a sinner. *Nedarim, 10a*

How to judge a man's character

299. R. Ilai said, "A man's character can be judged in three ways: *b'koso* ['by his cup'; i.e., by the way he drinks], *b'kiso* ['by his pocket';

---

[1] "Etymological support for this opinion is found in the Hebrew word for wine, *yayin*, which is the sound both of wine and of wailing" (Noah Jacobs, *Naming Day in Eden* [New York: Macmillan, 1969], p. 81).

[2] The expression *ki yithadam* ("when it is red") ends with the word *dam* ("blood").

[3] A Nazirite was a person, consecrated to God, who had taken a vow never to drink wine or cut his hair. See Num. 6:12ff. The vow could be permanent or for a period of thirty days. The practice, which existed mainly in the time of the second Temple, eventually disappeared.

i.e., how he uses his money], and *b'kaaso* ['by his anger'; i.e., how he controls his temper]." Others add, *b'tzahako* ['by his laughter'; i.e., by the way he laughs and what prompts him to do so].

Erubin, 65b

D. HEALTH

The need for sleep and rest

300. R. Judah said, "Night was created only for sleep."

Erubin, 65a

301. Samuel said, "Sleeping at dawn is like a steel edge on iron [i.e., strengthening]." *Berachoth, 62b*

302. R. Judah of Kfar Gibboraya said, "The best medicine for all ailments is silence [i.e., complete rest]." *Megillah, 18a*

Quick energy may be derived from sugar

303. Our rabbis taught, "If one feels faint due to fasting, he should eat honey or other sweet things because they restore light to the eyes [i.e., provide quick energy]." *Yoma, 83b*

Avoiding drugs and unnecessary pulling of teeth

304. Rab said to his son Hiyya, "Do not get into the habit of taking medicines and do not hasten to have the teeth pulled [for the pain may be temporary]." *Pesahim, 113a*

Treatment for indigestion

305. Rabina said, "For indigestion, take three hundred grains of long pepper and drink a hundred of them daily in wine."

Gittin, 69b

. . . for tapeworm

306. For tapeworm take a fourth of a cup of wine with a bay leaf. For white worms take a seed of Eruca, tie it in a piece of cloth, soak it in water and drink the juice. However, be careful not to swallow the seed, lest it pierce the bowels. *Gittin, 69b*

. . . for diarrhea and constipation

307. For diarrhea take fresh poley in water; for constipation take dried poley in water. *Gittin, 69b*

. . . for catarrh

308. For catarrh take gum-ammoniac in an amount equal to the size of a pistachio-nut. *Gittin, 69b*

. . . for asthma

309. For asthma—others say for heart palpitations—take three wheat cakes, soak them in honey, eat them and then drink some undiluted wine. *Gittin, 69b*

. . . for angina

310. For angina take mint in the amount of three eggs, with cumin and sesame in the amount of one egg of each. *Gittin, 69b*

. . . for an abscess

311. For an abscess take a measure equal to a fourth of a cup of wine with purple-colored aloe. *Gittin, 69b*

312. An abscess is the forerunner of a fever.[1] What is the remedy for it? Squeeze it between the thumb and middle finger with a snapping motion sixty times [to soften it] and lance it laterally, provided it does not have a white head. If it has, the remedy will not be effective. *Abodah Zarah, 28a*

. . . for poisoning

313. Samuel said, "If a man has been wounded by a Persian lance [tipped with poison] there is no hope for him. However, he should be given fat roast meat and strong wine, as this may keep him alive long enough for him to leave some final instructions." *Gittin, 70a*

How to cure a cold

314. Whenever the servants of R. Amram, the Exilarch, upset him, he would get sick with chills. They would then say to him, "What does the Master want brought to him?" He thought to himself, "Whatever I will ask of them, they will bring me the opposite." He therefore would say to them, "Bring me lean roasted meat and wine mixed with water." As he had foreseen, they brought him fat roasted meat and strong wine.

---

[1] While the association of an abscess with a fever was recognized, it was probably not known that the fever fights the infection. Some of the treatments here prescribed were obviously folk remedies and may have had little value.

Whenever Yalta, the Exilarch's daughter, learned that he was indisposed, she ordered a bath of hot water for him. When R. Joseph caught a cold, he would work with a hand-mill to warm his body. Whenever R. Shesheth was beset by a cold he would busy himself carrying logs. *Gittin, 67b*

A description of gout

315. Mar Zutra, the son of R. Nahman, said to his father, "What kind of a sickness is *podagra* ['gout']?" "It is like needles sticking in the flesh," he replied. Whence did he learn this? Some say that R. Nahman himself suffered with this ailment. Others say that he learned this from his teacher. *Sotah, 10a*

Signs of improving health

316. Six things are a good sign for one who is ill: sneezing, perspiration, open bowels, seminal emissions, sleep and dreaming.

Berachoth, 57b

Moderation in all things is recommended

317. Do not sit too much because this is bad for piles; do not stand too much because it is bad for the heart; do not walk too much because it is bad for the eyes. Spend a third of your time sitting, a third standing and a third walking. *Kethuboth, 111a*

Where excess is harmful

318. In eight things excess is harmful and moderation beneficial: travel, sexual intercourse, wealth, work, wine, sleep, hot water [for bathing] and bloodletting.[1] *Gittin, 70a*

The penalty for profligacy

319. Raba b. Joseph b. Hama said, "Barzilai the Gileadite was excessively profligate, and whoever is profligate ages rapidly."[2]

Sabbath, 152a

---

[1] Bloodletting was regarded as beneficial in medical practice even toward the close of the eighteenth century and may have hastened the death of George Washington.

[2] (2 Sam. 19:32ff.) When King David asks Barzilai to come to Jerusalem, the latter refuses because he is eighty years old and feeble. His advanced age is no proof of "aging rapidly," but Raba finds it convenient to hang his argument on this peg.

The state of mind affects bodily health

320. Rab said, "A sigh [sadness or melancholy] breaks half the body of an individual;[1] for Scripture states: (Ezek. 21:11) *Sigh therefore thou son of man, with the breaking of thy loins."* *Berachoth, 58b*

321. Three things reduce a person's strength: fear [anxiety], travel and sin. *Gittin, 70a*

The use of Scripture to cure illness is prohibited

322. R. Joshua b. Levi declared, "It is forbidden to try to cure oneself from illness by [reciting] verses from the Torah. [Use of such verses for] prevention is permissible."[2] *Shebuoth, 15b*

---

[1] Here and in the next passage the rabbis display some recognition of the impact of anxiety and depression on the bodily health of a person, as psychogenic factors in illness. See also item 139.

[2] This is in striking contrast with widespread use of Scriptural readings, even in our day, for healing purposes among some faith groups. The rabbis go so far as to deny resurrection to those who follow this practice (see item 771). The objection was based on the common use of Biblical verses as incantations of a magical nature, and the thought that this practice was an attempt to "test" God, which was forbidden in Deut. 6:16, which states *Ye shall not try* [test] *the Lord your God* (see item 131). The objection did not apply to prayers for continued health.

6

THE FAMILY

THE nuclear Jewish family traditionally has been noted for its cohesiveness. The sense of kinship with the extended family and loyalty to the larger family of Israel represented further expressions of this solidarity. The observance of the Sabbath and festival occasions, largely centered in the home, served not only to intensify religious commitment but also to strengthen family ties.

The rabbis regard marriage as both natural and good, as a fulfillment of the Biblical injunction, "Be fruitful and multiply" (Gen. 1:28). The unmarried individual is viewed as an incomplete person, and early marriage is strongly recommended. The marriage ceremony is designated as *kiddushin* ("sanctification"), testifying to the sacredness ascribed to the marital relationship. Children are looked upon as a blessing: a gift of God Who shares in their creation.

The atmosphere generated in the home receives special attention by the rabbis, and they indicate the need for love and trust between husband and wife as essential ingredients of a happy home life, cautioning against quarreling and strife. Parental authority and the child's need for guidance are assumed, with little evidence of a permissive approach to the raising of children. Parents are expected to provide their children with an education and prepare them for a useful vocation. Reciprocally, children are duty-bound to honor their parents, a life-long obligation mandated in the Ten Commandments.

Divorce, like drinking, was permitted; but like drunkenness, it was infrequent and discouraged. Women were not accepted as men's equals in some ways, but generally were treated with affection and respect. In the marriage-contract *(kethubah),* provision is made for the protection and financial security of the wife. The rabbis recognize a woman's right of consent in marriage and her right to initiate a divorce, neither of which is envisioned in the Torah legislation. Indeed, they even give consideration to her sexual needs.

The rabbis advocate remarriage following a divorce or upon the death of a spouse, and having children in a second marriage, even at an advanced age.

A. MARRIAGE

The custom of breaking a glass at weddings

323. Mar, the son of Rabina, held a marriage banquet for his son. When he saw that his guests became boisterous, he took a cup, worth four hundred *zuzim,* and shattered it.[1] Thereupon they were immediately quieted.

R. Ashi also made a marriage feast for his son. When he noticed that his guests became unruly, he broke a cup made of clear glass and they became subdued. *Berachoth, 30b*

How to praise a bride

324. Our rabbis discussed the question, "What do we sing [or recite] in praise of a bride at a wedding feast?" The school of Shammai declared that she should be described as she actually is [without exaggeration]. But the school of Hillel said, "We are to call her a beautiful and graceful bride." The disciples of Shammai then said to the disciples of Hillel, "Suppose the bride is lame or blind; should she too be described as 'a beautiful and graceful bride'? The Torah states (Exod. 23:7) *Keep thyself far from false speech!*"[2]

Thereupon the Hillelites replied, "When someone buys a poor bargain at the market, should we commend it in the eyes of the purchaser or should we point out its defects? Surely you will agree that one should commend it in the presence of the purchaser [so that he will not feel unhappy about it]!"

From this comes the saying of the Sages, "A man's disposition should always be pleasant in his dealings with others."

Kethuboth, 16b

---

1 Rashi identifies this as a goblet of white crystal. The Tosafists, twelfth- to fourteenth-century teachers whose comments appear on the outer margins of the Talmudic text, explain that this is the origin of the Jewish custom of breaking a glass at weddings. The custom is sometimes interpreted as a reminder of the destruction of the Temple in Jerusalem or of the fragility of life. A demonological origin for the practice has also been offered: that it was initially intended to drive away evil spirits by making a sudden loud noise.

2 The 1962 J.P.S. Bible reads *from a false charge.* The word here rendered as "speech" is *davar.* Its basic meaning is "word," but it can also mean "matter." See item 579.

Dancing with a bride

325. R. Aha used to place the bride upon his shoulders and dance. When the others asked him, "May we do the same?" he answered, "If she is like a mere beam on your shoulder [and does not incite impure thoughts] you may do so, but not otherwise."

Kethuboth, 17a

Weddings have priority over funerals or study

326. A funeral procession [literally, "the dead"] must make way for a bridal procession [literally, "before a bride"].[1] *Kethuboth, 17a*

327. The study of the Torah should be interrupted for a funeral procession, and also to escort a bride to the marriage service. It was said of R. Judah b. Ilai that he would interrupt his study of the Torah [only] for a funeral and to escort a bride to her wedding.

Kethuboth, 17a

328. One may sell a Torah scroll for the purpose of marriage.

Megillah, 27a

The importance of being married

329. R. Hisda extolled the greatness of R. Hamnuna before R. Huna. R. Huna then said to R. Hisda, "When you see R. Hamnuna, send him to me." When R. Hamnuna visited him, he noticed that R. Hamnuna wore no *sodrah* ["marriage-garment"].[2] "Why do you not wear a head-covering?" asked R. Huna. "Because I am not yet married," came the reply. Thereupon R. Huna turned his face away saying, "You shall not see my face until you are married."

This was in keeping with R. Huna's convictions, for he said, "If one is twenty years old and unmarried, all his days will be spent in sin." But is it really possible that someone would spend all his days in sin? We must rather say that he will spend his days in thinking sinful thoughts. *Kiddushin, 29b*

In praise of early marriage

330. R. Hisda said, "The reason that I am brighter than my colleagues is that I married at the age of sixteen; and had I married at

---

[1] The Hebraic affirmation of life is here discernible.
[2] A scarf or turban used by married men to cover their heads.

fourteen, I would have said to Satan,[1] 'I defy you' [literally, 'An arrow in your eye']." *Kiddushin, 29b*

331. Raba said to R. Nathan b. Ammi, "While your sons are still under your control—from sixteen to twenty-two or, according to others, from eighteen to twenty-four—try to get them married off."

Kiddushin, 30a

Does early marriage interfere with study?

332. R. Judah said in the name of R. Samuel, "One should first marry, and afterwards devote his time to the study of Torah." R. Johanan said, however, "How is it possible that when one has a millstone around his neck [a wife and children to support] he should study Torah?" [Hence he should study before he is married.]

The two opinions are not really contradictory. The former applied to Babylonia. There they used to leave their homes to study [and the burden of supporting a family did not exist].[2] The latter applied to scholars in the land of Israel [who lived with their families].

Kiddushin, 29b

When to take a wife

333. Our rabbis taught that the verse (Deut. 20:5) *He who has built a new house . . . has planted a vineyard . . . has betrothed a wife* presents us with a lesson in proper procedure.[3] One should first build a house, then plant a vineyard and, afterward, get married. *Sotah, 44a*

A wife provides a man with stability

334. R. Jose said, "Never have I called my wife by that word ['wife'], but I have always called her 'my home.'" *Sabbath, 118b*

335. R. Hiyya was often vexed by his wife, yet whenever he saw something nice he bought it for her. When Rab said to him, "She often annoys you [; why do you buy her gifts?]" R. Hiyya replied, "It

---

1 In the Bible, Satan generally connotes an adversary (1 Kings 5:18; 1 Sam. 29:4). In Job, he appears as the celestial prosecutor. Only later does he appear as an independent agent (1 Chron. 21:1). Early portions of the Talmud rarely mention him. Popular concepts of Satan may later have influenced the rabbis.

2 The wife remained with her parental family.

3 The Bible passage refers to those exempt from military service, but the verse is used here by way of analogy.

is enough that our wives raise our children and keep us from sin[ful thoughts]." *Yebamoth, 63a*

336. R. Hama b. Hanina said, "As soon as a man is married, his sins stop accosting him [literally, 'are stopped up']; for Scripture states: (Prov. 18:22) *He who has found a wife has found happiness, and has obtained favor from the Lord* [as one without sin]." [See also items 362 and 363.] *Yebamoth, 63b*

No man should remain unmarried

337. R. Tanhum said in the name of R. Hanilai, "One who has no wife lives without happiness, without blessing and without good. Without happiness, for Scripture states: (Deut. 14:26) *And thou shalt rejoice, thou and thy household*;[1] without blessing, for it states: (Ezek. 44:30) *To cause a blessing to rest on thy household*;[2] without good, for Scripture declares: (Gen. 2:18) *It is not good that man should be alone.*"
Yebamoth, 62b

338. R. Eleazar said, "A Jew [*Jehudi*][3] who has no wife is not considered a [complete] man; for Scripture states: (Gen. 5:2) *Male and female created He them, and called their name* [not 'his' name] *Adam* [i.e., the name applies to the couple]." *Yebamoth, 63a*

How a wife helps a man

339. R. Jose once met Elijah and asked him, "Scripture states: (Gen. 2:18) *I will make him a help meet for him.* In what way does a woman help a man?" And he answered, "A man brings in wheat; but can he chew wheat? He brings in flax; can he clothe himself with flax? [It is his wife who grinds the wheat and spins the flax.] Does this not show that she brightens his eyes and keeps him on his feet?"
Yebamoth, 63a

---

[1] The word *bayis,* meaning "home" or "household," is taken to refer to one's wife. See item 334 above. Tanhum interprets the verse to mean that one can rejoice only with a "household."

[2] Ezekiel speaks of bringing offerings to the priests, but the word "blessing" is here associated with a "household."

[3] Of the three common designations for the Jewish people—Hebrews, Israelites (or children of Israel) and Jews—the term "Jew" was the last to appear. It is derived from Judea or Judah, the name of the southern kingdom which survived the conquest of the northern kingdom of Israel by the Assyrians in 722 B.C.E. The three terms vary somewhat in their denotations and connotations with regard to the ethnic, nationalistic and religious identity of the Jewish people. In contemporary usage the term "Jew" is generally preferred as an indication of a primarily religious identification.

340. R. Eleazar said, "What does the passage (Gen. 2:23) *This is the bone of my bone and the flesh of my flesh* mean? We can infer from this that Adam did not find life fully satisfying until he cohabited with Eve [and they became one flesh]." *Yebamoth, 63a*

341. R. Hanina said that the words (Prov. 15:15) *All the days of the afflicted* refer to one who has a bad wife; but the words (ibid.) *he who has a cheerful heart* refer to one who has a good wife. R. Janai, however, said that *All the days of the afflicted* refers to one who is overly fastidious, while *he who has a cheerful heart* refers to one who has a good physical constitution. *Baba Bathra, 145b*

How to choose a wife

342. R. Papa said, "Always be quick to buy land, but be deliberate in taking a wife." *Yebamoth, 63a*

Investigating a woman's family

343. Raba said, "He who takes a wife should investigate her brothers; for Scripture states: (Exod. 6:23) *And Aaron took Elisheva, the daughter of Aminadab, the sister of Nachshon.* Why does Scripture speak of *the sister of Nachshon?* Since we are told that she was the daughter of Aminadab, is it not evident that she was also the sister of Nachshon? This is intended to teach us that one who is about to marry should investigate the [character of the] brothers of his prospective bride. It is taught [in a *baraitha*] that children usually resemble their uncles."

Baba Bathra, 110a

One should not marry for money

344. Rabba b. Adda said in the name of Rab, "Whoever marries a woman for her money will have degenerate children."

Kiddushin, 70a

The woman must consent to the marriage

345. R. Judah said in Rab's name, "A man is forbidden to give his daughter in marriage while she is still a minor [but must wait] until she has grown up and says, 'I wish to marry so-and-so.' " *Kiddushin, 41a*

Joining couples in marriage is not easy

346. Rabba b. bar Hana said in the name of R. Johanan, "Joining couples in marriage is as difficult as the parting of the Red [Reed]

Sea; for Scripture states: (Ps. 68:7) *God maketh the solitary to dwell in a household* [i.e., only God can do this]." *Sotah, 2a*

347. Is joining couples in marriage as difficult as the splitting of the Red Sea, as R. Johanan said? R. Judah declared in the name of Rab,[1] "Forty days before the birth of a child, a heavenly voice announces, 'The daughter of so-and-so shall marry the son of so-and-so.' " Hence, it is really prearranged!'

There is no contradiction here. The latter deals with a first marriage [ordained in heaven], while the former deals with a second marriage [which is not]. *Sotah, 2a*

One must honor his wife

348. R. Helbo said, "One should always be careful to honor his wife for the welfare of the household depends upon her; as Scripture states: (Gen. 12:16) *And He dealt well with Abram for her sake.* Indeed, Raba used to say to the people of his town of Mehuza, 'Revere your wives, so that you may prosper.' "

Baba Metzia, 59a

349. If one loves his wife as much as himself, and honors her more than himself,[2] leading his sons and daughters on the right path and marrying them off while they are yet young, to him does the passage apply (Job 5:24) *And thou shalt know that there is peace in thy tent.*

Yebamoth, 62b

One must not deceive his wife

350. Rab said, "One should always avoid deceiving his wife, for she is easily brought to tears." *Baba Metzia, 59a*

Cohabitation during menstruation is prohibited

351. A *min* ["dissenter"] said to R. Kahana, "Your law permits a man to be alone [*yihud*] with his wife during the days of her menstruation. Is it possible for flax and fire to be together without the flax burning?" But R. Kahana replied, "Scripture has testified for us, for it states: (Song of Songs 7:3) *Thy belly is like a*

---

[1] See item 17.

[2] One cannot generally be expected to love another more than himself. If one loves his wife as much as himself, great indeed is his love for her. However, one should not seek honor for himself and should, therefore, be able to honor his wife more than himself.

heap of wheat, set about with lilies; that is, even a fence of lilies is
sufficient [restraint] for us, and it will never be broken."[1]

Sanhedrin, 37a

Things that destroy a home

352. R. Hisda said, "Infidelity in a home is like a worm in a poppy
plant." R. Hisda also said, "Anger in a home is like a worm in a
sesame plant [both are destructive]." *Sotah, 3b*

On following a wife's advice

353. Rab said, "He who follows the advice of his wife will descend
into Gehinnom; for Scripture states: (1 Kings 21:25) *But indeed there
was none like unto Ahab . . . whom Jezebel, his wife, stirred up* [and who
died as a result]." But R. Papa objected, saying, "Do not people say,
'If your wife is short, bend down and listen to her [advice]?' "
This presents no contradiction. Rab speaks about matters of business [where the husband should take charge], while the popular saying refers to domestic affairs [the wife's domain]. According to others,
Rab speaks of spiritual matters, while the popular saying refers to
mundane affairs. *Baba Metzia, 59a*

Varying assessments of women

354. R. Simeon b. Johai said, "Women are of unstable tempera-
ment." *Sabbath, 33b*
355. R. Hisda said, "God endowed women with more understanding than men." *Nidah, 45b*
356. R. Hiyya said, "A woman is only for beauty and for having
children." R. Hiyya also said, "A woman primarily wants finery. If a
man wants to give his wife pleasure, he should clothe her in fine linen
garments." *Kethuboth, 59b*
357. The disciples of R. Shila said, "Women are compassionate."

Megillah, 14b

358. It is written in the Book of Ben Sirah [in the Apocrypha; see

---

[1] Cf. Ezek. 18:6, which praises a man who has not "come near to a woman in her impurity."
Lev. 15:24 prohibits cohabitation with a menstruant woman. In the Talmud, Niddah, 31b
reads: "Because a man may become overly familiar with his wife and thus repelled by her,
the Torah said that she should be a *niddah* ('menstruant') for seven clean days after her flow,
so that she should be as beloved (after her period) to her husband as on the day of her
marriage." It has been suggested that this served to strengthen the Jewish marriage.

chapter 16]: A good wife is a good gift; she should be given to one who fears [reveres] God. *Yebamoth, 63b*

359. Rab said to R. Hiyya, "How do women achieve merit? By sending their children to study Torah in the synagogue and their husbands to study in the academies, and by waiting patiently for their husbands to return." *Berachoth, 17a*

Polygamy is discouraged though permitted

360. Raba said, "A man may marry other wives in addition to the first, provided that he has the means to support them."[1]

Yebamoth, 65a

361. A man may not marry more than four wives, so that each may receive one marital visit a month.[2] *Yebamoth, 44a*

B. PROBLEMS IN MARRIAGE

The possibility of a bad marriage is recognized

362. Raba said, "See how splendid is a good wife and how evil is a bad wife! Scripture states: (Prov. 18:22) *Whoso hath found [matzah] a wife hath found happiness,* yet also declares (Eccles. 7:26) *And I find [motzeh] the woman more bitter than death.*" [The first verse applies to a good wife, the second to a bad one.] *Yebamoth, 63b*

363. [In comment on the above verses] R. Hanina said, "In the land of Israel, when a man got married he was asked, 'Found [*matzah*] or find [*motzeh*]?' because the past tense speaks of happiness while the present tense speaks of bitterness." *Berachoth, 8a*

A man gets the wife he deserves

364. R. Samuel b. Isaac reported that whenever Resh Lakish lectured on the subject of Sotah[3] he would say, "A wife is chosen [in heaven] for each man according to his deserts." *Sotah, 2a*

---

[1] See fn. to item 8; also item 376

[2] This standard was adopted by Mohammed (Koran, 4:3). In view of the feminine liberation movement, it is of interest that the sexual needs of women are here recognized. Indeed, the Mishnah (Kethuboth, 5:6) speaks of sexual neglect of a wife as grounds for her to seek a divorce. The qualifying period of neglect, in the opinion of the school of Hillel, was a week ("one Sabbath"); in that of the school of Shammai, two weeks ("two Sabbaths"). Others recommended one week for the wife of a workman and thirty days for the wife of a scholar who must leave town for study. See also fn. to item 370.

For other comments on sex in marriage, see items 261, 269, 274, 278, 318, 351 and 352.

[3] *Sotah* involved a woman suspected of adultery. See Num. 5:12ff.

365. R. Eleazar said, "What does (Gen. 2:18) *I will make him a help meet for him* [*ezer k'negdo*] mean? This means that if he is deserving, she will be a help [*ezer*] to him. If not, she will be an obstacle to him [*k'negdo*]."[1] *Yebamoth, 63a*

A bad wife is a great misfortune

366. Raba b. Mehasia said in the name of R. Hama b. Goria, who quoted Rab, "Rather any complaint, but not a complaint of the bowels; any pain, but not heart pain; any ache, but not headache; any evil, but not an evil wife!" *Sabbath, 11a*

When a man has an impossible wife

367. Rab was often annoyed by his wife. When he asked her to prepare lentils for him, she would cook peas. When he asked for peas, she would prepare lentils. After his son Hiyya grew up, Hiyya used to reverse the request of his father [so that Rab got what he wanted]. "Your mother has improved," he once remarked to his son. And Hiyya replied, "That is because I have been reversing your requests." Then Rab said to him, "This is as people say, 'Your offspring will teach you sense.' [I could have done the same!]" *Yebamoth, 63a*

368. Our rabbis taught that among those who cry out but are not heeded is the husband who is ruled by his wife [because he is too submissive]. *Baba Metzia, 75b*

369. Our rabbis taught that among those who will never behold Gehinnom is he who has a bad wife [because he has expiated his sins in this world by his patience]. *Erubin, 41b*

Conduct unbecoming a wife

370. We are told [in a *baraitha*] that R. Meir said, "Just as the habits of men differ when eating, so also do men's habits differ with respect to their wives. There are men who, if a fly falls into their cup, [overreact and] pour out the entire contents. In similar fashion, Papa b. Judah [was overcautious and] locked the door on his wife whenever he went out. There are others who [take normal precautions and] cast the fly out, then drink from the cup. Such is the behavior of a man who permits his wife to talk [only] with her brothers and relatives.

"Still others [exercise no caution and] consume the fly together

---

[1] The term *ezer k'negdo*, here translated as "a help meet [suitable] for him," can be literally rendered as "a help opposite him" or "against him" without violence to the text.

with the food. Comparable is the man who permits his wife to walk about in the street with her hair unfastened, to spin cloth outdoors, or to engage in similar unbecoming behavior. It is permissible to divorce such a wife; for Scripture states: (Deut. 24:1) *Because he hath found some unseemly thing in her* [he may divorce her]."[1] *Gittin, 90a*

Should divorce be made easy or difficult?

371. (Deut. 24:1) *If she find no favor in his eyes, because he has found some unseemly thing in her,* etc. The school of Shammai said, "A man may not divorce his wife unless he discovers that she is unfaithful to him."[2] The school of Hillel said, "He may divorce her even if she spoils his food."[3] *Mishnah Gittin, 9:10*

372. R. Judah said, "If one hates his wife, he should send her away [i.e., divorce her]." But R. Johanan said, "He is to be despised who divorces his wife." The two, however, do not really disagree. The latter refers to a first marriage while the former refers to a second marriage.

R. Eleazar said, "When one divorces his first wife, even the altar sheds tears; for Scripture states: (Mal. 2:13) *Ye cover the altar of the Lord with tears, with weeping and with sighing*, and the verse continues *Yet ye say, 'Wherefore?' Because the Lord hath been witness between thee and the wife of thy youth* [i.e., one's first wife], *against whom thou hast dealt treacherously, though she be thy companion and the wife of thy covenant.*"

Gittin, 90b

373. Raba said, "It is proper to divorce a bad wife; for Scripture states: (Prov. 22:10) *Drive away the scorner, and strife will depart; then will cease dissension and dishonor.*" *Yebamoth, 63b*

374. R. Shaman b. Abba said, "See how difficult it is [or should be] to obtain a divorce; for Abishag was permitted to be with King

---

[1] Because, in Biblical law, the husband has a right to repudiate his wife but she has no right to divorce him, the rabbis devised the *kethubah* ("marriage-contract"), stipulating the amount to be paid to her in the event of divorce or her husband's death. Remarkably, the rabbis go so far as to grant a woman the right of divorce not only if her husband neglects her sexually (see fn. to item 361) or takes an additional wife (see item 376), but even if he merely exacts degrading tasks (Kethuboth, 72a), unduly limits her freedom (Kethuboth, 48a) or prevents her from visiting her parents (Kethuboth, 71b).

[2] Cf. "Whoever shall put away his wife, except that it be for fornication, and shall marry another, committeth adultery" (N.T., Matt. 19:9).

[3] This suggests that if the bond between them is so fragile that it may be thus easily broken, divorce should be made possible. Hillel's view prevailed, and the possibility of divorce as a viable option tended to raise the level of the Jewish marriage relationship.

David [as a concubine], and he was not allowed to divorce one of his wives in order to marry her." [See 1 Kings 1:15.]

Sanhedrin, 22a

The distinction between wives and concubines

375. What is the distinction between wives and concubines? R. Judah said, "Wives are married by *kethubah* ['marriage-contract'] and *kiddushin* ['the marriage service'].[1] Concubines have neither of these." *Sanhedrin, 21a*

When a man takes an additional wife

376. R. Ammi said, "A man must give his wife a divorce, if she desires it, when he takes an additional wife, and must pay her the amount stipulated in her *kethubah.*" *Yebamoth, 65a*

Divorcing a wife who is sterile

377. The son of R. Judah HaNasi spent twelve years in study away from his wife. By the time he returned she had become sterile. On hearing of this, his father asked, "How shall we act in this matter? If she is divorced, people will say that this virtuous woman waited for him all these years in vain.[2] And if my son were to take an additional wife, people would say that one woman is his wife, and the other is his concubine."[3] He therefore prayed on her behalf, and she was healed. *Kethuboth, 62b*

C. WHEN A SPOUSE DIES

The death of a spouse is grievous indeed

378. There is a *baraitha* which declares that no one feels the death of a man more than his wife, and no one feels the death of a woman more than her husband. Surely no one feels the death of a man more than his wife; for Scripture states: (Ruth 1:3) *And Elimelech, Naomi's husband, died.*[4]

Similarly, no one feels the death of a woman more than her hus-

---

[1] The conferring of the *kethubah* originally preceded the marriage service. The two rituals are now generally combined.

[2] Divorce on the ground of prolonged infertility was permitted.

[3] See items 360, 375 and 376.

[4] Since he is identified here only as Naomi's husband, the implication is that Naomi mainly felt the loss.

band; for Scripture states: (Gen. 48:7) *And as for me, when I came from Paddan, Rachel died unto me.* [1] *Sanhedrin, 22b*

379. R. Alexandri said, "For him whose wife dies, the world is dark; as Scripture states: (Job 18:6) *The light shall be darkened in his tent, and his lamp will be quenched above him.*" R. Jose b. Hanina added, "His steps will also be shortened; for the passage continues: *The steps of his strength will be [come] straitened.*" And R. Abbahu declared, "His wisdom will also desert him; for the end of the passage reads *And his own counsel shall cast him down.*" *Sanhedrin, 22a*

God provides a deceased wife's successor

380. R. Isaac said, "The very same day on which Ruth came to the land of Israel [from her homeland Moab], the wife of Boaz [whom she later married] died. This serves to support the popular saying, 'Before a woman dies, her replacement for managing the household is already provided.'" [See Ruth 4:13.]

Baba Bathra, 91a

One's first wife is irreplaceable

381. R. Johanan said, "When a man's first wife dies, it is [as tragic] as if the Temple were destroyed in his days; as Scripture states: (Ezek. 24:10) *I will take away from thee the desire of thine eyes.*"

Sanhedrin, 22a

382. R. Samuel b. Nahman said, "There can be a replacement for everything, but not for the wife of one's youth; for Scripture states: (Isa. 54:6) *And a wife of one's youth, can she be rejected?*"

Sanhedrin, 22a

383. R. Judah taught his son R. Isaac, "One can find real joy [literally, 'quickening of spirit'] only with his first wife; as Scripture states: (Prov. 5:18) *Thy fountain will be blessed; and rejoice with the wife of thy youth.*" [It is in reference to the wife of one's youth that the word *blessed* is used.] *Sanhedrin, 22a*

Marrying for a second time

384. Resh Lakish said, "When a man marries a woman after his first wife, he remembers the deeds of the first [and may draw unfavorable comparisons]." [The concept of "three in a bed."]

Berachoth, 32b

---

[1] That is, it was Jacob who sustained the loss.

A widower ought to remarry

385. R. Nahman said in the name of R. Samuel, "Although a man already has children, he is nonetheless prohibited from remaining single [if widowed or divorced]; for Scripture states: (Gen. 2:18) *It is not good that man should be alone."* Yebamoth, 61b

D. RAISING CHILDREN

How long can a woman bear children?

386. R. Hisda said, "If a woman marries before the age of twenty, she can bear children until sixty. If she marries after twenty, she can bear children until forty. But when she marries after forty, she can no longer bear children." *Baba Bathra, 119b*

Scripture commands us to have children

387. R. Hamnuna said, "Isaiah the prophet came to him [King Hezekiah] and said to him, (Isa. 38:1) *'Thus saith the Lord: Set thy house in order, for thou shalt die, and not live.'* What is the meaning of *for thou shalt die, and not live?* [Why the seeming repetition?] *For thou shalt die* refers to this world; *and not live* refers to the life hereafter.

"The king asked, 'Why am I to be punished so severely?' Isaiah replied, 'Because you have not fulfilled the commandment to beget children.' Hezekiah then said to him, 'The reason is, that I have seen by the aid of the Holy Spirit that worthless children will issue from me.'[1] And Isaiah answered, 'What have you to do with the secrets of the All-Merciful? That which you have been commanded to do, you should do. Let the Holy One do whatever is pleasing to Him.' "

Berachoth, 10a

388. R. Joshua b. Levi said, "A man who has no children is accounted as dead; for Scripture states: (Gen. 30:1) *Give me children, or else I die.*[2] We are also taught in a *baraitha* that there are four persons who are considered as dead: the pauper, the leper, the blind and he who is childless." *Nedarim, 64b*

389. (Ps. 55:20) *Those who leave no successors* [literally, "changes"] *fear no God.* R. Johanan and R. Joshua b. Levi differed on the meaning

---

[1] An allusion to Manasseh, king of Judah from c. 692–641 B.C.E. (See 2 Kings 21:1–18; 2 Chron. 33:1–20.) During his reign, there was a relapse from the reforms of his father Hezekiah. Rabbinic literature declares that the acts of Manasseh were responsible for the destruction of Jerusalem.

[2] These words are spoken by Rachel to her husband, Jacob.

of this verse. According to one, a son was meant; according to the other, a disciple. *Baba Bathra, 116a*

On having children at an advanced age

390. R. Joshua said, "Although a man took a wife when he was young, he should nonetheless marry again [if widowed or divorced] at a later age. Even if one already has children from an earlier marriage, he should nevertheless try to have children at an advanced age; for Scripture states: (Eccles. 11:16) *In the morning* [early years] *sow thy seed, and in the evening* [later years] *let not thy hand rest; for thou knowest not which will succeed, whether this or that, or whether both will be alike good.*"

Yebamoth, 62b

God is a partner in the child

391. Our rabbis taught that there are three partners in a child: God, the father and the mother. *Kiddushin, 30b*

Fortunate is he whose children are males

392. Bar Kappara said, "The world cannot exist without both males and females. But fortunate is he whose children are males, and unhappy is he whose children are females. The world cannot exist without spice-dealers and tanners. But fortunate is he who is a spice-dealer, and woe unto him who is a tanner!" [A tanner is malodorous.]

Baba Bathra, 16b

393. (Ben Sirah 43:9–10) A daughter is a vain treasure for a father. Because of the worry she causes him, he does not sleep at night. When she is a minor, he is concerned that she may be seduced; when she comes of age, that she may sin; when she is an adult, that she may not marry; and after she is married, that she may have no children.

Sanhedrin, 100b

Sons provide assurance of immortality

394. R. Pinhas b. Hama said, "What does the passage (1 Kings 11:21) *And when Hadad learned in Egypt that David slept with his fathers, and that Joab, the captain of the host, had died* mean? [Why *slept* in one case, and *died* in the other?] The answer is that David left sons, but Joab did not leave sons; therefore of Joab the word *died* is used."

But did not Joab also leave sons? There is the verse (Ezra 8:9) *Of the sons of Joab, Obadiah,* etc. We must therefore say that David, who left a son like himself, is referred to as having slept; but Joab did not leave a son like himself, and is therefore mentioned as having died.

Baba Bathra, 116a

But some prefer girls over boys

395. R. Hisda said, "If the first child is a girl, this is a good omen for the future children." He also said, "As for me, I prefer girls over boys." [His own daughters married eminent scholars.]

Baba Bathra, 141a

All of one's children should be treated equally

396. Raba b. Mechasia said in the name of R. Hama b. Guria, who quoted Rab, "A man should never show preference for one child over his other children. Because of two *selaim* ['coins'] worth of silk which Jacob bestowed upon Joseph in preference to his other sons [by giving him 'a coat of many colors'], the brothers became jealous of him, [placed him in an abandoned well] and brought about the migration of our ancestors to Egypt." [Gen. 37:3ff.] *Sabbath, 10b*

We must be careful of what we say to our children

397. People say, "What a child speaks in the street, he has heard from his father or mother." [Parents influence their children's speech and behavior.] *Sukkah, 56b*

398. R. Zera declared, "A person should never tell a child that he will give him something and not keep his promise, for he thereby teaches his child to lie; as Scripture states: (Jer. 9:4) *They have taught their* [children's] *tongues to speak lies.*" *Sukkah, 46b*

One should not terrorize his children

399. R. Hisda said, "A man should not frighten his children excessively." *Gittin, 6b*

Exercising control over children

400. The Tannaim [teachers during the Mishnaic period] differ in a *baraitha* about the explanation of the verse (Prov. 22:6) *Train up a child in the way he should go.* R. Judah and R. Nehemia interpret this to refer to different ages. One says that it refers to the years up to and including sixteen to twenty-two. The other says it refers to the years up to and including eighteen to twenty-four.

Kiddushin, 30a

Supporting one's children

401. (Ps. 106:3) *Happy are those who observe justice, who do charity* [righteousness] *at all times.* Is it possible to give charity continuously? Our rabbis of Jabneh—some say it was R. Eliezer—explained that this refers to one who supports his children while they are minors. But R. Samuel b. Nahmani said, "This refers to one who raises an orphan boy and girl in his home and enables them to marry." *Kethuboth, 50a*

402. We are taught in a *baraitha* that it is meritorious to support one's daughters [beyond their minority], and all the more so sons who occupy themselves with study. Such was the opinion of R. Meir. But R. Judah said, "It is meritorious to support sons who are engaged in study, but even more so to support one's daughters [beyond their minority] because of their possible humiliation [if reduced to begging, which is more shameful for a woman]." [See also item 171.]

Baba Bathra, 141a

403. (Lev. 19:29) *Profane not thy daughter, to make her a harlot.* R. Eliezer said, "This refers to one who marries off his young daughter to an old man." But R. Akiba said, "This refers to one who leaves his daughter unmarried until she enters the age of womanhood [since she might become unchaste if not married]." *Sanhedrin, 76a*

Teaching one's son a vocation

404. Just as one is duty-bound to educate his son, so is he obligated to teach him a vocation.[1] According to some, one is even required to teach his son how to swim for it may some day save his life.

Kiddushin, 30b

405. R. Judah said, "If one does not teach his son a vocation, it is as if he teaches him to steal." *Kiddushin, 30b*

E. HONORING PARENTS

One must honor his parents as he honors God

406. Our rabbis taught that Scripture places honoring one's parents on a par with honoring God.[2] Scripture states: (Exod. 20:12) *Honor thy father and thy mother* and speaks also of honoring God. Scripture teaches: (Prov. 3:9) *Honor the Lord with thy substance.* So too does Scripture place the fear [reverence] of parents on a par with the

---

[1] For observations on the choice of a vocation, see items 207, 208 and 209.
[2] Parents are regarded as partners of God in a child (see item 391).

fear of the Lord; for it states: (Lev. 19:3) *Ye shall fear every man his father and mother,* and also says with regard to God: (Deut. 6:13) *Thou shalt fear the Lord thy God.* Kiddushin, *30b*

407. Our rabbis taught that when a man honors his father and mother, the Holy One says, "I ascribe [as much] merit to him as if I dwelt with them and it was I that was being honored." When a man distresses his parents, the Holy One says, "It is well that I have not dwelt with them, for if I had dwelt with them I would have been distressed." *Kiddushin, 30b et seq.*

How to honor one's father and mother

408. R. Judah said, quoting Samuel, that R. Eliezer was once asked, "How far should one go in honoring his father and mother?" He replied, "Just see what a Gentile of Ashkelon, Dama ben Nathina, did. The Sages wanted to buy a jewel from him for the *ephod* [a sacred ritual object],[1] but the key [to the safe where it was kept] was under the pillow of his father [who was asleep]. Dama refused to disturb him [and lost the sale].

"The following year the Holy One rewarded him with the birth of a red heifer.[2] When the Sages offered to buy it, he said to them, 'I know that I could ask of you any amount of money, and you would pay the price. However, I only want you to make good the loss I sustained in honoring my father.'"

R. Hanina declared that if one who is not commanded to honor his parents does so, and is so richly rewarded, how much more certain is the reward of one who is commanded to do so![3]

R. Dimi said, "Dama ben Nathina was once dressed in gold-embroidered silk garments, seated among the noblemen of Rome, when his mother appeared. She tore his robe, slapped him and spat in his face, but he did nothing to put her to shame. Indeed, when her slippers fell off, he handed them back to her to save her the trouble of retrieving them." *Kiddushin, 31a*

---

[1] The upper garment worn by the Temple priests was called an *ephod*. An embroidered *ephod*, ornately decorated, was worn by the high priest. The shoulder pieces were held together by two onyx stones, each engraved with the names of six tribes of Israel (Exod. 28:4ff.)

[2] A red heifer was rare and brought a large price. Regarding its use, *for a water of sprinkling* as a purification from sin, see Num. 19:2ff.

[3] The reward for fulfilling God's commandments is here regarded as an earthly one.

The father is first to be honored

409. The son of a widow asked R. Eliezer, "If a father says, 'Bring me a drink of water,' and the mother says, 'Bring me a drink of water,' who should be obeyed first?" He replied, "Delay honoring your mother, and honor your father first, for both you and your mother are duty-bound to honor your father."[1] *Kiddushin, 31a*

410. Rabbi said, "A son honors his mother more than his father for she sways him [gently] by words; thus [to compensate], the Holy One placed honoring the father before honoring the mother [in the Ten Commandments]. . . . A son fears his father more than his mother; therefore the Holy One placed the fear of the mother before that of the father."[2] *Kiddushin, 30b, 31a*

How Abimi honored his father

411. Abimi, the son of R. Abbahu, declared, "One may feed his father pheasant, yet deserve the punishment of a disrespectful son, while another may set his father to work at a hand-mill, yet be rewarded in the World to Come [i.e., the attitude of the son toward his father is what counts]."

Said R. Abbahu, "Abimi, my son, has followed this precept as it should be observed." Abimi himself had five ordained sons during his father's lifetime. Yet when R. Abbahu came to his door, Abimi would hasten to open the door himself, saying, "I am coming." Upon one occasion, his father asked him for a glass of water. While he was getting it, the old man fell asleep, and Abimi, re-entering the room, stood by his father's side with the glass of water in his hand until his father awoke. [It was more important to respect his father's sleep than to obey his request.] *Kiddushin, 31a*

How to correct one's father

412. Samuel said to R. Judah, "Genius! Do not express yourself in such terms to your father! There is a *baraitha* which says that if a son sees his father transgressing what is written in the Torah, he must not say to him, 'Father, you have transgressed the law,' but should simply say, 'Father, such-and-such is written in the Torah' [stating the Biblical law] and he himself will detect his mistake." *Sanhedrin, 80b*

---

[1] In the Ten Commandments we read, (Exod. 20:12) *Honor thy father and thy mother*. This places the father first.

[2] (Lev. 19:2) *Ye shall fear every man his mother and his father*. See item 415 and fn.

Honoring one's mother

413. Whenever R. Tarphon's mother wanted to go to bed, he would bend down and she would step on his back to climb into bed. Whenever she wanted to leave the bed, he would bend down for her to step on him. One day he happened to mention this, and his colleagues said to him, "You have not really done much to honor your mother. Did she ever throw a pocketful of money into the sea in your presence without your causing her shame for her action?"

Kiddushin, 31b

414. When R. Joseph would hear the footsteps of his mother, he would immediately rise up and say, "Let us arise at the arrival of the *Shechinah." Kiddushin, 31b*

The difference between honoring and fearing parents

415. Our rabbis asked, "What does 'fear' [of parents] mean, as distinguished from 'honor'?"[1] They answered that "fear" [reverence or respect] means that one is not to sit in a parent's seat nor stand in his or her place; not to contradict the words of parents nor make a decision contrary to their opinion [i.e., to avoid offending them]. "Honor" refers to [such positive acts as] supplying parents with food and drink, assisting them in putting on their garments, helping them tie their shoes and taking them out and bringing them home.

Kiddushin, 31b

The question of honoring grandparents

416. R. Abba b. Jacob reared R. Jacob, his grandson. Once the grandfather said to him, "Bring me some water to drink." But the boy replied, "I am not your son [i.e., the duty to honor parents does not here apply]." *Sotah, 49a*

---

[1] The Hebrew for "honor" is *kavod*. The word for "fear" is *yirah*, which connotes reverence or respect. See item 410.

7

THE STUDY OF TORAH

TORAH study is regarded by the rabbis as basic to the education of a Jew and deserving of his lifelong attention. Through their devotion to the study of Torah, the Jews became a literate people early in their history. This tradition of study—once limited to Jewish males and restricted to Hebrew texts—ultimately led to a reverence for all learning.

The term "Torah" has both a specific and a more general meaning in rabbinic usage. While it refers more specifically to the Pentateuch, the rabbis frequently employ the word more broadly to include all of Scripture, not always distinguishing between the two usages. Here, however, a distinction is drawn between "the Torah" in the narrower sense of the term and "Torah" where the expanded meaning is intended.

The rabbis enlarge the concept of "Torah" even further, to embrace the injunctions of the Talmudic Halachah as well, in an attempt to establish the authority of the "oral Law." Indeed, the school of Rabbi Ishmael goes so far as to declare that both the Torah and the Halachah were given to Israel at Mount Sinai, with the understanding that only the former was to be committed to writing while the latter was to be transmitted orally.

Rabbinic insistence on the validity of the "oral Law" was opposed not only by the Sadducees and the Samaritans, but was also attacked by the Karaites in a "Back to the Bible" movement in the eighth century. Despite such resistance, however, Talmudic formulations of Jewish faith and practice represented the mainstream of Jewish religious expression for over a thousand years, until the political emancipation of the Jews toward the close of the eighteenth century.

Following the emancipation, the Reform movement in Judaism emerged, applying new "scientific" approaches to the study of Scripture and questioning, for example, the divine origin and mandatory observance of the dietary laws. But, as will be seen, the rabbis of the Talmud had much earlier raised even more fundamental questions, daring even to ask whether Moses really wrote all of the Torah, challenging cherished assumptions.

Today, long after the rise of Reform Judaism and the subsequent development of the Conservative and Reconstructionist movements, Orthodox Judaism, built upon Talmudic teachings, is still very much alive. Indeed, there is now in the United States an organization of Orthodox Jewish scientists.

A. THE TORAH AS DIVINE REVELATION

The Torah existed before the creation

417. R. Eleazar said, "Were it not for the Torah, the heavens and the earth would not exist;[1] for Scripture states: (Jer. 33:25) *If it were not for My covenant* [i.e., the Torah] *I would not have appointed day and night and the ordinances of heaven and earth." Pesahim, 68b*

All of creation depends upon the Torah

418. Resh Lakish said, "The Holy One made a condition with the works of creation, saying to them, 'If Israel accepts the Torah you will endure; if not I will again reduce you to chaos.' " [See items 425 and 426.] *Sabbath, 88a*

It is essential to human existence

419. R. Judah asked in the name of Samuel, "Why is it stated: (Hab. 1:14) *Thou makest men as the fishes of the sea* in Scripture? Why are men compared to fishes? This is to teach us that just as the fishes of the sea perish when they come upon dry land, so do men perish [spiritually] when they depart from the words of the Torah." [See also item 428.]
Abodah Zarah, 3b

Its words hold the power of life and death

420. R. Hananel b. Papa said, "What does the verse (Prov. 8:6) *Hear! For of noble things will I* [the Torah] *speak* mean?[2] Why are the

---

[1] Eleazar regards the Torah as the blueprint for the creation of the entire cosmic order, preceding its creation. Cf. "In the beginning was the Word" (N.T., John 1:1). See also *U.J.E.,* s.v. *"Logos."*

[2] Wisdom, speaking here, is identified by Hananel with the Torah, the source of all wisdom.

words of the Torah compared to those of a nobleman? Just as the latter has the power of life and death over us, so do the words of the Torah have that power over us [depending upon whether or not they are heeded]." *Sabbath, 88b*

The Torah is the answer to all evil

421. Raba said, "The Holy One created man's evil inclination, but created the Torah to overcome it." *Baba Bathra, 16a*

The giving of the Torah on Mount Sinai

422. R. Joshua b. Levi said, "When Moses ascended to heaven, the ministering angels said to the Holy One, 'Sovereign of the Universe, what has one born of woman to do among us?' 'He has come to receive the Torah,' was the divine response. 'What!' they exclaimed. 'Are You about to bestow upon man that cherished treasure which has been with You for nine hundred and seventy-four generations before the world was created?'

"Moses then said to Him, 'Sovereign of the Universe, what is written in the Torah which You are about to give me?' And God said, (Exod. 20:2) *'I am the Lord thy God who brought thee out of the land of Egypt'* [etc., reciting the Ten Commandments]. Moses then said to the angels, 'Did you go to Egypt and serve Pharaoh? It is also written *Thou shalt have no other gods beside Me.* Are you living among nations that worship idols [so that you need such instruction]?'

"Then Moses added, 'It is written *Remember the Sabbath day to keep it holy.* Do you engage in work that you need to rest? It is also written *Honor thy father and thy mother.* Have you a father and a mother? And it is written *Thou shalt not murder; thou shalt not commit adultery; thou shalt not steal.* Does jealousy exist among you or any evil impulse?' Thereupon the angels conceded that the Holy One was right [in giving the Torah to humanity]." *Sabbath, 88b*

The Torah is intended for all peoples

423. R. Judah, son of R. Hiyya, declared, "The nature of the Holy One differs from that of mortal men. When a man prescribes a remedy, it may benefit one individual but injure another. But God gave the Torah to Israel as a source of healing for all." *Erubin, 54a*

424. In the academy of R. Ishmael it was taught that (Jer. 23:29) *Like a hammer that breaketh the rock in pieces* means that just as a hammer shatters a rock into many pieces, so was every utterance of the Holy

One rendered [simultaneously] into seventy languages. [See also item 458.] *Sabbath, 88b*

All the nations except Israel refused the Torah

425. R. Johanan said, "The Holy One offered the Torah to every nation and every people, but none accepted it until He came to Israel, and Israel received it." [See item 418.] *Abodah Zarah, 2b*

How Israel accepted the Torah

426. (Exod. 19:17) *And they stood at the foot of* [literally, "beneath"] *the mountain*. R. Dimi b. Hassa said, "We learn from this verse [when rendered literally] that the Holy One arched the mountain over the people of Israel like a tent and said to them, 'If you accept the Torah, all is well; but if not, then here shall your grave be.' " [R. Aha b. Jacob objects to this notion.] Thereupon Raba declared, "At the time of Ahasuerus [King of Persia, who married Esther, a Jew], Israel accepted the Torah voluntarily; for Scripture states: (Esther 9:27) *The Jews confirmed it as a duty, and took upon themselves,* [1] which shows that they confirmed what they had taken upon themselves long before [i.e., their acceptance of the Torah]." *Sabbath, 88a*

God rejoiced when Israel accepted the Torah

427. R. Zeira—others say R. Hanina b. Papa—declared, "The way of God is not like that of mortal men. If a man sells a precious thing to a fellowman, the seller is saddened [at parting with something valuable] and only the purchaser is happy. But this is not the case with the Holy One. When He gave the Torah to Israel He rejoiced, saying, (Prov. 4:2) *For good doctrine do I give unto you.*" *Berachoth, 5a*

Israel cannot survive without the Torah

428. The [Roman] government issued a decree forbidding Israel to study the Torah. R. Akiba, in defiance of that decree, set up assemblies in public places and lectured to them on the Torah. Papa b. Judah said to him, "Akiba, are you not afraid of the government?"

R. Akiba replied, "Are you Papus, known as 'the Wise'? Let me

---

[1] The verse continues, *that they would keep these two days* [of Purim] . . . *every year.* The seeming redundancy of the phrases *confirmed it as a duty* and *took upon themselves* is taken by Raba to signify the affirmation of acceptance of the Torah as well as the promise to observe Purim annually. See item 437 and fn.

answer you with a parable. A fox, walking on the riverbank, saw the fishes swimming to and fro, and said to them, 'Why do you scurry about?' 'Because we fear the nets that are spread out for us,' they replied.

" 'Come ashore then,' said the fox, 'and live with me, just as your ancestors lived with my ancestors.' But they answered, 'Are you indeed called the wisest of the beasts? You are not wise at all, but very foolish. If we are in danger here in our natural environment, how much more would we be in danger on shore!' So it is with us. If we are in danger when we study the Torah, regarding which Scripture states: (Deut. 30:20) *It is thy life and the prolongation of thy days,* how much greater would be the danger if we were to stop studying the Torah!"[1] *Berachoth, 61b*

Cherishing the Torah properly

429. R. Judah commented on the verse (Deut. 27:9) *Be attentive and hearken O Israel; this day art thou become a people.* He asked, "Was the Torah really given to Israel on that day? The fact is that forty years [of desert wandering] already had elapsed [when these words were spoken]. This was said in order to teach us an important lesson: that the Torah should always be as dear to us as if it had this very day been given to us on Mount Sinai." [See also item 478.] *Berachoth, 63b*

The words of the Torah are compared to a fire

430. Rabbah bar Hana said, "Why are the words of the Torah compared to a fire? Scripture states: (Jer. 23:29) *Is not My word like a fire? saith the Lord.* This is to teach us that just as a fire cannot burn by itself [without something to burn], so too the words of the Torah do not remain with one who is alone [i.e., they must be shared by discussion]." *Taanith 7a*

. . . to a tree

431. R. Nahman b. Isaac said, "Why are the words of the Torah compared to a tree? Scripture states: (Prov. 3:19) *It is a tree of life to those that lay hold of it.* The Torah is compared to a tree in order to teach us that just as a small twig may kindle a larger branch, so does a lesser scholar sharpen the understanding of a greater one by his questions. This is what was meant by R. Hanina when he said, 'I have

---

[1] The allegory of the fishes is applied more universally by R. Judah in item 419.

learned much from my teachers, and more from my colleagues, but most from my students.' " *Taanith, 7a*

. . . to a fig tree

432. R. Hiyya b. Abba commented in the name of R. Johanan on the verse (Prov. 27:18) *Whoso guardeth the fig-tree will eat of its fruit.* Said he, "The Torah is like a fig tree. Just as a fig tree yields its fruit to one who searches it [since its fruit is often concealed by its leaves], so does the Torah yield [renewed] inspiration to one who continually examines it." *Erubin, 54a*

433. Our rabbis taught: Why is the Torah compared to a fig tree? In all fruits there is some part that is inedible. In dates there are pits; in grapes there are seeds; in pomegranates there are husks; but the whole of the fig is edible. Similarly, in the words of the Torah there is no refuse. *Erubin, 54a,b*

. . . to water

434. R. Hanina b. Idi said, "Why are the words of the Torah compared to water? Scripture states: (Isa. 55:1) *Ho, everyone that thirsteth, come ye for water.* This teaches us that just as water descends from a higher to a lower place, so can the words of the Torah be retained only by one with a humble spirit."

Taanith, 7a

. . . to water, wine and milk

435. R. Oshiya said, "Why are the words of the Torah compared to the three liquids—water, wine and milk? Scripture states: (Isa. 21:14) *To him that is thirsty bring ye water;* and also (Isa. 55:1) *Yea, come buy without money and without price wine and milk.* This teaches us that just as these liquids can best be kept in common utensils, such as wooden or earthen vessels, so the Torah can only be retained by those who are of a humble spirit."

Taanith, 7a

. . . to a bosom

436. R. Samuel b. Nahmani said, "What is the meaning of the verse (Prov. 5:19) *Let her bosom satisfy thee at all times?* The reference here is to the Torah. Just as the breast supplies milk as often as the suckling approaches it, so is it with the Torah. Whenever one draws near it he finds new meaning in it." *Erubin, 54b*

All Jewish teaching is derived from the Torah

437. Our rabbis taught: Forty-eight prophets and seven prophetesses spoke prophecies for Israel, yet they neither subtracted from nor added to what was written in the Torah, except for the injunction to read the Book of Esther annually on the Feast of Purim."[1]

Megillah, 14a

Hillel presents the essence of the Torah

438. A Gentile once appeared before Shammai and said, "I want to be converted to Judaism, but only on the condition that you teach me all of the Torah while I stand on one foot." Shammai drove him off. The Gentile then went to Hillel, who agreed to his request immediately and said to him, "That which is hateful unto thee, do not do unto another.[2] This is the whole Torah; the rest is commentary. Go and study."[3] *Sabbath, 31a*

The authorship of the Torah

439. Mar said, "Joshua [successor of Moses] wrote not only the book bearing his name but also the last eight verses of the Torah [which refer to the death of Moses]." We are also taught in a *baraitha* that while Moses gave us the Torah, the last eight verses were written by Joshua, beginning with (Deut. 34:5) *And Moses, the servant of God, died there.*

Is it possible that Moses could have written that he died after his death [or even before he died]? We must therefore agree that up to this point Moses did the writing, but that from this verse on, Joshua did.[4] *Baba Bathra, 15a*

440. R. Simeon said, "Is it possible that the Holy Scroll would not

---

[1] A late book of the Bible, the Book of Esther tells of the deliverance of the Jews of Persia from the plot of Haman, who sought to destroy them. The anniversary of that event has been observed ever since as the Festival of Purim. See item 426 and fn.

[2] Thought to be based on (Lev. 19:18) *Thou shalt love thy neighbor as thyself,* this is the presumable source, in negative terms, of the Golden Rule, "Do unto others as you would have others do unto you." This appears in the New Testament as "All things whatsoever ye would that men should do unto you, do ye even so unto them" (Matt. 7:12; Luke 6:31). See also items 880, 881, 882 and 883 on the Golden Rule in practice.

[3] Note that while Hillel presents this as the essence of the Torah, he nonetheless stresses the importance of study. For another incident about Hillel and a convert, see item 446.

[4] This may be an adumbration of modern Biblical scholarship. Item 440 defends the more traditional view.

have been complete to the last letter when it was presented to Israel? Yet we read: (Deut. 31:26) *Take this book of the Law,* etc., as if it had been completed at that point [while we know that it was not]. We must therefore assume that up to this verse [rather than Deut. 34:5, suggested in item 439], the Holy One dictated to Moses, and Moses repeated it as he wrote it down; but that from this verse on [and including the death of Moses] God dictated and Moses wrote with tears in his eyes [without repeating God's words]."

Baba Bathra, 15a

441. (Num. 15:31) *Because he hath despised the word of the Lord.* Our rabbis taught that this refers to one who says that the Torah is not [entirely] from heaven, even to one who agrees that the Torah is from heaven except for as much as a single verse which Moses spoke on his own accord. *Sanhedrin, 99a*

When the Torah itself may be violated

442. Scripture states: (Ps. 119:126) *It is time to act for the Lord;* [therefore] *they have violated Thy law.* [1] This means that when the time comes to act for the Lord, the Torah itself may [for the moment] be violated. *Yoma, 69a*

The most important commandment in all of Scripture

443. Micah reduced the Biblical commandments to three: (Mic. 6:8) *It hath been told thee O man, what is good, and what the Lord doth require of thee: Only to do justly, to love mercy, and to walk humbly with thy God.* Isaiah reduced them to two: (Isa. 56:1) *Thus saith the Lord, Keep ye justice, and do righteousness.* But Amos reduced them to one: (Amos 5:4) *For thus saith the Lord unto the house of Israel: Seek ye Me and live.*

Makkoth, 23b

444. R. Kappara asked, "Which verse contains the primary elements of Scripture? It is the verse (Prov. 3:6) *In all thy ways acknowledge Him, and He will direct thy path.*" *Berachoth, 63a*

445. Rabbi said, "The commandment of circumcision is more important than all the other injunctions of Scripture; for the Scriptures

---

[1] Here the rabbis reverse the actual meaning, which would require interpolation of the word "because" instead of "therefore." They were intent upon deriving Scriptural support for disobeying the injunctions of the Torah itself under conditions of great danger or need. For example, while no work could be done on the Sabbath, in obedience to the Ten Commandments, it was permitted in order to save a life.

state: (Exod. 24:8) *Behold the blood of the covenant* [i.e., circumcision] *which the Lord hath made with you in agreement with all these words.*"[1]

Nedarim, 31b

The sanctity of the "unwritten Law"

446. A Gentile once came to Shammai and asked him, "How many Torahs do you have?" To this Shammai replied, "We have two: the written Law and the unwritten Law [i.e., the Torah and the rabbinic Halachah]." The visitor then declared, "The written Law I can accept; but the oral Law I do not recognize. Make me a proselyte on the condition that you will teach me only the written Law." Thereupon Shammai rebuked the man sharply and sent him on his way.

The Gentile then came to Hillel, and Hillel agreed to make him a proselyte [on this condition]. On the first day of instruction, Hillel taught him the *aleph, beth, gimel* and *daleth* [i.e., the first four letters] of the Hebrew alphabet. The next day Hillel reversed the order of these letters. "You did not teach me so yesterday!" said the prospective convert. "True," replied Hillel, "but have you not relied upon me for instruction [in Hebrew]? Why then don't you rely on me with regard to [the validity of] the oral Law?" [See also item 438.]

Sabbath, 31a

447. R. Simeon b. Lakish asked, "Why does Scripture state: (Exod. 34:27) *Write thou these words* [of the Torah], then continue, (ibid.) *for after the tenor* [literally, 'by the mouth'] *of these words I have made a covenant with thee and with Israel?*" The school of Shammai said that this indicates that only the words of the Torah were to be written, but not the [equally valid] Halachic teachings.[2] *Gittin, 60b*

448. R. Johanan said, "The Holy One made a [written] covenant with Israel only because of [*bishvil*] the oral Law. This is implied in

---

[1] The intent here is that circumcision both validates and perpetuates all of the injunctions of the Torah. It is enjoined upon all Jewish males and traditionally takes place on the eighth day after birth. Abraham, the very first Jew, is reported to have circumcised his son Isaac on the eighth day (Gen. 21:4). Abraham himself is said to have been circumcised (Gen. 17:23).

[2] The Mishnah and Gemara were not originally intended to be recorded. The school of Shammai finds support in the cited verse, which appears to be somewhat redundant, for the oral transmission of the Halachah as a complementary part of the Torah covenant. Involved here is the literal rendition of the Hebrew *al pi* as "by the mouth" rather than "after the tenor." This is taken as a reference to the oral Law. See also item 448.

(ibid.) *for after the tenor* ['by the mouth'] *of these words I have made a covenant with thee and with Israel.*"[1] *Gittin, 60b*

B. ADULT LEARNING

The importance of study of the Torah

449. Rab—some say it was R. Samuel b. Martha—declared, "The study of the Torah is more important than the rebuilding of the Temple [in Jerusalem]." *Megillah, 16b*

Torah study is a lifelong pursuit

450. Rabbi Akiba said, "Even though one studied the Torah in his youth, he should continue to do so in old age." *Yebamoth, 62b*

It sustains us in our later years

451. R. Nehorai said, "I will put aside all worldly occupations and will teach my son only the Torah; for all other pursuits are productive only during a man's younger years, and when he becomes old he is exposed to hunger if he cannot perform his tasks. Absorption in the Torah, however, improves a man when he is young and gives him a good and lasting hope in his old age." *Kiddushin, 82a*

It should continue until death

452. R. Jonathan said, "A person should not withhold himself from the house of study and from words of Torah even at the hour of death." *Sabbath, 83b*

Setting aside time for study

453. Raba said, "Set a fixed [regular] time for study of the Torah."
Erubin, 54b

454. R. Tanhum b. Hanilai said, "It is advisable to divide one's years in three parts: one for the study of Scripture, the second for Mishnah and the third for Gemara." But how does one know how long he will live? This therefore must refer to dividing one's days.
Abodah Zarah, 19b

---

[1] Johanan goes a step further than the school of Shammai, stating that the Torah itself was created only as support for (*bishvil*) the Halachah, to be transmitted orally.

There is no excuse for not studying the Torah

455. When the poor, the rich and the licentious man shall appear for the divine judgment, the poor man will be asked, "Why have you not studied Torah?" If he answers that he was poor and had to work for a living, he will be answered, "Were you then poorer than Hillel the Elder?"[1]

Concerning Hillel the Elder, it is said that he went to work every day and earned a *tarpeik*,[2] of which he gave half to the porter at the academy for his admission, and by the other half did he and his family subsist. One day he did not earn anything, and the porter refused to admit him. He thereupon climbed to the roof and swung himself onto a skylight window, where he sat down and could hear the words spoken by Shemaiah and Abtalion.[3] This happened on a Friday, during the winter season, and as he sat there it began to snow. Before long, the snow had completely covered him.

Down below in the academy, Shemaiah said to Abtalion, "Why is it that we usually have light at this hour, but now it is dark? Is it such a cloudy day?" They raised their eyes, and saw the figure of a man at the skylight window. They went up, and there found Hillel, covered with a layer of snow. They took him down, washed him, rubbed him with oil and placed him before a fire, remarking, "Such a man deserves that even the Sabbath be violated for him."[4]

When the rich man is asked, "Why did you not study the Torah?" he may answer that he was a rich man, with many properties and no time for study. Then he will be asked, "Were you richer than R. Elazar b. Harsum?" Of the latter it was said that his father had bequeathed him a thousand towns and a thousand ships at sea, yet he used to put a bundle on his shoulder and travel from town to town and country to country in order to study Torah.

Once some of his own servants encountered him and, not recognizing him,[5] set him to hard labor. He said to them, "Let me go, I pray you, in order that I may study." Thereupon they said, "We swear by

---

[1] Hillel I, founder of the School of Hillel, lived in the first century B.C.E. He is sometimes called Hillel the Elder to distinguish him from Hillel II (c. 350 C.E.).

[2] A *tarpeik* was half of a *denar*.

[3] Shemaiah and Abtalion are referred to as "great men of the generation" (Pesahim, 66a). Abtalion is the earliest sage in whose name Aggadic observations have been recorded.

[4] In attending to his needs, they were delayed beyond sundown, when the Jewish Sabbath begins.

[5] He never saw his servants because he was always engaged in study.

the life of R. Elazar b. Harsum that we will not let you go befo
do some work." He then paid them a large sum of money in order
that they should let him go and study.

When the licentious man is asked, "Why did you not study the
Torah?" he may reply that he was handsome and was influenced by
his sensual appetites. Then he will be asked whether he was more
subject to sexual temptation than was Joseph. It is told of Joseph [Gen.
39:7] that Potiphar's wife tried to seduce him every day by her talk.
Also, the clothes she put on in the morning [to attract his attention]
she did not wear again in the evening.

"Listen to me and do what I ask of you," she pleaded with him, but
he refused. "I will imprison you!" she threatened. But he replied, (Ps.
146:7) *"The Lord releaseth the prisoners."*[1] "I will bring you low," she
warned him. But he answered, (ibid.) *"The Lord raiseth up those who
are bowed down."* She said to him, "I will blind you," but he replied,
(Ps. 146:8) *"The Lord causeth the blind to see."* She then offered him a
thousand talents of silver, but he still refused her entreaties (Gen.
39:10) *to live with her, to be near her.*

Thus the example of Hillel will serve to convict the poor man who
did not study; that of Elazar b. Harsum will convict the rich; and that
of Joseph will bring about the conviction of the voluptuous man.

Yoma, 35b

One should study despite one's limitations

456. Raba said, "One should study even though one may forget
what he has learned. One should study even though he does not fully
understand the material." *Abodah Zarah, 19a*

The habit of study leads to love for it

457. R. Judah said in the name of Rab, "A man should engage in
study of Torah and in meritorious deeds even if it is not for their own
sake; for by doing so, he will [ultimately] learn to love the study of
Torah and performance of good deeds for their own sake." [One
cultivates a "taste" for them.] *Pesahim, 50b*

---

[1] Joseph is depicted as quoting Biblical passages from a period much later than his own. Here
the rabbinic principle that "there is no earlier or later in the Torah" is extended to include
the Book of Psalms to justify the anachronism.

The words of the Torah may be variously interpreted

458. The school of R. Ishmael explained the verse (Jer. 23:29) *Is not My word like a hammer that breaketh the rock in pieces?* by saying that just as a hammer causes numerous sparks to flash, so is a Scriptural verse subject to many interpretations.[1] *Sanhedrin, 34a*

Torah passages must be understood in context

459. R. Kahana said, "When I was eighteen years old, I was well versed in the Talmud, but I did not know until now that a [Torah] passage must not be taken out of context." What does he mean to tell us by this statement? That a man must first study the whole Torah before he reasons about it [i.e., the more one studies the whole, the better one understands its parts].

Sabbath, 63a

Knowing the Torah requires reverence for God

460. Rabba b. R. Huna said, "Whoever possesses knowledge of the Torah without having reverence for God is like a treasurer who has been entrusted with the inner keys of the treasury but from whom the outer keys are withheld. How is he to enter?" [One may know its text yet fail to grasp its spirit.] *Sabbath, 31a*

When a Gentile studies the Torah

461. R. Meir said, "Whence do we know that even a Gentile who is occupied with the study of the Torah is equal to a [Jewish] high priest? From the passage (Lev. 18:5) *Ye shall therefore keep My statutes and Mine ordinances, which if a man do, he shall live by them.* This does not specify a priest, Levite or [even an] Israelite,[2] but peaks broadly of *a man.* Thus it may be inferred that a Gentile too, if he studies the Torah, is equal to a high priest."

Abodah Zarah, 3a

Studying in the company of scholars

462. R. Ashi [the redactor of the Talmud] said, "He who enjoys learning in the company of scholars derives the fruit of all their scholarship." *Makkoth, 10a*

---

[1] The observation applies to the very verse quoted here. For a different interpretation of that verse, see item 424. The reader will find other examples which illustrate the point.

[2] Three categories of Jews who traditionally have descending rank in ritual matters, such as being called to the pulpit when the Torah is read publicly. See item 977.

Two questions should not be asked together

463. Two questions must not be asked simultaneously. If two questions are asked together, only the first is to be answered.

Yoma, 73a

On dozing in a house of study

464. R. Zera said, "If one dozes in a house of study, his wisdom will be rent to pieces; for Scripture states: (Prov. 23:21) *And drowsiness clothes a man in rags.*"[1] *Sanhedrin, 71a*

One should not study in the street

465. Rabbi told his disciples not to study in the public streets, citing the verse (Song of Songs 7:2) *The roundings of thy thighs are like the links of a chain.* Just as the thigh [suggested Rabbi] is concealed, so also should the Torah be studied in privacy.[2] *Moed Katan, 16a*

The Torah must not be used for self-aggrandisement

466. R. Eleazar b. Zadok said, "Do good deeds in the name of your Maker [i.e., because this is God's will and not for the sake of reward] and converse in words of Torah for their own sake. Do not make the Torah [through mastery of it] a crown with which to exalt yourself; nor shall you make of it a spade to dig with [i.e., a means of livelihood]." *Nedarim, 62a*

467. We are taught in a *baraitha* that (Deut. 30:20) *To love the Lord thy God, to hearken to His voice, and to cleave unto Him* means that a man should not say, "I will study the Scriptures so that I may be called a learned man; I will study so that I may be called *Rabbi*, I will teach so that I may become a senior scholar with a seat in the academy." One should engage in study for the love of learning, and honor will come in due course. *Nedarim, 62a*

468. R. Alexandri said, "Those who occupy themselves with the Torah for its own sake cause peace to reign in the heavenly household [i.e., among the angels] and in the [human] household here below."

Sanhedrin, 99b

---

[1] The analogy here is that just as inadequate attention to one's work leads to poverty, so does one forego a wealth of learning and receive only a "ragged" education through inattentiveness at study.

[2] *Torah* is a feminine noun, and the Torah is here likened to a bride, whose full beauty is revealed only in privacy.

oad versus concentrated learning

469. Raba said in the name of R. Sechora, who quoted R. Huna, "What does the verse (Prov. 13:11) *Wealth gotten by vanity will diminish; but he that gathereth little by little will increase it* mean? If a person studies broadly [i.e., many subjects at one time] his learning will decrease; but if he gathers knowledge slowly [i.e., subject by subject] his learning will increase." *Erubin, 54b*

Secular studies are discouraged

470. One may ask, "Since I have studied all of the Torah, may I now study Greek philosophy?" Scripture answers: (Josh. 1:8) *This book of the Torah shall not depart out of thy mouth, but thou shalt meditate therein day and night.* Go and find out at which time it is neither day nor night, and you can devote that time to the study of Greek philosophy.[1] *Menahoth, 99b*

471. Cursed be the man who has his son taught Greek philosophy.

Baba Kamma, 82b

Study of the Greek translation of the Torah is permitted

472. R. Judah said, "Though our Sages permitted the use of Greek, this applied only to the translation of the Torah and nothing else. This was because of the episode involving King Ptolemy,[2] who ordered that the Torah be translated into Greek. We are told that Ptolemy brought seventy-two elders from Jerusalem [to Egypt] and put them into seventy-two separate rooms, without telling them why he had brought them to his capital city.

"He then visited each room separately and said to each elder, 'Translate for me the Torah of Moses from memory.' The Holy One caused them to think as with one mind, and they produced identical texts."[3] *Megillah, 9a*

---

[1] It is intriguing that the rabbis praise the beauty of the Greek language, referring to it in the words, (Megillah 9b) "The most beautiful possession of Japheth (the Greeks) shall dwell in the tents of Shem (Israel)." According to Gen. 9:27, Japheth *shall dwell in the tents of Shem;* that verse is the basis for the comment. The Greeks are elsewhere called Javan, after the son of Japheth. Japheth was one of the sons of Noah and the presumed ancestor of the Greeks. See item 622 and fn.

Jewish attraction to the dominant culture is ancient as well as contemporary, and has always been greeted with mixed reactions.

[2] Presumably King Ptolemy Philadelphus of Egypt, 285–247 B.C.E.

[3] The Greek translation, known as the Septuagint, was regarded as divinely inspired.

The greatness of knowledge

473. R. Ammi said, "Great is knowledge, for it is the theme of the first benediction in the weekday blessings." He also said, "Knowledge is of such great importance that it [the word] was placed between the two names of God in the verse (1 Sam. 2:3) *For a God of knowledge is the Lord.*"[1] *Berachoth, 33a*

474. Abaye said, "We have a tradition that none may be called poor except one who is poor in knowledge." In the West [i.e., the land of Israel] they used to say, "Whoever has knowledge has everything; but whoever has not this, what has he? Whoever acquires knowledge, what more does he need? But if one has it not, of what use are his other acquisitions?" *Nedarim, 41a*

Study versus good deeds

475. R. Tarphon and the elders were at the home of Netza in Lud [Lydda] when the question was raised, "Which is more important, study or good deeds?" R. Tarphon said that good deeds were more important, but R. Akiba said that study is greater. Then they agreed that study is greater, for study [of the sacred texts] results in good deeds.

They further declared that he who does not have a knowledge of Scripture and of the Mishnah cannot be considered a cultured man.

Kiddushin, 40b

C. EDUCATING CHILDREN

The duty of educating one's children

476. Our rabbis taught that he who instructs his child in the Torah[2] is among those who enjoy the fruit of their labors in this world while the capital remains for them in the World to Come [i.e., they will be doubly rewarded]. *Sabbath, 127a*

Teaching someone else's child

477. R. Samuel b. Nahmani said in the name of R. Jonathan, "He who teaches the Torah to his neighbor's son will be rewarded with a seat in the Academy on High; as Scripture states: (Jer. 15:19) *Behold,*

---

[1] The two names are *Elohim* ("God") and *Jahve* ("the Lord"). The 1917 J.P.S. Bible renders this: *For the Lord is a God of knowledge,* which would invalidate the comment.

[2] Children were originally taught by their fathers. See item 479.

thus saith the Lord. . . . Thou shalt stand before Me. And if one teaches
the Torah to the son of an *am ha-aretz* ["ignorant man"], even if the
Holy One had ordained an evil decree against the whole world, He
would annul it. For Scripture states: (ibid.) *And if thou bring forth the
precious from the vile, thou shalt be as My mouth* [i.e., a spokesman for
God, thus able to change His decree]." [See also item 238.]

Baba Metzia, 85a

On teaching a grandson

478. R. Joshua b. Levi said, "If one teaches the Torah to his grandson, it is regarded by Scripture as if the grandson had received his
instruction [directly] at Mount Sinai; for Scripture states: (Deut. 4:9)
but make them known [i.e., the words of the Torah] *unto thy children and
thy children's children;* (Deut. 4:10) *the day thou didst stand before the Lord
thy God at Horeb* [Sinai], . . ."[1] *Kiddushin, 30a*

How universal Jewish education began

479. (Isa. 2:3) *For out of Zion shall go forth the Law* [Torah] *and the
word of the Lord from Jerusalem.* In comment on this verse, R. Judah said
in the name of Rab, "Truly, that man must be remembered for blessing whose name is Joshua b. Gamla, for were it not for him, Israel
would have forgotten the Torah."

In former times, the child who had a father received instruction
from his father; for Scripture states: (Deut. 11:19) *And ye* [not others]
shall teach them [i.e., the words of the Torah] *to your children.* But the
fatherless child did not study the Torah at all. Later, an ordinance was
instituted that teachers for the children were to be appointed in Jerusalem; for Scripture states: (Isa. 2:3) *For out of Zion shall go forth the Law
and the word of the Lord from Jerusalem.*

Thereafter, the child who had a father was brought to Jerusalem for
instruction; but the fatherless child was not brought to Jerusalem. It
was therefore further decreed that schools for primary instruction
should be established in the principal communities of each province.
Even so, children were sometimes brought for study when they were
already sixteen or seventeen years old, and when the lads were
rebuked by their teachers, they rebelled and left.

Finally, R. Joshua b. Gamla decreed that primary schools should
be set up throughout the provinces, even in the small towns, and

---

[1]Joshua here builds on a *non sequitur* in the Hebrew text.

that children should be sent to school at the age of six or seven.

Baba Bathra, 21a

Every Jewish community must have a school

480. Resh Lakish said in the name of R. Judah the Nasi, "I have a tradition from my ancestors that any town that has no school will eventually be destroyed." Rabina said that [the tradition was that] the town should be placed under a ban [until a school was provided].

Sabbath, 119b

Children must not be kept from school

481. Resh Lakish said in the name of R. Judah HaNasi, "Children should not be kept out of school even for the rebuilding of the Temple." *Sabbath, 119b*

482. R. Hamnuna said, "Jerusalem was destroyed only because people neglected to send their children to school." *Sabbath, 119b*

Children at study sustain the world

483. Resh Lakish said in the name of R. Judah HaNasi, "The world could not endure if it were not for the breath of children at study." [Study was conducted orally.]

"What about my breath and yours?" R. Papa asked Abaye. And Abaye replied, "The breath that emanates from one who may have sinned is not [as pure as] the breath of one who is incapable of sinning." *Sabbath, 119b*

The principle of the "double learning bond"

484. Samuel said to R. Judah, "You must open your mouth when you study Scripture and when you study Mishnah, so that the material may stay with you." [The auditory impression reinforces the visual.][1] *Erubin, 54a*

Why some students find study difficult

485. Resh Lakish said, "If you find a student whose lesson seems to him as hard as iron, it is because the material is not properly systematized in his mind." *Taanith, 7b*

---

[1] The study of Hebrew texts by reading them aloud also enhances the understanding of the material or its interpretation. The intonations used provide the vowels and punctuation which are missing, resulting in the so-called Talmudic singsong.

486. Raba said, "When you encounter a student whose lesson seems to him as hard as iron, it is because his teacher has not adequately explained the material to him." *Taanith, 8a*

The importance of repetition

487. R. Eliezer said, "It is the duty of a teacher to repeat a lesson with his student four times." But R. Akiba said, "Whence do we infer that one must review the lesson with his student until he masters it? Scripture states: (Deut. 31:19) *and teach it to the children of Israel,* followed by *put it in their mouths* [i.e., so that they can explain it]."

Erubin, 54b

488. R. Joshua b. Karha said, "If one studies Torah and does not review it again and again, he is like one who sows without reaping [i.e., without benefitting from his labors]." *Sanhedrin, 99a*

489. Hillel said, "One who reviews his lesson one hundred times is not like one who reviews it one hundred and one times."

Hagigah, 9b

The falseness of literal translation

490. We are taught in a *baraitha* that R. Judah said, "Whoever translates a Biblical verse word for word [literally] is considered a falsifier [since idiomatic expressions cannot be translated literally].[1] And whoever offers multiple explanations of a Biblical verse [some of which may not be accurate] is to be regarded as one who blasphemes and reviles the Lord." *Kiddushin, 49a*

Recommended educational procedures

491. Rab said to [the schoolmaster] R. Samuel b. Shilath, "Take no pupils until they are six years of age. From six and upward, stuff them with knowledge as you would feed an ox." Rab also said to him, "When you punish a child, use only a shoelace [i.e., do not hurt him]. If this causes the child to behave, well and good; if not, seat him next to a diligent student [whose progress he will witness and strive to emulate]." *Baba Bathra, 21a*

492. R. Huna said in the name of Rab, who quoted R. Meir, "A teacher should always employ conciseness of expression with his pupil [avoiding confusing verbosity]." *Pesahim, 3b*

---

[1] The principle applies also to the public translation of the Torah reading into the vernacular at synagogue services, a custom which continues to this day.

493. Rab said, "The number of pupils to be assigned to each teacher should be limited to twenty-five. If there are fifty, we must appoint two teachers. If there are forty, we appoint an assistant [plus the teacher]."[1] *Baba Bathra, 21a*

How to select a teacher

494. Raba said, "If there is a teacher who can perform his duties passably well but there is another who is even better, the former must not be replaced by the latter, lest he [the second] relax his efforts and become indolent [because he no longer fears competition]." But R. Dimi of Nehardea said, "On the contrary, he [the second] will become all the more diligent for rivalry among scholars increases wisdom." [The second will not want to be similarly replaced.]

Raba also said, "If there are two teachers, one of whom is fast but inexact while the other is exact but slower, the one who is faster though inexact should be appointed as the errors will [in time] be corrected by themselves." But R. Dimi said, "On the contrary, the one who is slow but exact should be appointed because an error implanted in the mind of a child remains there forever."

Baba Bathra, 21a

Who has priority in study?

495. Our rabbis taught that if one wants to study the Torah himself, and also has a son who requires instruction [but has the means for only one of them to study], the father is to be given preference over his son. But R. Judah said, "If his son is a bright and retentive student, then his son should be given preference for his study will be more lasting." [He will outlive his father.]

R. Jacob, the son of R. Aha b. Jacob, was sent by his father to study with Abaye. When he returned, the father saw that his son's study was not as fruitful as it should have been. He therefore said to his son, "I would do much better than you. You stay here and I shall go and study." *Kiddushin, 29b*

---

[1] This principle is now followed in some public schools. It was recently advocated by the Chancellor of the New York City school system, Frank J. Macchiarola ("The Sherrye Henry Program," RKO-General, Inc., radio station WOR, New York, January 17, 1979).

8

THE LIFE OF PIETY

THE absorption of the rabbis in the study and teaching of Scripture was matched by their personal piety. They discerned the directing hand of God in their own lives and in the varied experiences of their people. Prayer was as natural to them as breathing, and they regarded private devotion and public worship as incumbent upon all members of the Jewish community.

The rabbis of the Talmud contributed greatly to the development of the synagogue and to the liturgy of this institution, though the origins of the synagogue—a word derived from the Greek and meaning "assembly"—are quite ancient. Synagogues existed long before the destruction of the second Temple, and are known to have existed in Egypt in the third century B.C.E. Indeed, Ezekiel, living in Babylonia in the sixth to fifth century B.C.E., speaks of such a meeting place as a "small sanctuary" (Ezek. 11:16).

The synagogue served a threefold purpose as a house of assembly (*beth ha-knesseth*), a house of study (*eth ha-midrash*) and a house of prayer (*beth ha-tefilah*). The pageantry of the Temple service was replaced by prayer, the "service of the heart" (*avodah she-balev*). This required neither a sacrificial altar nor an established hereditary priesthood. Any member of the Jewish community was permitted to conduct the service, and every Jewish male was expected to be qualified to do so.

The Talmud deals in detail with both the substance and sequence of prayers prescribed for private and public worship, and sets the structure for the *Siddur,* the Jewish prayerbook. In the Aggadah we find occasional passages dealing with prayer and worship in more general terms.

A. PRIVATE PRAYER

Prayer is the service of the heart

496. We have been taught (Deut. 11:13) *To love the Lord your God, and to serve Him with all your heart.* What is the service of the heart? Prayer. *Taanith, 2a*

497. R. Ammi said, "A man's prayer is not answered unless he prays from the heart; for Scripture states: (Lam. 3:41) *Let us lift up our hearts with our hands unto God in the heavens.*" *Taanith, 8a*

498. Our rabbis taught that when a man prays he should direct his heart to heaven. *Berachoth, 31a*

One must be aware before Whom one prays

499. R. Eliezer said, "When you pray, know before Whom you are standing, and in this way you will achieve the World to Come." [See chapter 14.] *Berachoth, 28b*

500. R. Hana b. Bizna said in the name of R. Simeon the Pious, "He who prays should always believe the *Shechinah* is before him; for Scripture states: (Ps. 16:8) *I have set the Lord always before me.*"
Sanhedrin, 22a

Prayer can win God's mercy

501. R. Eleazar said, "Why may the prayer of the righteous be compared to a shovel?[1] Just as a shovel moves grain from one place to another, so does the prayer of the righteous turn the dispensation of the Lord from anger to mercy." *Sukkah, 14a*

502. R. Helbo said, "If one has the fear [reverence] of the Lord, his words will be heard." *Berachoth, 6b*

Prayer should not be interrupted

503. A pious man was once praying on the road when he was encountered by a prince, who greeted him saying, "Peace unto you!" The pious man did not answer. The prince waited until he had finished his prayers, then said to him, "Good for nothing! In your Torah it states: (Deut. 4:9) *Only take heed to thyself, and guard thy soul*

---

[1] A play on words is involved here. In Gen. 25:21, Isaac entreats God that Rebecca might have a child. The verb "entreat" (*vayeathar*) is from the root *athar*, which is spelled like the word *ether*, meaning "a shovel." Eleazar relates the two homiletically. The intent is that God can be "moved" to show mercy.

[life] *diligently.* Scripture also states: (Deut. 4:15) *Take ye therefore good heed of your souls.* When I greeted you, why did you not reply? If I were to order your head cut off, who would hold me accountable?"

"Wait," said the pious man, "and I shall appease your anger with a parable. If you had been standing before a mortal king and someone greeted you, would you have answered him?" "No," the prince replied. "If you had done so," continued the pious man, "what would the king have done to you?" "He would have had my head cut off," said the prince. The man then said to him, "If you were to act thus before a mortal king, how much more cautious must I be when I stand in the presence of the King of kings, Who endures throughout eternity?" The prince was thereupon appeased, and the pious man went peacefully home. *Berachoth, 32b*

504. R. Johanan said, "Would that a man could pray all day."

Berachoth, 21a; Pesahim, 54b

Continuing to pray even when prayer seems unavailing

505. R. Hama b. R. Hanina said, "Even if a man sees that his prayers go unanswered, he should continue to pray; for Scripture states: (Ps. 24:14) *Wait for the Lord; be strong and let thy heart be of good courage; yea, wait thou for the Lord.*"[1] *Berachoth, 32b*

On knowing what to pray for

506. In the days of R. Samuel b. Nahmani, both famine and pestilence prevailed, and the Sages raised the question, "What shall we pray for? Shall we pray for both to cease? This is too much to ask. Let us therefore pray for the abatement of the pestilence, and we shall put up with the famine."

However, R. Samuel b. Nahmani said to them, "Not so. Let us rather pray for relief from the famine; for when the All-Merciful provides sustenance He provides it for the living; as Scripture states: (Ps. 145:16) *Thou openest Thy hand and satisfiest the desire of every living creature* [for sustenance]."[2] *Taanith, 8b*

---

[1] The word "wait" is repeated, suggesting continued waiting.

[2] Since God provides sustenance for all of His creatures, He would surely answer the prayer for food, so they would not have to put up with the famine. And because He can provide sustenance only for the living, He would of necessity spare them from the danger of death through the plague.

The private prayer of R. Eleazar

507. R. Eleazar would say on concluding his prayers, "May it be Thy will, O Lord our God, to cause love and brotherhood, peace and friendship to abide among us. Mayest Thou make our borders rich in disciples and prosper our latter end with good prospect and hope, and set a portion for us in Paradise. Bestow upon us a good companion and a good impulse in Thy world. May we be filled with pious thoughts on waking, and mayest Thou be pleased to grant us the satisfaction of our desires." *Berachoth, 16b*

. . . of Mar

508. Mar, the son of R. Huna, would add the following prayer after finishing his daily devotions: "O my God, guard my tongue from evil and my lips from speaking guile. To such as curse me, let my soul be dumb; yea, let my soul be to all as dust. Open my heart to thy Torah, and let my soul pursue Thy commandments. Deliver me from any mishap, from evil inclinations and from the various perils that beset mankind. If any plot harm against me, speedily make their counsel of no effect and frustrate their designs. Do it for the sake of Thy name, for the sake of Thy right hand, for the sake of Thy holiness, for the sake of Thy Torah, so that Thy beloved ones may be delivered. O save with Thy right hand and answer me. May the words of my mouth and the meditations of my heart be acceptable unto Thee, my Rock and my Redeemer."[1]

Berachoth, 17a

. . . of R. Zera

509. R. Zera, upon concluding his prayers, would add, "May it be Thy will, O Lord our God, that we sin not, nor bring upon ourselves shame or disgrace before our fathers." *Berachoth, 16b*

. . . of Rab

510. At the close of his prayers Rab would add, "May it be Thy will, O Lord our God, to grant us long life; a life of peace, a life of good, a life of blessing, a life of sustenance, a life of bodily vigor, a life free from sin, from shame and confusion, a life of riches and honor, in which we may demonstrate love of Torah and fear of

---

[1] The last sentence is from Psalm 19:15 and is part of the Amidah, a prayer recited in private and public worship.

heaven, a life in which Thou wilt fulfil the good desires of our heart."[1] *Berachoth, 16b*

Praying on behalf of another

511. Raba, the son of Hanina the Elder, said in the name of Rab, "Whoever is in a position to pray on behalf of another and does not do so is to be called a sinner; for Scripture states: (1 Sam. 12:23) *Moreover, as for me, be it far from me that I should sin against the Lord by ceasing to pray in your behalf."* Berachoth, 12b

512. Raba said to Rabbah b. Mari, "Whence can we derive that whoever prays for a fellowman while himself being in need of prayer will be answered first? From the words (Job 42:10) *And the Lord changed the fortune of Job when he prayed for his friends."* Baba Kamma, 92a

Facing toward Jerusalem at prayer

513. If one is in the East [during prayer], he should face toward the West; in the West, he should face east; in the South, he should face north; in the North, he should face south. It is thereby established that all of the household of Israel directs its heart to one place [Jerusalem].[2] *Berachoth, 30a*

Standing on a low place

514. R. Jose b. Hanina said in the name of R. Eliezer b. Jacob, "A man should never stand on an elevated place while praying, but upon a low place [as a sign of humility]; for Scripture states: (Ps. 130:1) *Out of the depths have I called Thee, O Lord."* Berachoth, 10b

One should not pray in a dirty place

515. We have a *baraitha* supporting R. Hisda's opinion that if one is walking in a filthy alley he should not recite the *Shema*.[3] Moreover, if one is reciting his prayers while walking, and finds himself in a filthy street, he should stop. *Berachoth, 24b*

---

[1] This prayer is now recited on the Sabbath of the new moon. For the prayer of Rabbi Akiba, see item 32.

[2] The Bible (Dan. 6:11) states that Daniel prayed three times a day facing Jerusalem. Synagogues are traditionally built facing Jerusalem, and pious Jews in America often mount a plaque, known as a *Mizrah* (Hebrew: "East"), on an east wall in their homes to show which way to turn in prayer.

[3] The *Shema* is a declaration of the unity of God, and is regarded as the watchword of the Jewish faith. It appears in Deut. 6:4.

Nor should one pray in an abandoned building

516. R. Jose said, "Once when I was walking, I entered into one of the ruins of Jerusalem to pray. Elijah [the prophet] appeared and watched me at the door until I finished my prayers. After I had finished, he said to me, 'Shalom, my teacher,' to which I replied, 'Shalom, my teacher and my guide.' 'My son,' said he, 'why did you enter this ruin?' 'To pray,' I answered. 'You could have prayed along the road,' he said. 'I was afraid lest I be interrupted by travelers,' said I. 'You should then have prayed a shorter prayer,' he replied.

"From this incident I concluded three things: first, it is not safe to enter a ruin; second, it is permitted to pray while on the road; third, a man on the road [having no place to pray] has the right to shorten his prayers." *Berachoth, 3a*

Any language may be used in prayer

517. One can pray in any language if necessary.[1] *Sotah, 31a*

Even God prays

518. R. Johanan said in the name of R. Jose b. Zimra, "Whence do we know that the Holy One also prays? Scripture states: (Isa. 56:7) *Even these will I bring to My holy mountain, and make them joyful in My house of prayer.* We learn from this [i.e., God's reference to His house of prayer, through use of the word *My*] that the Holy One also engages in prayer."

How does God pray? R. Zutra b. Tubia said in the name of Rab, "He prays in the following fashion: 'May it be My will that My mercy may overcome My anger; and may My spirit of compassion rule over My attribute of justice, so that I may deal with My children with loving-kindness and forego strict judgment.' " *Berachoth, 7a*

B. PUBLIC WORSHIP

One should pray when the community prays

519. R. Isaac said to R. Nahman, "Why does not the master come to the synagogue to pray?" "Because I am not feeling well," replied R. Nahman. "The master should in that case gather ten men [as

---

[1] But Hebrew was regarded as most appropriate. Prayerbooks today frequently contain both Hebrew and the vernacular.

required for a quorum to conduct public worship]¹ in his own house, and then pray," said R. Isaac.

"It is too difficult a task for me," said R. Nahman. "If so," replied R. Isaac, "why does not the master direct the sexton [of the synagogue] to inform him when a quorum is assembled for prayer [in the synagogue, so that he might pray at the same time that they do]?"

"Why are you so meticulous about this?" asked R. Nahman. "Because," said R. Isaac, "R. Johanan declared in the name of R. Simeon b. Johai that the verse (Ps. 69:14) *But as for me, I direct my prayer unto Thee, O Lord, in an acceptable time* [i.e., a favorable time] means that one should pray when the community prays."

R. Jose b. Hanina said, "This can also be derived from the verse (Isa. 49:8) *In an acceptable time have I answered thee* [i.e., if one prays in *an acceptable time*—when the public prays—his prayers will be answered]." *Berachoth, 7b*

520. Abba Benjamin said that a man's prayers are only heeded by God when offered in a synagogue [i.e., at communal prayer].

Berachoth, 6a

521. Abaye said that a person should always associate himself with the community in his prayers. How then should one pray? One should pray, "May it be Thy will, O Lord our God, to conduct us in peace," etc. [The plural forms "our" and "us" are to be used rather than "my" or "me."] *Berachoth, 29b*

The need for a quorum at worship

522. R. Eliezer went into a synagogue [to pray] and did not find ten men there, so he freed his slave [i.e., indentured servant] and completed the requisite number.² *Berachoth, 47b*

523. R. Johanan said, "Whenever the Holy One enters a synagogue and does not find ten persons there, he becomes upset;³ for Scripture states: (Isa. 50:2) *Wherefore, when I came, was there no man? When I called there was no answer?*" *Berachoth, 47b*

---

¹ See items 522 and 523.
² The requirement of ten men for a *minyan*, or quorum, is presumably derived from Gen. 18:32, where God promises Abraham that He will not destroy Sodom if as few as ten righteous men are to be found there. See also items 116 and 117.
³ In the absence of a *minyan*, some important parts of the service are omitted.

Why the sexes are separated at worship

524. Our rabbis taught that originally the women sat inside the Temple court and the men outside, but some levity took place. It was therefore decreed that the women should sit outside the Temple court and the men within. But levity still arose, so it was ordained that women should sit above [i.e., in a balcony] and the men below.[1]

Sukkah, 51b

Arriving at the synagogue early and staying late

525. R. Joshua b. Levi said to his children, "Always arrive at the synagogue early and remain late, in order that your years may be lengthened." R. Aha, the son of Hanina, when asked which Biblical verse supported this concept, quoted the verse (Prov. 8:34) *Happy is the man who hearkeneth unto Me, watching daily at My gates, waiting at the posts of My doors,* which is followed by the words *For whoso findeth Me findeth life* [i.e., length of years]. *Berachoth, 8a*

526. R. Helbo said in the name of R. Huna, "One who leaves the synagogue should not hurry [literally, 'take long steps']." Said Abaye, "This applies only upon leaving. Upon going to the synagogue it is meritorious to hurry; for Scripture states: (Hos. 6:3) *Let us know and hasten to serve the Lord.*" *Berachoth, 6b*

The centrality of the synagogue

527. Resh Lakish said, "Whoever has a synagogue in his town and does not go there to pray is considered a bad neighbor; for Scripture states: (Jer. 12:14) *Thus saith the Lord, as for all Mine evil neighbors that touch* [i.e., interfere with] *the inheritance which I have caused My people Israel to inherit.* Moreover, he brings exile upon himself and upon his children; for Scripture states: (ibid.) *Behold, I will pluck them up from their land, and pluck up the house of Judah from among them.*"

Berachoth, 8a

528. Raba b. Mehasia said in the name of R. Hama b. Goria, who quoted Rab, "Any city whose rooftops are higher than the synagogue will ultimately be destroyed; for Scripture teaches us (Ezra 9:9) *to set up* [*l'romem:* 'to exalt'] *the house of our God and* [or] *to repair the ruins thereof* [i.e., destruction will be the lot of a city where this is not done]." *Sabbath, 11a*

---

[1] Such separation is no longer general practice. Even some modern Orthodox congregations have mixed seating.

Replacing an old synagogue structure

529. R. Hisda said that an old synagogue must not be torn down until a new synagogue has been constructed to take its place. Some say that this is to avoid the possibility of neglecting the matter [of building a new one]. But others say that this is to prevent any interruption of [public] worship [while the new edifice is being built].

Baba Bathra, 3b

C. BLESSINGS

How Abraham taught others to bless God

530. Our father Abraham would cause everyone who passed by to utter the name of God. How did he accomplish this? After they had eaten and drunk [as his guests], they would rise in order to bless Abraham [for his hospitality]. But Abraham would say to them, "Have you eaten anything which is mine? You have eaten only that which belongs to the God of the whole universe! Therefore you should thank, praise and bless Him Who by the spoken word brought the whole world into existence." *Sotah, 10b*

How David blessed God

531. Five separate times did David speak the words (Ps. 103:1, 2,22; 104:1,35) *Bless the Lord, O my soul.* For what reason did he say this five times? R. Simeon b. Pazzi said, "He did so in order to relate the soul of man to the Holy One; for just as God fills the whole universe, so does man's soul suffuse his whole body.[1] Just as God sees but cannot be seen, so does the soul perceive yet cannot be perceived. Just as God nourishes all of humanity, so does the soul sustain the whole body. Just as God is pure, so is the soul pure. And just as God dwells in a place hidden from all men, so does the soul dwell in a secret place. Therefore let the soul, which has these five attributes, bless Him who possesses these same attributes."[2]

Berachoth, 10a

---

[1] Bernard Bamberger suggests that the idea that God pervades the universe as the soul pervades the body seems to have been a rabbinic borrowing from the Stoics ("Philo and the Aggadah," *Hebrew Union College Annual* 48 [1977]:78).

[2] Regarding the soul, see also items 758–762.

Blessing God for the pleasures of life

532. R. Hanina b. Papa said, "He who experiences any pleasure in this world without saying a blessing is considered as if he had robbed the Holy One [Who made it possible]." *Sanhedrin, 102a*

. . . and for the beauties of nature

533. R. Judah said, "Whoever takes a walk in the month of Nissan [springtime] and beholds the blossoming trees should say, 'Blessed art Thou Who hast made Thy world lacking in naught, and produced therein goodly creatures and lovely trees to give delight to the children of men.' " *Rosh Hashanah, 11a*

534. Rab[1] declared that it is forbidden to say, "How lovely is this Gentile woman!" But it was pointed out that when R. Simeon b. Gamaliel stood on the steps of the Temple mount and saw a Gentile woman of great beauty he exclaimed, (Ps. 104:24) *"How manifold are Thy works, O Lord!"* [in seeming defiance of Rab's statement]. However, there is no contradiction here. R. Simeon b. Gamaliel praised God by reciting a passage of Scripture [without referring to a woman's beauty], and a Master [R. Judah, in item 533] has taught us that one who sees beautiful things such as lovely trees should say, "Blessed be He Who hath created such things in this world" [in praise of God and not of His created object].

Abodah Zarah, 20a

Special occasions for expressing gratitude

535. R. Judah said in the name of Rab, "Four kinds of people are duty-bound to thank God: those who have returned safely from a sea voyage; those who have returned from the desert; those who have recovered from a serious illness; and those who have been released from prison [i.e., captivity]."[2] *Berachoth, 54b*

536. He who beholds a king of Israel should say, "Blessed be He Who shares His glory with those who revere Him." If one sees a king of another people he should say, "Blessed be He Who shares His honor with one who is flesh and blood." Upon seeing a wise man of Israel one should say, "Blessed be He Who shares His wisdom with one who reveres Him." And upon seeing a wise man of another

---

[1] This title was given to Abba Aricha (175–247).

[2] The relevant blessings for this and the next selection are to be found in the traditional *Siddur.*

people one should say, "Blessed be He Who gives of His wisdom to those of flesh and blood." *Berachoth, 58a*

Blessing God for whatever happens to us

537. One must bless God for the evil [which befalls him] as well as for the good [since God is our true Judge].[1] *Berachoth, 33b*

538. R. Meir said, "Whence do we derive that just as one blesses God for good tidings, so should one bless God for evil tidings as well? Scripture states: (Deut. 8:10) *And thou shalt eat and be satisfied, and bless the Lord thy God for the good land which He hath given thee.* This implies that He is your Judge, whatever His decree."

Berachoth, 48b

Avoiding verbosity in blessing God

539. A disciple prayed in the presence of R. Hanina, saying, "O God, Who art great, mighty, awesome, magnificent, strong, exalted, valiant, powerful, real and honored. . . ." R. Hanina waited until he had finished, then said to him, "Have you indeed exhausted all the praises of your Master? Why do you employ so many terms of adulation? There are only three expressions of praise [i.e., "great," "mighty" and "awesome"] used in the [first blessing of the] eighteen benedictions in the prayer service. Even these words we would not dare to utter had not Moses our Teacher spoken them in the Torah [Deut. 10:17], and had not the men of the Great Synagogue ordained their use.[2] Yet you have uttered many words of praise, and seemed inclined to continue to do so. This is like one who compliments an earthly ruler upon possessing a million silver *denars* when he actually has a million gold *denars.* Would not such intended praise really be an insult rather than an expression of honor?"

Berachoth, 33b

---

[1] The words "Blessed be the true Judge (*Baruch dayan emeth*)" are recited to this day at a funeral service by the family.

[2] The "Men of the Great Synagogue (*anshe knesseth hagedolah*)" constituted the legislative body established by Nehemiah upon the return from Babylonian exile. See the Book of Nehemiah, also *U.J.E.*, s.v.

The importance of saying "Amen"

540. R. Jose said, "He who responds with 'Amen' [completing a blessing] is greater than the one who recites the blessing."[1] "By heaven, that is so," said R. Nehorai, "for we find that ordinary soldiers may begin a battle, but it is the skilled troops who win the victory."[2] *Nazir, 66b*

Cherishing the blessing of a common man

541. R. Eleazar said in the name of R. Hanina, "Never should the blessing of a common man be considered insignificant in your estimation; for two great men of their generation were blessed by simple men, and their blessings were fulfilled. They were David and Daniel.

"David was blessed by Araunah; for Scripture states: (2 Sam. 24:23) *And Araunah said unto the king: 'The Lord thy God accept thee'* [or, 'May the Lord thy God accept thee with favor']. Daniel was blessed by Darius; for Scripture states: (Dan. 6:17) *'Thy God, Whom thou servest continually, He will deliver thee'* [or, 'May thy God . . . deliver thee']."[3] *Megillah, 15a*

How Rab's blessing was fulfilled

542. R. Huna once appeared before Rab wearing a rope as a belt [girdle]. When Rab noticed this, he asked R. Huna, "Where is your silken sash?" And R. Huna replied, "I had no wine for *kiddush* and pawned it to buy wine."[4] Thereupon Rab said, "May it be God's will that you shall be covered with silken robes!"

Some time later, at the wedding of his son Rabbah, R. Huna [who was quite short in stature] took a nap on a bed, and his daughters-in-law [unwittingly] threw their silken robes over him so that he was

---

[1] The original meaning of "Amen" is "firm" or "straight"; thus it is taken to mean "True!" or "So may it be!" In "Amen" is implied an oath, a promise and a prayer for fulfillment (Marcus Jastrow, *Dictionary of the Talmud* [New York: Shapiro, Vallentine & Co., 1926], s.v. "Amen.")

[2] This is a reference to the Roman practice of using seasoned veterans to complete the victory after the enemy had been weakened.

[3] The bracketed renditions represent the subjunctive of wish or blessing. In Hebrew there is no distinction between "will" and "may." Note that Darius, who was king of Persia, is here referred to as a "simple" man.

[4] *Kiddush* is the blessing recited over wine on the Sabbath and on Jewish festival occasions. The word means "sanctification" and is related to *kaddish* (the prayer in memory of the dead) and *kiddushin* (the marriage ceremony).

completely covered. When Rab subsequently heard that his blessing had been fulfilled in this manner he said to R. Huna, "When I blessed you, why did you not answer, 'And the same to the Master' [so that your blessing too might have been fulfilled]?"[1] *Megillah, 27b*

---

[1] The thought here is that Huna's blessing of Rab, who was very tall, would have been all the more fruitful since much more silk would be required to cover him. Rab was of course jesting. The use of humor was not uncommon. Rabbah, for instance, was said to have started his lectures with humor (Pesahim, 117a). Other examples of humor appear in items 181, 290, 470 and 765.

9

THE RULE OF LAW

THE rabbis of the Talmud were concerned with the quest for justice, not only as teachers and preachers valuing justice as an ideal, but also more directly as the judges of their people. The scattered Jewish communities functioned as ethnic enclaves within the larger body politic. As semiautonomous communities, they had their own schools and academies, and also their own courts in which rabbis served as judges.

The scope of Jewish law, as the rabbis perceived it, is not easily described in conventional categories. An esteemed teacher of Judaism, Hirschel Revel, has explained that "All relationships between man and God, between man and his fellowmen, as well as all actions pertaining to man's spiritual and physical welfare, are regulated either directly by the Torah or by applications of principles contained in it."

However, Jewish law may be said to be of two kinds: religious law, which pertains to the practice of the Jewish faith, such as the observance of the dietary laws, festivals and fast days; and civil law, involving such matters as damages, theft or litigation about property. Although the Jews lost the right of jurisdiction in the area of criminal law even before the destruction of the second Temple, two tractates of the Talmud—Sanhedrin and Makkoth—deal with capital crimes and offenses meriting corporal punishment, i.e., flogging. Since these transgressions are also covered by Biblical legislation, they too invite rabbinic comment.

Throughout the centuries, rabbinic courts continued to function in such family and interpersonal matters as marriage and divorce, arbitration of disputes, etc., and are still to be found in cities with a large Jewish population in America and elsewhere. Based upon the principle that "the law of the land is law" (Gittin, 10b), they operate within the framework of the secular legal code, and their jurisdiction is regarded as binding by Jews with a strongly traditional approach to their faith.

The observations cited here are of course peripheral to the more detailed treatment of justice and the legal process in the Halachah.

A. JUSTICE

Why Scripture does not explain its laws

543. R. Isaac said, "Scripture does not give the reason for its laws because in the two instances where Scripture did so the greatest man of his generation stumbled over those laws. We read: (Deut. 17:17) *He shall not acquire many wives, that his heart not turn away.* Yet Solomon said to himself, 'I shall take many wives, and my heart shall not be turned away.' Thereafter we read: (1 Kings 11:14) *And it came to pass . . . that his wives turned away his heart after other gods.*

"Scripture also states: (Deut. 17:16) *He shall not acquire for himself many horses, nor cause the people to return to Egypt* [the great horse market] *in order to multiply horses. . . .* (Deut. 17:20) *to the end that he shall prolong his days in his kingdom, he and his children, in the midst of Israel.* Yet subsequently we read: (1 Kings 10:29) *And a chariotteam came up and went out of Egypt for six hundred shekels of silver."* [Horses were bought from Egypt despite this injunction.] *Sanhedrin, 21b*

God finds ways to achieve justice

544. (Esther 2:21) *In those days, while Mordecai was sitting in the king's gate, Bigthan and Teresh became wroth, and sought to lay hands on King Ahasuerus.* R. Hiyya b. Abba said in the name of R. Johanan, "The Holy One causes masters to be angry against their servants in order to do justice. He also causes the wrath of servants against their masters to achieve justice."[1] *Megillah, 13b*

---

[1] God caused Bigthan and Teresh to be angry against the king so that Mordecai, who overheard their plotting, could be rewarded for saving the king's life by being raised to high estate instead of hanged (as Haman had planned). Conversely, in the case of Joseph (Gen. 41:12), Pharaoh became angry at his butler, and threw him into prison. There the butler met Joseph, who had been jailed, and was instrumental in securing Joseph's release and later rise to eminence.

Cf. ". . . by knaves, as by martyrs, the just cause is carried forward." (R. W. Emerson, "Montaigne," *Emerson's Works* [New York: Three Sirens Press, n.d.], vol. 2, p. 346.)

God judges the judges

545. Judges must be aware before Whom their judgment is being rendered, and Who will punish them [for bad judgment]; for Scripture states: (Ps. 82:1) *God standeth in the congregation of God; in the midst of judges doth He judge* [i.e., God is present at the judgment].[1] And concerning Jehosaphat, Scripture states: (2 Chron. 19:6) *Consider what ye do; for ye judge not for man, but for the Lord.* Sanhedrin, 6b

A judge will be held accountable for faulty judgment

546. R. Samuel b. Nahmani said in the name of R. Jonathan, "If a judge orders the transfer of money from one party to another contrary to the law, then the Holy One will hold him responsible; for Scripture states: (Prov. 22:23) *Rob not the poor because he is poor, neither crush the afflicted in the gate* [in court]; *for the Lord will plead their cause, and despoil the life of those who despoil them.*" Sanhedrin, 7a

547. Whenever Rab went to hold court he would say, "Of my own volition do I go forth to face death [i.e., divine punishment for faulty judgment], and the needs of my own household do I put aside. Empty-handed do I return to my home. May I always be as pure at my return as at my going forth." *Sanhedrin, 7b*

548. R. Samuel b. Nahmani said in the name of R. Jonathan, "A judge should always feel as if a sword lay between his thighs, and as if Gehinnom were open beneath him." *Sanhedrin, 7a*

He must be sure of his judgment

549. R. Jeshia—according to others, R. Nahman b. Isaac—asked, "What is does the verse (Jer. 21:12) *Exercise justice in the morning, and deliver him who is robbed out of the hand of the oppressor* mean? Do judges serve only in the morning, and not all day? This means that if the matter is as certain to you as the [coming of the] morning, then decide; but if it is not, then do not." [See also item 835.]

Sanhedrin, 7b

The importance of equity

550. R. Johanan said that Jerusalem was destroyed because of wide-spread insistence upon the exact letter of the [Biblical] law. Were they then to have judges who were untrained arbitrators? He meant rather

---

[1] For a different interpretation of the same verse, see item 552.

that they based their judgments [strictly] on Biblical law.

Baba Metzia, 30b

551. A judge who passes judgment in true equity [*din emeth l'ami-tho*]¹ for even a single hour is considered by Scripture as if he were a partner of God in the work of creation [i.e., the moral order depends on equity]. *Sabbath, 10a*

552. R. Nahman said in the name of R. Johanan, "A judge who decides a case in accordance with true equity causes the *Shechinah* to dwell in the midst of Israel; for Scripture states: (Ps. 82:1) *God standeth in the congregation of God; in the midst of judges doth He judge* [when equity is truly served].² And the judge who decides a case not in accordance with true equity causes the *Shechinah* to depart from Israel; for Scripture states: (Ps. 12:6) *'Because of the oppression of the poor, because of the sighing of the needy, now will I arise* [depart]*', saith the Lord.*"

Sanhedrin, 7a

Small and great cases merit equal consideration

553. (Deut. 1:17) *The small as well as the great shall ye hear.* Resh Lakish said, "This means that you must treat a case involving one *p'ruta* [i.e., the smallest coin] as attentively as a case involving one hundred *manoth* [coins of gold and silver]." But is this not self-evident? It means rather that if two cases come before you, one involving only a *p'ruta* and the other a hundred *manoth*, you must not say, "This is a minor case, and I shall attend to it later."

Sanhedrin, 8a

It is hard for a judge to avoid partiality

554. R. Ishmael, the son of R. Jose, had an *aris* ["tenant-gardener"] who brought him a basket of fruit every Friday [as payment for rental]. Once he delivered it on a Thursday, whereupon the rabbi asked him the reason for bringing it a day earlier. He replied, "Since I have a lawsuit coming up before you today, I thought I might save myself the trip tomorrow." Hearing this, the rabbi refused to accept the basket of fruit even though it was rightly his, and he also refused to act as judge in the case. Instead, he designated two other judges.

---

¹ Literally, *din emeth l'amitho* means "a judgment of truth according to its truth"; i.e., a judgment in which judicial interpretation of the law is involved in order that the law may be applied in the most benevolent way to suit the specific circumstances of the case.

² For another interpretation of this verse, see item 545. Here the *Shechinah* is said to be present only when equity is achieved.

While they were hearing the evidence in the case, he paced back and forth saying to himself, "If the gardener were wise, he might say such-and-such in his own behalf." He was at one point on the verge of speaking out in defense of his tenant-farmer when he checked himself, saying, "Oh, the despair that awaits those who take bribes! If I, who have refused a bribe of that which is my own, feel partial, how perverted must become the disposition of those who receive real bribes!" [See also items 558–562.]

Kethuboth, 105b

555. Mar, the son of R. Ashi, declared, "I feel unfit to sit in judgment on a learned man for I love him as I love myself and no man can conceive himself to be wrong." *Sabbath, 119a*

One may not judge a friend or an enemy

556. R. Papa said, "A man should never serve as a judge in a case involving his intimate friend or his hated enemy. In the case of a friend, because he will never find any fault in him; in that of an enemy, because he will never find any good in him." *Kethuboth, 105b*

557. (Deut. 1:17) *Ye shall not respect persons in judgment.* R. Judah said, "This means that you shall not favor anyone because he is your friend." R. Eliezer said, "It means that you shall not discriminate against anyone [even if he is your enemy]."

A former host of Rab had a case to bring before him. When he came to Rab, he said to him, "Do you remember that you were a guest in my home?" "Yes," answered Rab, "but why have you come to see me?" "I have a case to try," said the man. Thereupon Rab declared, "I am not fit to judge your case," and he appointed R. Kahana to serve instead. *Sanhedrin, 7b*

Why judges are prohibited from accepting gifts

558. Raba said, "What is the reason that a judge is prohibited from accepting gifts? Because a man who receives a gift becomes as friendly toward the donor as he is toward himself, and a man never sees any wrong in himself." *Kethuboth, 105b*

The temptation to accept bribes

559. R. Abbahu said, "How blind are the eyes of those who accept a bribe! If a man feels a pain in his eyes, he goes to a doctor, whom he pays, even though it is uncertain whether the doctor can save him from blindness. Yet judges will accept bribes as small as a *p'ruta* and blind their own eyes; as Scripture states: (Exod. 23:8) *For a gift blindeth them that have sight.*" *Kethuboth, 105a*

560. Scripture states: (Deut. 16:19) *Thou shalt take no gift, for a gift blindeth the eyes of the wise.* How much more would this be true of the eyes of the foolish! The verse continues, (ibid.) *And perverteth the words of the righteous.* How much more would this apply to the words of the wicked! *Kethuboth, 105a*

Bribery need not always be monetary

561. (Exod. 23:8) *And thou shalt take no gift* [*shohad*] does not refer to monetary bribes only,[1] but to verbal bribes also since the verse does not say, "And thou shalt take no gain."

How is it possible to bribe someone in any other way [than by money]? Samuel once got into a ferryboat to cross a river, and someone lent him a helping hand to keep him from falling. Thereupon Samuel asked him, "What have I done for you that you are so attentive to me?" The man replied, "I have a lawsuit coming up before you." Then Samuel answered, "I hereby disqualify myself from presiding in the case." *Kethuboth, 105b*

562. Amemar once sat in judgment when someone stepped forward and removed some feathers that were clinging to his hair. The judge asked the man, "What service have I performed for you?" The man replied, "I have a case coming up before the master." Amemar then said to him, "You have disqualified me from serving as the judge in your case." *Kethuboth, 105b*

Bad judges produce a troubled society

563. We are taught that R. Jose b. Elisha said, "If there is a generation overwhelmed by many troubles, go and investigate the judges of Israel, for retribution comes upon us because of the [corrupt] judges of Israel; for Scripture states: (Mic. 3:9) *Hear this, O ye heads of Jacob, and princes of the house of Israel, that abhor justice and make crooked all that is straight.*"[2] *Sabbath, 139a*

564. R. Eleazar b. Malai said in the name of Resh Lakish, "What does the passage (Isa. 59:3) *For your hands are defiled with blood, and your*

---

[1] The verb root of *shohad* means "to win the favor of," which need not involve a bribe.

[2] The passage continues in verse 12, *Therefore shall Zion for your sake be plowed as a field, and Jerusalem shall become heaps.*

fingers with iniquity; your lips have spoken falsehood and your tongue uttereth deception mean?

"*For your hands are defiled with blood* refers to the judges. *And your fingers with iniquities* refers to the scribes of the judges [who write false documents]. *Your lips have spoken falsehood* refers to the lawyers [who teach people to lie]. *And your tongue uttereth deception* refers to the litigants themselves." *Sabbath, 139a*

The case of Ima Shalom

565. Ima Shalom, the wife of R. Eliezer and sister of Rabban Gamaliel, met a philosopher who was also a judge and had a reputation for not taking bribes. She and Rabban Gamaliel wanted to put him to the test so she came before him, bringing along a golden lamp as a gift.

"I wish to inherit half of my father's estate," said Ima Shalom to the judge. And he replied, "I will order that you be given half of it." "But," she continued, "our Torah states that when a son survives, a daughter may not inherit."[1] To this, the judge replied, "Since you of the household of Israel have been exiled from your land, the law which Moses gave you has been superseded, and new laws prevail. In these laws [i.e., in the New Testament] it is stated that daughters may inherit equally with sons."[2]

The next day Rabban Gamaliel came before the judge [with his sister], bringing a Libyan ass as a gift [and said that he did not want his sister to share in the estate]. The judge thereupon declared, "After your sister left, I consulted the law a bit further, and found that it states: 'I did not come to abolish or add to the Mosaic law';[3] and it is written therein that a daughter does not inherit where there is a son."

Then Ima Shalom said to the judge, "May God make your light as bright as a lamp [hinting at her bribe of the previous day]." Whereupon Rabban Gamaliel declared, "An ass came along and kicked over the lamp [extinguishing it]." *Sabbath, 116a*

566. Rabbi said, "A woman who is supported by her brother [on

---

[1] Deut. 21:16 reads, *then it shall be, in the day that he causeth his sons to inherit that which he hath.*

[2] Actually, there is no passage in the Gospels stating specifically that a son and a daughter do inherit alike (see Soncino translation).

[3] N.T., Matt. 5:17. It is noteworthy that the Talmud here includes a reference to the words of Jesus.

the death of their father] is entitled to inherit a tenth of her father's estate [i.e., she should, upon marriage, receive a tenth of the estate as a dowry]."[1] *Nedarim, 39b*

One should respect the judges of his own day

567. Scripture states: (Deut. 17:9) *And thou shalt come unto the priests, the Levites, and unto the judges that shall be in those days.* [What is the meaning of the words *in those days?*] Would one go to a judge who did not live in his own days? This is intended to teach us that one should respect the decisions of a judge of his own time. Indeed, Scripture states: (Eccles. 7:10) *Say not thou, 'How was it that the former days were better than these?'*[2] *Rosh Hashanah, 25b*

Compensation for the time spent by a judge

568. R. Judah said in the name of R. Assi, "Those who served as judges in Jerusalem received up to ninety-nine *manoth* as a salary from the Temple funds." Karna [a judge of the exile] used to take an *istira* [a silver coin] from both litigants before he would hear a case. On what basis did he do this? Is there not a verse in which (Exod. 33:8) *And thou shalt take no gift* is stated? Since he took the same amount from each, this was merely payment for the time he was taking from his own affairs, and he was therefore entitled to it."

R. Huna acted in a similar manner. Whenever he went to hold court he would say, "Get me a man to irrigate my field in my place and I will take up your case." *Kethuboth, 105a*

B. THE LEGAL PROCESS

The importance of dispensing justice

569. R. Assi said, "We should not think that passing judgment is merely intended to create peace [between the litigants] and nothing more . . . [for] the pursuit of justice is as important as the study of Torah [i.e., both are in themselves sublime pursuits regardless of the benefits they bring]." *Berachoth, 6a*

---

[1] See Num. 27 for the story of the daughters of Zelophehad, an early instance in which exclusive male inheritance of a father's estate is challenged. See also item 565.

[2] While this verse is here applied to judges, its intent is more general: that one should not glorify the past.

Sharing the responsibility of passing judgment

570. R. Joshua b. Levi said, "If ten judges sit in a case,[1] the responsibility for the verdict is shared by all of them." But is that not self-evident? This is intended to include even a disciple who is present with his teacher [though he shares only in the discussion and not in the decision]. *Sanhedrin, 7b*

571. R. Huna used to gather ten disciples from the academy whenever a case came before him, explaining, "I do this in order that each of us may carry a chip of the beam [i.e., bear part of the responsibility for the verdict]." *Sanhedrin, 7b*

A disciple must speak up for justice

572. R. Joshua b. Karha said, "Whence do we infer that if a disciple is present when a case comes before his teacher and he discerns a point in defense of the poor or a point against the rich, he must not keep silent? Scripture states: (Deut. 1:17) *Ye shall not be afraid of any man* [even if he is your teacher]." R. Hanina concurred, declaring, "One must not withhold his words [where justice is involved] out of respect for anyone." [See also item 85.]

Sanhedrin, 6b

When a judge may refuse a case

573. Resh Lakish said, "If two people bring a case before you, one being powerful [who can harm you], you may say to them (either before you hear the case or even thereafter, but before you know which way the judgment lies), 'I am not obligated to judge this case,' because the powerful man may cause you harm. But if you have heard the case, and know which way the judgment lies, you are not permitted to say, 'I am not obligated to judge the case,' for Scripture states: (Deut. 1:17) *Ye shall not be afraid of any man.*" *Sanhedrin, 6b*

Conflicting views of arbitration

574. R. Eliezer b. R. Jose the Galilean said, "A court is forbidden to attempt an arbitration, and the judge who makes such settlements offends. He who praises arbitration despises the Lord; for Scripture

---

[1] We are told that a court must have at least three judges (Sanhedrin, 2b). However, this practice was not followed if both litigants agreed beforehand to accept the decision of a single judge.

states: (Ps. 10:3) *And he who blesseth an arbiter* [*u'botzea berech*] *contemns the Lord* [*nietz Adonoy*].[1] The law must cleave through the mountain [i.e., justice must be done]; for Scripture states: (Deut. 1:17) *The judgment is God's* [i.e., must not deviate from the Law of the Torah]."

Sanhedrin, 6b

575. R. Joshua b. Karcha said, "Arbitration is meritorious; for Scripture states: (Zech. 8:16) *With truth and judgment of peace judge ye in your gates.* How is *judgment of peace* to be understood? Often, when there is [strict] justice, there is no peace [between the litigants, for one is judged to be wrong]. And where there is peace there is no [strict] justice. The passage must therefore refer to arbitration which brings peace [through the judicial process]."

The endorsement of arbitration can be seen in the actions of King David, about whom Scripture states: (2 Sam. 8:16) *And David did what was just and charitable unto all his people.* How can these two terms [*just* and *charitable*] be reconciled? What is just is not [necessarily] charitable, and if charitable, then it is not [necessarily] just. We must therefore conclude that the passage refers to arbitration which contains elements of both justice and charity.

Sanhedrin, 6b

576. R. Simon b. Menasia said, "If two people bring a case before you, prior to the hearing of their claims and even thereafter, but before you are sure which way the judgment lies, you may say to them, 'Go and arbitrate between yourselves.' But after you have heard the case and are aware in whose favor the verdict inclines, you must not advise them to arbitrate; for Scripture states: (Prov. 17:14) *As one letteth loose* [a stream of] *water, so is the beginning of strife; therefore, before it is enkindled, leave off the contest.* That is, before the case is considered, you may advise them to leave off; but after the contest has been kindled, you must not advise them to leave off." [See also item 67.]

Sanhedrin, 6b

---

[1] The 1917 J.P.S. Bible reads *And the covetous boasteth himself though he contemn the Lord.* The translation offered above is Eliezer's interpretation of the Hebrew. The word *botzea*, rendered in the J.P.S. translation as "covetous," has a root meaning of "cut," and is read by Eliezer as an "arbiter," one who "cuts the difference" between litigants. *Botzea* is taken as the object of the verb *berech*, which is read as "he who blesseth" instead of "boasteth himself."

The accused should be permitted to confront his accuser

577. Scripture states: (1 Sam. 1:15) *And Hannah answered and said, 'No, my lord.'* [1] R. Eleazar said in comment on this verse, "From this we learn that if one is wrongly accused of anything, he should so inform his accuser." *Berachoth, 31b*

Treating the litigants alike

578. Our rabbis taught that the verse (Lev. 19:15) *In righteousness shalt thou judge thy neighbor* means that the court should not allow one litigant to sit while the other stands; and one should not have the privilege of speaking at length while the other is denied that privilege.

Another interpretation may be added: Always try to judge a person on the side of virtue. [2] [See items 100 and 110.] *Shebuoth, 30a*

579. Whence do we infer that if a scholar and an ignorant man have a lawsuit, the former may not attend the court in advance of the other to be heard because it might appear [even if it is not true] that he is prejudicing the case [in his favor]? Scripture states: (Exod. 23:7) *Keep thee far from* [even the suspicion of] *a false matter.* [3]

Whence do we infer that if one party appears in tatters and the other in expensive garments, the latter is told, "Either dress like him or clothe him in a manner similar to the way you are dressed?" Scripture states: (ibid.) *Keep thee far from a false matter. Shebuoth, 30b, 31a*

How an oath should be administered to litigants

580. An oath taken by one who comes before the court must be spoken in a language he understands, and the court must say to him before he takes his oath, "Be aware that the whole world trembled when the Holy One said on Mount Sinai, (Exod. 20:7) *Thou shalt not take the name of the Lord thy God in vain.* Also, concerning all the transgressions named in the Torah, Scripture states: (Exod. 34:7) *Forgiving iniquity, transgression and sin.* But concerning a false oath, Scripture declares: (Exod. 20:7) *The Lord will not hold him guiltless who*

---

[1] Hannah dared to protest Eli the priest's accusation of drunkenness. He had seen her lips move in prayer but had not heard her words.

[2] Giving the individual the benefit of the doubt, or judging him innocent until he is proved guilty.

[3] The words *a false matter* are here applied to anything that might produce a distinction between the litigants, even the way they dress (see next paragraph). Regarding *a false matter,* see item 324 and fn.

taketh His name in vain [i.e., he will not be forgiven]."

Shebuoth, 38b

The court procedure in Jerusalem

581. R. Nehemiah said, "It was the custom of the fair-minded [i.e., the judges in Jerusalem] to let the litigants enter and listen to their claims. Then they let the witnesses enter and heard their testimony. After that, they would clear the court and would discuss the case fully." *Sanhedrin, 30a*

The responsibility of serving as a witness

582. He who can give evidence in a case concerning his fellowman and does not testify is free from the judgment of man but is subject to the judgment of God. *Baba Kamma, 56a*

583. Our rabbis taught that there are three persons whom the Holy One despises: the man who says one thing with his mouth and another in his heart; he who knows evidence in favor of his fellowman and does not testify; and he who sees something improper in [the actions of] his fellow-man and testifies as the only witness against him. *Pesahim, 113b*

Signing documents as witnesses

584. It has been taught in a *baraitha* that it was customary for pure-minded people in Jerusalem not to sign a document as a witness unless they knew who was to sign along with them. They would also not sit in judgment on a case unless they knew who was to preside with them. *Sanhedrin, 23a*

Relatives of the litigants cannot testify

585. What does the verse (Deut. 24:16) *The fathers shall not be put to death for the children, neither shall the children be put to death for the fathers* mean? If this is intended to teach us that fathers should not be put to death for sins committed by their children and vice versa, behold it is explicitly stated: (ibid.) *Every man shall be put to death for his own sin!* This verse is therefore intended to mean that fathers should not be condemned for an offense through the testimony offered by their children, and vice versa.[1] *Sanhedrin, 27b*

---

[1] Certain other relatives are also prohibited from testifying, and the principle is applied not only to cases involving capital punishment but in other situations as well. This illustrates how the rabbis were able to elaborate upon Biblical legislation through the process of interpretation.

Judges should keep silent after the verdict

586. Whence do we know that a judge, after leaving the court, must not say, "I was for the acquittal of the defendant, but my colleagues were against me, and they were in the majority"? Scripture states: (Lev. 19:16) *Thou shalt not go up and down as a talebearer amongst thy people.* And another verse states: (Prov. 11:13) *He that walketh about as a tale-bearer revealeth secrets* [i.e., matters that should be kept secret]. *Sanhedrin, 31a*

Compensation for mental anguish

587. (Mishnah) Although the offender pays pecuniary damages, he is not fully pardoned until he asks forgiveness of the plaintiff. (Gemara) Our rabbis taught that monetary compensation for mental anguish [*bosheth:* "shame" or "disgrace"] is the [limited] concern of the court, but indicated that there can be no assuagement of injury to one's feelings [*tzaar:* "suffering"], for which all of the best rams in the world would not suffice, unless [in addition to monetary compensation] forgiveness is asked of the plaintiff.[1]

Baba Kamma, 92a

Capital punishment

588. (Mishnah) A Sanhedrin [the highest court] which executes a person only once in seven years is considered wicked. R. Eleazar b. Azariah said, "Even a Sanhedrin that does so only once in seventy years [is wicked]." Both R. Tarphon and R. Akiba declared, "If we were in the Sanhedrin, a death sentence would never be imposed." To this R. Gamaliel replied, "Such scholars would only increase bloodshed in Israel."[2] *Makkoth, 7a*

The meaning of circumstantial evidence

589. What is the meaning of a supposition [circumstantial evidence]? The court says to the witness, "Suppose you saw one man pursuing another toward an abandoned house, and you ran after them. Then you saw in the hand of one of them a bloody sword, and saw the victim writhing in pain. If so, you have seen nothing [for the

---

[1] A distinction is drawn here between the defamation of one's character as it affects one's public reputation and the suffering it causes the individual privately.

[2] The juxtaposition here of items 587 and 588 is intended to show the wide range of rabbinic legal concern, from matters in which neither monetary nor bodily injury is sustained to murder.

man was not attacked in your presence, and circumstantial evidence is not enough]."

Indeed, there is a *baraitha* to this effect. Simeon b. Shetach said, "I once saw a man pursue another, and ran after him. Then I beheld a bloody sword in his hand, and saw the victim writhing. I said [to the pursuer], "Wicked creature, who has attacked this man, you or I? Yet I can do nothing, since Scripture states: (Deut. 17:6) *Upon the testimony of two . . . be put to death.* However, He Who knows the very thoughts of men shall take revenge on you.' "[1] *Sanhedrin, 37b*

The "cities of refuge" in Biblical times

590. We are taught [in a *baraitha*] that R. Eliezer b. Jacob said, "The word 'refuge' was posted at every crossroads so that he who had slain a man inadvertently might know the way to take [to escape from avengers]."[2] *Makkoth, 10a*

Why the Talmud cites individual judicial opinions

591. (Mishnah 4) Why are the opinions of both Shammai and Hillel stated when the opinion voiced by one of them does not in the end prevail? This is intended to teach later generations that one must not insist upon his own opinion, since even our most distinguished ancestors did not [always] prevail in their views. *Eduyoth, 2b*

The process of appeal

592. (Mishnah 5) Why is mention made of the opinion of a single individual, as well as that of the majority of scholars, when the decision is invariably in accord with the majority? This is done in order that if a subsequent court should happen to approve of that [individual] opinion, it may base its decision thereon.

However, no court may annul the decision of another court unless that court is superior in both erudition and number of judges. If it is greater in only one of these respects, in either erudition or number of judges, it cannot annul. It must be superior in both regards.[3]

Eduyoth, 2b

---

[1] Not only is the evidence circumstantial, but the testimony would come from a single individual.

[2] Six cities of refuge were designated by Scripture (Josh. 20) where one who had taken a life inadvertently could not be seized by relatives of the slain man for vengeance.

[3] This not only helped to insure the validity of appeal judgments but also served to reduce the burden of litigation.

On the proper administration of justice

593. Our rabbis taught that the verse (Deut. 17:20) *Justice, justice, shalt thou pursue* means that a judge should follow R. Huna of Lod and Rabban Johanan b. Zakkai of Brur Hiel [i.e., strive to emulate their procedures].[1] *Sanhedrin, 32b*

---

[1] The word "justice" is here personified as "judges," and its repetition is taken to refer to two distinguished jurists. It is interesting that the judges of the Supreme Court of the United States are called "Justice."

10

THE TWO ISRAELS

THE term "Israel" is used by the rabbis to refer to the people of Israel, descended from Jacob, who first bore that name (Gen. 32:29). This designation, today as in the past, is intended to include the whole Jewish people, identifying that people as an enduring entity in time. However, the same term is also applied by the rabbis to the land of Israel, called Palestine by the Romans and often referred to as the Holy Land.

While the people of Israel and the land of Israel are not identical, they are not unrelated, and the close connection between them is indicated by Scripture itself. The Bible links the people of Israel with the land of Israel by repeatedly associating the Chosen People with the Promised Land. Thus the rabbis of the Talmud regard both the land of Israel and the people of Israel as unique instruments for the achievement of God's purpose.

The land of Israel is perceived as the land of the Patriarchs and Prophets; Jerusalem, the city of David, as the place where the Temple once stood; and the people of Israel as God's "own treasure from among all peoples" (Exod. 19:5), called upon to serve as a "light unto the nations" (Isa. 42:6).

The rabbis are persuaded that the land of Israel, which has played so prominent a part in their people's past, is destined to make further contributions to the forging of the Jewish future and the shaping of the fate of humanity. They encourage their people, scattered among the nations, to hold fast to the vision of a return to that land, meanwhile living in accordance with God's commands and serving as His witnesses among the peoples of the earth, awaiting the day of redemption when the people of Israel and the land of Israel will at last be reunited.

A. THE LAND OF ISRAEL

The land of Israel was created first

594. Our rabbis taught that the land of Israel was created first, and the rest of the world only later;[1] for Scripture states: (Prov. 8:25,26) *Before the hills was I brought forth, while as yet He had not made the earth, nor the fields.*[2] *Taanith, 10a*

It is compared to a deer

595. R. Hisda said, "What does the verse (Jer. 3:19) *And give thee a pleasant land, the goodliest heritage* [*nahalath zvi*][3] *of the nations* mean? Why is the land of Israel compared to a deer? Just as the hide of a deer, once it is removed, cannot thereafter contain its body, so too is the land of Israel unable to hold all of its produce [i.e., its fruits burst from their storehouses]."

This may be interpreted differently. Just as the deer is the swiftest of animals, so does the fruit in Israel ripen more quickly than it does in other lands. *Kethuboth, 112a*

Visiting the land is meritorious

596. R. Jeremiah b. Abba said in the name of R. Johanan, "Whoever walks [as little as] four cubits on the soil of the land of Israel is assured of a place in the Hereafter."[4] *Kethuboth, 111a*

Burial in the land of Israel

597. R. Anan said, "Whoever is buried in the land of Israel is considered as if he were buried under the Temple altar."[5]

Kethuboth, 111a

One should prefer to live there

598. A man should choose to live in the land of Israel, even in a town where the majority are non-Jews, rather than outside the land

---

[1] See item 40, where Jerusalem, and particularly the Temple mount, is declared to have been created first.

[2] Here Wisdom, personified, is the speaker. The passage is applied, in this instance, to the land of Israel, where Wisdom, as knowledge of God, is said to dwell. See item 602.

[3] A play on words is involved. The primary meaning of *zvi*, here rendered as "goodliest," is "a deer." Thus *nahalath zvi* becomes for Hisda "the heritage of a deer."

[4] Note that four cubits is only seventy-two inches. On the Hereafter, see chapter 14.

[5] Some devout Jews still ask to be buried in the land of Israel, where the resurrection is expected to take place. See item 774.

of Israel among a majority of Jews.[1] Whoever lives in the land of Israel is like one who has a God, while one who lives outside the land of Israel is like one who has no God; for Scripture states: (Lev. 25:38) *To give unto you the land of Canaan,* [there] *to be unto you a God.*[2]

But is it conceivable that whoever lives outside the land of Israel has no God? [Is it not possible to worship God anywhere?] We must infer from this verse that whoever lives outside the land of Israel is constantly tempted to serve idols. *Kethuboth, 110b*

Those living in Israel live without sin

599. R. Eleazar said, "Whoever lives in the land of Israel lives without sin; for Scripture states: (Isa. 23:24) *And the inhabitant shall not say, 'I am sick'; the people that dwell therein shall be forgiven their iniquities.*"[3] *Kethuboth, 111a*

Rabbi Judah disagrees

600. R. Judah said, "Whoever lives in the land of Babylonia is considered as though he lived in the land of Israel."

Kethuboth, 111a

601. R. Judah said in the name of Samuel, "All other lands are *issah*[4] in comparison with the land of Israel; but the land of Israel is *issah* compared to Babylonia." *Sanhedrin, 71a*

The greatness of Jerusalem

602. Ten measures of wisdom came into the world at the time of the creation. The land of Israel received nine, and one was left for the rest of the world. Ten measures of beauty came into the world. Jerusalem received nine, and one was left for the rest of the world. [See item 594 and fn.] *Kiddushin, 49a*

---

[1] For a different view, see items 600 and 601. The issue is now debated between American and Israeli Jews.

[2] The second part of the verse is treated as being dependent on the first.

[3] Moral sickness is taken as the intended meaning since the verse speaks of forgiving iniquities.

[4] Jastrow's *Dictionary of the Talmud,* s.v. "issah," defines it as "a mixed family, a family suspected of containing an alien mixture." The statement, attributed to Samuel, an Amora of the first Babylonian generation, indicates not only the wide dispersal of the Jews but also the frequency of intermarriage and acceptance of non-Jews into the Jewish fold. See also items 987 and 988.

Going on pilgrimage to Jerusalem is a duty

603. R. Dostai b. Janai said, "Why are the hot springs of Tiberias not located in Jerusalem instead? For the simple reason that those who make a pilgrimage to Jerusalem during the festivals[1] should not say, 'Were it for nothing else than to bathe in its hot springs that we visited Jerusalem, it would have been enough.' Their pilgrimage to Jerusalem would then no longer be a matter of duty [but of pleasure]."

Pesahim, 8b

Jerusalem in this world and the next

604. Rabbah said in the name of R. Johanan, "Jerusalem in the World to Come will not be like the Jerusalem of this world. In the Jerusalem of this world, all who wish to enter may do so, but in the Jerusalem of the World to Come [*Yerushalayim shel ma'alah*: 'the heavenly Jerusalem'] only those who are invited to do so may enter." [See chapter 14.] *Baba Bathra, 75b*

B. THE PEOPLE OF ISRAEL

The character of the people of Israel

605. King David [is reputed to have] said, "The people of Israel are recognized by three characteristics: they are compassionate, chaste and charitable." *Yebamoth, 9a*

606. R. Simeon b. Lakish said, "Three [of God's creatures] are distinguished for their boldness: Israel is the boldest of all peoples, the dog among animals and the cock among birds." *Betzah, 25b*

Israel lives under God's providence

607. R. Johanan declared that the people of Israel does not come under the influence of the stars and planets.[2] He said, "Whence do

---

[1] The three festivals during which Jews were obligated to make a pilgrimage to Jerusalem were Pesach, Shabuoth and Sukkoth.

[2] Sorcerers, diviners, magicians and soothsayers as well as astrologers were common in the ancient world. Astrology is specifically denounced in Isa. 47:13. The point made here is reinforced in item 608.

It is intriguing that astrology still has so strong a hold on the minds of so many. Recently a newspaper dropped its column on astrology, since it was felt that the column no longer had much reader interest. The flood of protests in letters to the editor brought about its return. It is also to be noted that the telephone company is now offering (at a price) horoscopes by phone!

we infer that Israel is not subject to planetary influences? Scripture states: (Jer. 10:2) *Thus saith the Lord, 'Learn not the way of the nations, and be not dismayed at the signs of heaven; for* [although] *the nations are dismayed at them.'* Other peoples may be dismayed by them, but not Israel." *Sabbath, 156a*

608. R. Judah said in the name of Rab, "Whence do we know that Israel is not subject to planetary influence? Scripture states: (Gen. 15:5) *And He brought him forth abroad,* etc. [God brings Abraham outdoors and tells him that his seed shall be as numerous as the stars.] Then Abraham said to the Holy One, 'Sovereign of the Universe! I have examined my constellation [i.e., the constellation under which he was born], and I have found that I am not destined to have a son.' But the Lord said to him, 'Cease your astrological calculations for Israel does not stand under planetary influence. What makes you think so? Is it because the planet Jupiter is in the West [i.e., your planet is in decline]? I shall cause it to return to the East.' " *Sabbath, 156a*

609. R. Hanina said, "A man's intelligence is determined by chance [*mazal*], and by chance are his riches acquired; but the destiny of Israel is not determined by chance."[1] *Sabbath, 156a*

Israel is compared to a dove

610. Israel is like a dove, of which Scripture states: (Ps. 68:14) *The wings of the dove are covered with silver, and her pinions with the shimmer of gold.* How is Israel like a dove? Just as the dove defends herself with her wings [and not with her beak], so does Israel defend itself with its Torah [and not by armed might]. *Sabbath, 49a*

. . . to an apple tree

611. R. Hama b. Hanina said, "What does the verse (Song of Songs 2:3) *Like an apple tree among the trees of the wood, so is my beloved among the sons* mean? Why is Israel compared to an apple tree?[2] Because, just as an apple tree produces its buds first, then its leaves, even so did Israel say [upon receiving the Ten Commandments] first 'We will obey' and then 'We will hearken.' " [One would normally hear first

---

[1] The primary meaning of *mazal* is a "constellation" or "planet," but its derived meaning is "chance" or "destiny." See *Dictionary of the Talmud,* s.v. "mazal." Whether it is employed here in its original usage or in the latter meaning, Rabbi Hanina insists that God alone determines the fate of Israel.

[2] The two lovers in Song of Songs were regarded by the rabbis as being God and Israel. Israel, God's beloved, is depicted as *an apple tree among the trees of the wood.*

and then obey, but Israel was eager to do God's will.]

Sabbath, 88a

. . . to the Ethiopians

612. (Amos 9:7) *Are ye not like the children of the Ethiopians unto Me, O children of Israel?* [What does Scripture mean by this?] The children of Israel were not called Ethiopians; they were called Israel. In what respect were they then like the Ethiopians? This passage serves to teach us that just as the Ethiopians differ from others by the color of their skin, so do the people of Israel differ from all other peoples in the goodness of their deeds.[1] *Moed Katan, 16b*

. . . to stars and sand

613. (Gen. 22:17) *I will multiply thy seed as the stars of the heavens, and as the sand which is upon the shore.* The Jews are compared to the stars and to grains of sand [not because they are numerous, but rather] because when they fall [morally], they sink as low as the sands of the sea; and when they rise, they rise to the very stars of the heavens.

Megillah, 16a

It is forbidden to count the people of Israel

614. R. Isaac said, "It is forbidden to count the people of Israel, even for [the purpose of] fulfilling a commandment." R. Ashi, however, disagreed with him.

R. Eleazar said, "Whoever numbers Israel [by taking a census] violates a prohibitory law; for Scripture states: (Hos. 2:1) *The number of the children of Israel shall yet be like the sands of the sea, which can* [may] not be measured nor numbered."[2] *Yoma, 22b*

Poverty is becoming to Israel

615. Elijah said to Ben He He, "What does the verse (Isa. 48:10) *Behold, I have refined thee, though not as silver; I have proved thee in the furnace of affliction [oni]* mean? We may infer from this that the Holy One pondered all the desirable traits to determine which would be

---

[1] This is a rather limited perception of the Biblical passage, which has classically expressed the equality of all races. Perhaps unknown to the rabbis, a black Jewish community has long existed in Ethiopia. They are known as Falashas.

[2] The verse is here interpreted as a prohibition. Translating "can" as "may" conveys that idea. In Jewish folklore, it is unsafe to count any group of people as this may invite Satan to diminish their number by death. It is significant that R. Ashi disagreed. See also item 228.

best for the people of Israel, and He found that none was more suitable than poverty [*aniuth*]."[1] Samuel—according to others, R. Joseph—declared, "This is in accord with the popular saying, 'Poverty becomes Israel, like a red harness on a white horse.'" *Hagigah, 9b*

Why God provided manna for Israel daily

616. The disciples of R. Simeon b. Johai asked him, "Why did not the manna descend for Israel [during their desert wanderings] all at once, in sufficient quantity for a whole year?" He answered, "I will explain this by means of a parable. This is like the case of a human king, who ordered that his son's rations should be supplied only once a year.

"The son therefore came to see his father only once a year, and the king was disturbed by this. He then ordered that his son's rations should be provided on a daily basis instead. Could his son do anything other than visit his father daily? So it was with Israel. Whoever had several children was concerned about them, and said to himself, 'Suppose no manna will descend tomorrow. All of my children may die of hunger!' Consequently, all Israelites directed their hearts daily toward their heavenly Father."[2]

According to others, the reason for supplying it daily was that Israel should have it fresh each day. Still others say that this was in order that they should not have to carry it on their way [and be hampered in their movements]. *Yoma, 76a*

Why God favors the people of Israel

617. The ministering angels said to the Holy One, "Sovereign of the Universe! Your Torah states: (Deut. 10:17) *Who shows no favor to persons and taketh no bribes.* Yet You favor Israel; as the Torah states: (Num. 6:26) *The Lord will show His favor unto thee!*" To this God replied, "Why shall I not show favor unto Israel? For I wrote in the Torah which I gave them: (Deut. 8:10) *And thou shalt eat and be satisfied* [i.e., eat plentifully] *and bless the Lord.* But they are so obedient and observant that even if they eat as little as an olive or an egg, they recite the grace after meals." *Berachoth, 20b*

---

[1] The same Hebrew root is used for "poverty" and "affliction," and poverty was regarded as unfortunate. However, as recognized by the proverb which follows, in periods of prosperity the Israelites tended to forget God.

[2] See also item 259.

618. (Deut. 7:7) *The Lord did not set His love upon you nor choose you because ye were more in number than any people.* The Holy One said unto Israel, "I love you because, even when I overwhelm you with honor, you humble yourselves before Me. I gave honor to Abraham, yet he declared: (Gen. 18:27) *Who am I but dust and ashes?* I did the same for Moses and Aaron, yet they said: (Exod. 16:7) *And what are we?* I gave honor to David, yet he stated: (Ps. 22:7) *But I am a worm, and not a man.*

"The other peoples behave quite differently. When I gave prestige to Nimrod, he said: (Gen. 11:4) *Come, let us build us a city* [in a spirit of arrogance]. And Pharaoh, whom I made ruler of Egypt, stated: (Exod. 5:2) *Who is the Lord?" Hullin, 89a*

619. Israel is loved by the Lord even more than [are] the ministering angels because Israel sings praises to God every hour, while the ministering angels sing His praises but once a day. *Hullin, 91b*

620. The divine Attribute of Justice[1] pleaded before the Holy One, saying, "Sovereign of the Universe! What is the difference between Israel and all other peoples that You give special honor to Israel?" The Holy One answered, "Israel studies the Torah and the others do not." *Megillah, 15b*

God is compassionate even when afflicting Israel

621. Resh Lakish said, "God does not afflict Israel without first providing the cure." [See also item 29.] *Megillah, 13b*

622. R. Hiyya said, "What does the verse (Job 28:23) *God alone understandeth her way, and He knoweth her place* mean? God knew that Israel could not bear the harsh decrees of the Syrians [Javan] and of the Arabs [Ishmael], and He therefore exiled Israel into Babylonia [a more suitable place]."[2] *Pesahim, 87b*

623. R. Johanan said, "God sent them into their native land. This may be likened to a man who has become angry with his wife. Where does he send her? Back to her mother's home."[3] *Pesahim, 87b*

624. Ulla said, "The reason why Israel was sent to Babylonia is that they might eat dates [which are cheaply available in Babylonia], and

---

[1] Exod. 34:6, 7 assigns certain attributes to God. Among them are Justice and Mercy.

[2] Javan, son of Japheth (Gen. 10:2), was the reputed progenitor of the Greeks. Here their successors, the Syrians, are intended. Ishmael was the name of Abraham's son (Gen. 16:15) who was the ancestor of the Arabs (Ishmaelites). The Talmud also refers to the Aryan races (Greeks, Persians, et al.) as Japheth (see fn. to item 470).

[3] Abraham came from Ur of the Chaldees, i.e., Babylonia.

thus the more easily study the Torah [without exerting themselves at earning a livelihood]." *Pesahim, 87b*

625. R. Simeon b. Johai said, "See how much the Holy One loves the people of Israel! Wherever they were exiled, the *Shechinah* accompanied them. When they were in Egypt, the *Shechinah* was with them; for Scripture states: (1 Sam. 2:27) *Did I reveal Myself to the house of thy father, when they were in Egypt . . . ?* And when they were taken into Babylonian captivity, the *Shechinah* went with them; for Scripture states: (Isa. 43:14) *For your sake have I sent* [My *Shechinah*] *to Babylon.*"[1] *Megillah, 29a*

All Israelites are responsible for one another

626. Scripture states: (Lev. 26:37) *And they shall stumble one over* [or because of] *another.* We may infer from this verse that all Israelites are responsible for one another. This applies when there is an opportunity to protest against a misdeed and no protest is made [i.e., he who fails to protest shares in the guilt].[2] *Sanhedrin, 27b*

Sharing the anguish of the people

627. One must share in the distress of the community. We find that Moses shared the distress of his people; for Scripture states: (Exod. 17:12) *But when the hands of Moses became heavy, they took a stone, and put it under him, and he sat thereon.* Did not Moses have a pillow or a bolster upon which he could have sat? He did, but Moses thought, "Since Israel is in trouble, I must share in their difficulties." He who shares in the anguish of his people will live to see the relief of the community. *Taanith, 11a*

External threat produces internal growth

628. (Esther 3:10) *And the king drew off his signet ring from his hand, and gave it to Haman.* R. Abba b. Kahana said, "The transfer of the ring [authorizing Haman to destroy the Jews] had a greater effect on the Jewish people than forty-eight prophets and seven prophetesses

---

[1] The verb "sent" normally requires an object, here supplied.

On God's compassion for Israel, see also items 28 and 29.

[2] The words "All Israelites are responsible for one another" are often quoted to urge mutual aid rather than protest, in support of schools and other Jewish institutions. The Hebrew reads: *kulam arevim zeh la-zeh*; literally, "all are bound up with one another," which has of course this broader implication.

who preached to the people of Israel that they should mend their ways. The warnings of these forty-eight prophets and seven prophetesses did not cause the people of Israel to improve their behavior, but the threat posed by Haman did."[1] *Megillah, 14a*

How God holds Israel to account

629. R. Abbahu introduced R. Safra to the *minim* [dissidents][2] as a great man. They thereupon exempted him from taxes for a period of thirteen years. Some time later, they met him and asked him to explain the verse (Amos 3:2) *You only have I loved, of all the families of the earth; therefore will I visit upon you all your iniquities.*

"If one is angry," they asked, "will he let out his anger on a friend?" He could not explain the verse, and they abused him. Subsequently, R. Abbahu asked them why they had done this and they replied, "You presented him to us as a great scholar, but he cannot explain a passage of Scripture." Abbahu replied, "I said that he was a master of Talmud, but I did not say that he was a scholar in the study of Scripture!"

They then asked him, "If that is so, how does it happen that you are so familiar with Scripture?" To this, he replied, "Because those of us who have to deal with you [non-Jews] usually pay greater attention to the Bible." "Well then," they said, "suppose you explain this passage to us." To this, he responded, "I will do so with a parable. There was once a creditor who had two debtors. One was a close friend while the other was a personal enemy. From his friend he demanded regular payments, in small sums [that were easy to manage], but from his enemy he required a single payment of the whole sum at one time."[3] *Abodah Zarah, 4a*

The "agony and ecstasy" of being God's people

630. R. Johanan b. Zakkai said, "Fortunate are you, O Israel; for as long as you perform the will of God, no nation or people can have

---

[1] Esther 4:3 states that there was *fasting, and weeping, and mourning; and many put on sackcloth and ashes.* Such behavior was associated with repentance for sin, and is so construed here.

[2] In this instance, these were Judeo-Christians, who served as government tax collectors. Jews had taxed themselves a half-shekel yearly for maintaining the Temple; when the Temple was destroyed, the Romans confiscated this tax and diverted it to their own coffers.

[3] This refers to the Hereafter. Israel pays for its sins on a pay-as-you-go basis, while other peoples will be made to pay for their sins all at once.

any power over you! But when you fail to perform the will of God, you are delivered into the hands of a people which oppresses you; even to the very beasts of that nation!"[1] *Kethuboth, 66b*

All other peoples are also God's creatures

631. R. Johanan declared, "The Holy One proclaims, 'Israel and all of the nations of the world are My creatures. Why then should I destroy one for the sake of another [i.e., destroy any nation because of the wrongs suffered by Israel]?'" *Sanhedrin, 98b*

On the dispersion of Israel

632. R. Eleazar said, "The Holy One exiled Israel among the nations only for the purpose of acquiring proselytes; for Scripture states: (Hos. 2:25) *And I will sow her* [Israel] *unto Me in the land.* Surely a man sows a *seah* to harvest many *kor* [i.e., one sows little in order to harvest much more]!"

R. Johanan made the same inference from [ibid.] *And I will have compassion upon her that hath not obtained compassion.* Pesahim, 87b

The world needs the people of Israel

633. R. Joshua b. Levi said, "Scripture states: (Zech. 2:10) *For as the four winds of heaven have I spread you abroad.* What did the Holy One mean by this? Why does the verse read *as* [like] *the four winds* rather than 'upon the four winds'? We must understand the verse to mean that [the four winds were not a device for dispersing Israel, but that] just as no place in the world is without wind, so also the world cannot exist without the people of Israel [in dispersion everywhere]."[2]

Taanith, 3b

The greatness of the coming redemption of Israel

634. (Jer. 23:7) *Behold, days are coming, saith the Lord, when they shall no more say, 'As the Lord liveth, Who brought up the children of Israel out of the land of Egypt'; but 'As the Lord liveth, Who brought up and Who hath led forth the seed of the house of Israel out of the north country, and out of*

---

[1] The concept of *mea culpa* is here implicit. Jews, trusting God's providence, have often tended to blame themselves, not only for Roman oppression but even for Nazi bestiality.

[2] Joshua perceived a universal role for the Jewish people in dispersion. So, too, the philosopher Philo of Alexandria (b. about 20 B.C.E.) described his people as "a nation destined to become consecrated above all others to offer prayers forever on behalf of the human race, that it may be delivered from evil and participate in what is good" (*Life of Moses* 1:49).

all the countries whither I had driven them'; and they shall dwell in their own land.

The Sages declared that this [the mention of Egypt] is intended to teach us that the memory of the redemption from Egypt will not be entirely eradicated [from the minds of the Jewish people], but that the redemption [from other lands] still to come will be regarded as even more significant, and the redemption from Egypt will seem to be only secondary.

An analogy may be found in the verse (Gen. 35:10) *Thy name shall not be called any more Jacob, but Israel shall be thy name.* The name Jacob was not entirely abandoned [after Jacob wrestled with the angel and his name was changed], but Israel became the primary designation and Jacob the alternate. [So will the coming redemption be mentioned more often than the redemption from Egypt.] *Berachoth, 12b*

635. R. Johanan said, "The day on which the reunion [return] of the exiles will take place will be as great as the day on which the heavens and the earth were created."[1] *Pesahim, 88a*

The redemption of Israel cannot be obstructed

636. R. Johanan said, "Woe unto that nation which may try to prevent the redemption of Israel when the Holy One will bring it to pass for his children! Who can prevent a lion from coming together with his lioness when they seek one another?"[2] *Sanhedrin, 106a*

The future of Israel is assured

637. In comment on the verse (Jer. 11:16) *The Lord called thy name a leafy olive tree, fair with goodly fruit,* R. Isaac said, "Just as the olive tree produces its best fruit at an advanced age, so will Israel flourish most in days yet to come." *Menahoth, 53b*

---

[1] The day of redemption was associated with the coming of the Messiah (see chapter 14c). With his advent, the hope for a restoration of the Jewish nation and the dream of universal justice and righteousness would both be realized.

[2] Here Johanan compares God to a lion and Israel to His lioness. Similar imagery is used in Hos. 5:14 and Amos 3:4,8.

11
MARTYRS AND MIRACLES

THE Jews in their dispersion were frequently subjected to the all too human "dislike of the unlike." Indeed, in the Bible itself, Haman, the Prime Minister of ancient Persia, says to King Ahasuerus, "There is a certain people scattered abroad . . . in all the provinces of thy kingdom; and their laws are different from those of every people; . . . therefore it profiteth not the king to suffer them" (Esther 3:8).

This view, abetted by religious, economic or political considerations, took a dreadful toll of Jewish lives during the centuries from Haman to Hitler, for which records of Jewish martyrdom abound. Some of the victims were men of renown whose names have been preserved in various lists of martyrs. Probably the oldest of such lists is that of the Ten Sages who died for their faith during the reigns of Trajan and Hadrian, a period of intense persecution.

Accounts of Jewish martyrdom are also contained in the Talmud. The story is told of the woman and her seven sons who went to their death because of their refusal to bow down to idols. The heroic figures of Rabbi Akiba and Hanina b. Teradion are described as accepting death rather than restrictions on their teaching, and two young people taken captive as slaves die rather than be forced to flout their people's religious requirements.

While they were often the victims of the whims of foreign potentates, the Jews remained convinced of God's concern for their welfare. It is therefore not surprising that elements of the miraculous appear in the Talmud as a source of comfort and an expression of faith. What is perhaps more remarkable is the fact that reports of miracles are sometimes cautiously received or their very credibility questioned.

178

A. THE SUPREME SACRIFICE

The woman and her seven sons

638. (Ps. 44:23) *For Thy sake are we killed all day long; we are counted as sheep for the slaughter.* R. Judah said, "This refers to the woman and her seven sons. They were brought before the tyrannical conqueror [Antiochus][1] one by one, beginning with the eldest. The ruler commanded the boy to bow down before an idol, but the youth said, 'It is written in our Torah: (Exod. 20:2) *I am the Lord thy God.*' He was immediately led out for execution.

"The second son was brought in and told to bow before the idol. But he replied, 'It is written in the Torah: (Exod. 20:3) *Thou shalt have no other gods before Me.*' His death followed his brave words. When the third son was brought in and commanded to worship the idol, he answered, 'The Torah states: (Exod. 20:4) *Thou shalt not make unto thee a graven image.*' In the same manner was he executed. Similar homage was demanded of the fourth son, but he responded, 'Our Torah states: (Exod. 20:5) *Thou shalt not bow down unto them.*' And he too was slain.

"The fifth lad, when ordered to bow before the idol, surrendered his life with the watchword of Israel: (Deut. 6:4) '*Hear O Israel, the Lord our God, the Lord is One!*' When the sixth son was asked to serve the idol, he calmly replied, 'The Torah declares: (Deut. 4:39) *Know therefore this day, and reflect in thy heart, that the Lord He is God, in the heavens above and on the earth beneath; there is none else.*' And he was put to death.

"Then the seventh son was brought before the tyrant, and the same command to serve the idol was addressed to him. But the youngest child answered, 'Never will we exchange our God for any other; for our Torah states: (Deut. 26:17) *Thou hast this day acknowledged the Lord.* Moreover, the Torah adds: (Deut. 26:18) *And the Lord hath acknowledged thee this day to be His own treasure.*'

"The king offered to spare his life if he would, for the sake of appearances, stoop and pick up a ring which had been dropped on purpose. 'Alas for you, O Caesar!' answered the boy; 'if you are so

---

[1] This account appears in the Apocrypha (Second Book of Maccabees) with Antiochus Epiphanes (Antiochus IV) as ruler of the Syrian empire. He ruled from 175–164 B.C.E., and tried to unify his empire through a common faith. He forbade the teaching of the Torah, the practice of circumcision and the observance of the Sabbath. The story is associated with the Hanukkah festival, commemorating the success of the Jewish revolt under the leadership of Judah the Maccabee. In Jewish tradition, the woman is known as Hannah.

zealous for your own honor, how much more zealous ought we to be for the honor of the Holy One!'

"As he was led away to execution, his mother asked and received permission to give him a farewell embrace. 'Go, my son,' she said to her only surviving child, 'and tell Abraham that he built an altar for the [intended] sacrifice of only one son [Gen. 22:2] while I have sacrificed seven sons.' Then she turned aside, threw herself from the roof, and perished. Thereupon a heavenly voice proclaimed her to be (Ps. 113:9) *A joyful mother of children* [in the next world]."

Gittin, 57b

The story of Rabbi Akiba

639. R. Akiba at one time was a lowly shepherd employed by Ben Kalba Shebua.[1] The latter's daughter observed that Akiba was a very pious and gifted individual. She said to him, "If I marry you, will you enter an academy to study Torah?" And he replied, "Indeed." Then they were married, and he went off to an academy. When her father learned of this, he ordered her to leave his house and vowed that she would receive no benefit from his estate.

Akiba spent twelve years at the academy, and upon his return he led with him twelve thousand disciples. As he approached his wife's house, he overheard an old woman say to his wife, "How long are you going to lead the life of a widow?" His wife replied, "If my husband were to listen to me, he would remain at the academy twelve more years." R. Akiba thereupon said to himself, "Since she has given her consent, I will act accordingly."

He thereupon returned to the academy and spent twelve more years there. Then he came home, bringing with him twenty-four thousand disciples. His wife, informed of his arrival, went out to meet him. When she reached him, she prostrated herself before him and kissed his feet. His attendants wanted to push her away, but R. Akiba said to them, "Leave her alone, for all of my learning and all of yours [i.e., all that you have received from me] is due to her."

Her father, who regretted his earlier action, was informed that a great scholar had arrived in town, and said, "I shall go to see him. Perhaps he will nullify the vow which I have made against my daugh-

---

[1] Akiba b. Joseph, who died about 135 C.E., was a distinguished Jewish scholar, generally regarded as one of the founders of rabbinic Judaism and the systematizer of Jewish law. Ben Kalba Shebua was a rich man of Jerusalem at the time of Vespasian's siege.

ter." And he went to meet him. When the visiting scholar asked Ben Kalba Shebua whether his original intention had been to make the vow against her, even if she had married a great scholar, he replied, "Not even if her husband knew as little as one chapter of the Torah or just one Halachah."

Then R. Akiba said, "I am the man your daughter married." Kalba Shebua thereupon prostrated himself at R. Akiba's feet and kissed them and assured Akiba of half of his fortune.

R. Akiba's daughter did the same with [her husband] Ben Azai. And this is in accordance with the popular saying, "Ewe follows ewe [Eve follows Eve]." As the mother acts, so does her daughter.

Kethuboth, 62b; Nedarim, 50a

640. Our rabbis taught that when R. Akiba was confined to prison [by the Romans, for teaching Torah],[1] R. Joshua Hagarsi served as his attendant. Every day he brought into the prison a pre-scribed amount of water. One day the warden, finding that he had brought a larger amount of water than usual, said to R. Joshua, "What a great amount of water you have brought today! Do you intend to use it to soak [and thereby undermine] the prison walls?" The warden then poured out half of it and left only the rest.

When R. Joshua came in to see R. Akiba, the latter [seeing how little water he had brought] said to him, "Joshua, do you not know that I am very old, and my life depends on you?" R. Joshua then related what had happened.

"Give me water to wash my hands," said R. Akiba. "But there is barely enough to drink, let alone for washing the hands," answered R. Joshua. Then R. Akiba said to him, "What am I to do? He who neglects washing the hands before eating is considered guilty of sin. It is better for me to die from hunger than to act contrary to the thinking of my colleagues."

It is related that he did not taste food until he had enough water to wash his hands. And when the Sages heard of this incident, they said, "If he was so strict in his old age, how strict he must have been in his younger years! And if he was so strict in prison [where water

---

[1] The Jews revolted when Hadrian ordered a pagan altar built on the Temple site, and the Roman government issued decrees against Jewish practices and the teaching of Judaism. Akiba is believed to have backed Bar Kochba in the unsuccessful revolt against Rome of 132–135 C.E.

was hard to obtain], how much more so must he have been at home!"

Erubin, 21b

641. When R. Akiba was arrested and imprisoned, Papus was also arrested, and he was placed in the same prison. "Papus, what brought you here?" asked R. Akiba. Papus replied, "You are fortunate in that you have been arrested for teaching Torah. Woe is me, that I was arrested for no good reason at all!"

R. Akiba was led forth for execution at the time of the morning *Shema*.[1] As they tore his flesh with iron currycombs, he continued his morning devotions. His disciples asked him, "Rabbi, how long will you continue?" He answered, "All my life I have wondered how I could fulfill the ordinance [*Thou shalt love the Lord thy God*] *with all thy soul,* which means even if your soul is taken from you. I did not know whether I would ever be able to fulfill this commandment. Now that the occasion has finally come to do so, shall I not accept the opportunity?"

With a prolonged sound he uttered the word *one* [*ehad*], and his soul departed. A heavenly voice then declared, "Blessed art thou, Akiba, that thy soul departed with the word *ehad* [proclaiming the unity of God]." *Berachoth, 61b*

The martyrdom of R. Hanina

642. The Romans found R. Hanina b. Teradion teaching the Torah in public [contrary to the Roman decree]. He was thereupon wrapped in the Torah scroll, and twigs were placed around him and set on fire. Tufts of wool soaked in water were put over his heart, so that his soul might not depart too soon. His daughter, standing by, said to him, "Father, is this just, what I see done to you?" He answered, "If I alone were being burned, it would indeed be hard for me to bear. But since I am being burned with the Torah scroll, I feel certain that He Who will take revenge for the sacred scroll will take revenge for me as well."

As the flame increased, his disciples asked him, "What do you see now?" And he replied, "I see the parchment burning, and its letters flying heavenward." They then said to him, "Rabbi, open your mouth, so that the smoke may suffocate you." But he answered, "It is far better that my soul should be taken by Him Who gave it to me

---

[1] Deut. 6:4–10 begins with *Hear O Israel, the Lord our God, the Lord is one* and continues with *And thou shalt love the Lord thy God with all thy heart and with all thy soul and with all thy might.*

[in His own time] than that I should cause it to depart more quickly."[1]

Then the executioner said to him, "Rabbi, if I increase the fire and take the tufts of wet wool from your heart, will you assure me of life in the World to Come?" To this, he replied that he would.[2] The executioner thereupon increased the fire and took away the moist tufts of wool from over Hanina's heart, and Hanina's soul departed from him. The executioner himself then jumped into the flames, and at this very moment a heavenly voice was heard, saying, "Both the executioner and Hanina are destined for life in the World to Come."

When Rabbi heard about this, he wept and said, "Truly, there are those who achieve eternal life in a moment [through a single act], while there are others who achieve immortality only through the efforts of a lifetime." *Abodah Zarah, 18a*

The tragedy of the two young captives

643. R. Judah said in the name of Rab, "The son and daughter of R. Ishmael b. Elisha were both taken captive,[3] but by two different captors. One day the two men happened to meet, and one of them said, 'I have a young male slave whose beauty cannot be equalled anywhere in the world.' The other replied, 'I have a maiden slave whose beauty is unsurpassed by anyone. Let us have them marry each other, and we will divide their children between us.' And they placed the two young people in the same [unlighted] room [cater-corner from each other].

"When the youth and the maiden were [separately] informed about the proposed marriage, the son of R. Ishmael [who could not clearly see his sister] declared, 'I am of a priestly family, the son of high priests. Shall I marry a slave?' And the girl [who did not recognize her brother] protested in like manner, 'I am of priestly lineage, a daughter of high priests. How can I marry a slave?'[4]

---

[1] This reflects the rabbinic attitude toward suicide or euthanasia in hastening the death of an individual.

[2] Hanina's acceptance of the removal of the wet wool from over his heart does not contradict his refusal to open his mouth so that the smoke might suffocate him. In that instance, he would have been hastening his death; here he allows removal of the wool because the wet wool artificially prolongs life. One may not end life, but need not artificially prolong it.

[3] Ishmael, their father, as a youth was taken captive to Rome. For the account of his rescue, see item 832.

[4] Deut. 10:8 declares that the tribe of Levi is to minister at God's altar. This honor is attributed to the tribe's loyalty during the incident of the golden calf. Members of the priesthood were

"Both of them wept through the night. When the dawn came and they recognized each other, they embraced and wept again, until their souls departed from them. To this episode one may apply the words of Jeremiah, (Lam. 1:16) *For these things I weep; Mine eye, mine eye runneth down with water* [tears]." *Gittin, 58a*

B. HEAVENLY INTERVENTION

Honi Hamagel prays for rain

644. It once happened that the greater part of the month of Adar [roughly, March] had passed, and no rain had yet fallen. Honi Hamagel ["the circle-drawer"] was therefore requested to pray for rain. He prayed, but no rain came. He then drew a circle around him, as Habakkuk had done when he said: (Hab. 2:1) *Upon my watch will I stand.* He stood in the center of it and said, "Sovereign of the Universe! Thy children have always looked up to me as one who is close to Thee. I swear, therefore, by Thy great name, that I shall not move from this spot until Thou shalt have compassion upon Thy children." Thereupon the rain began to descend in single drops.

"Rabbi," his disciples said to him, "it would appear that the rain is falling only [in token fashion] to release you from your vow." He therefore pleaded before God again, saying, "It was not for this that I prayed, but for rain enough to fill the wells and cisterns!" Then the rain began to fall with great force, each drop containing no less than a *lug* [cup] of water. The disciples now said to him, "Rabbi, we believe the rain is strong enough to destroy the whole world!"

Thereupon he again pleaded before God, saying, "Not for such rain have I prayed, but for rain that would be a blessing." The rain then descended in the more usual manner. But the people of Jerusalem were obliged to seek refuge on the Temple mount because of the great accumulation of water. So they came to Honi and said, "Rabbi, just as you prayed that the rain should descend, pray now for it to cease."

But Honi replied, "We are not permitted to pray for a cessation of [what is] good. However, bring me a bullock for a praise-offering

---

to follow certain regulations with regard to clothing, trimming the hair and entering into marriage. The objection to the marriage plans was based on such considerations rather than the rejection of incest (which was expressly forbidden in Lev. 18:9), since they had not yet recognized each other. The import of the story is that the refusal by the young people to violate the priestly regulations saved them from the greater sin of incest.

[*par hodaah*]."[1] When it was brought, he put both hands upon it and said, "Sovereign of the Universe! Thy people, which Thou hast brought up out of Egypt, can endure neither too much misfortune nor too much good fortune. Let it be Thy will that the rain may cease so that Thy people may be happy." Then a wind came up and dispersed the clouds, and the sun began to shine. When the people left the Temple mount, they saw that it was completely covered with mushrooms. *Taanith, 23a*

How Abba Helkiya prayed for rain

645. Abba Helkiya was a grandson of Honi Hamagel. When there was a drought, the rabbis would come to him to ask that he pray for rain. Once the rabbis sent a delegation of two young colleagues to him with the request that he pray for rain. They went to his house, but did not find him there. They then went out to the field and found him hoeing. When they greeted him, he did not acknowledge the greeting nor even turn to look at them, so they waited.

Toward sundown, he started back to his house. He took with him a piece of wood, and placed the wood and his hoe on one shoulder, throwing his cloak over the other. On the way back to his house, he did not wear his shoes, but just as he came to a small stream, he put them on. When he came to a thorny path, he raised his garments.

As he approached his house, his wife met him, dressed in fine clothing. She entered the house first, then he and the two young men entered, in that order. He sat down at the table to eat, but did not invite his visitors to eat with him. When he portioned out bread for his children, he gave the older child a single piece, and the younger child two pieces.

Then he turned to his wife and whispered, "Let us go to the upper floor and pray [secretly] for rain. I know that these young men have come to ask that I pray for rain, and if it please the Almighty to grant our request, it will not appear [to them] that this came about through our intervention." They then went to the upper room, and Abba Helkiya stood in one corner and his wife in another while they prayed.

Soon a raincloud appeared in the sky from the direction where his wife was standing. When they saw this, they came down, and he said

---

[1] Various types of animal sacrifice, intended to strengthen the bond between man and God, existed in ancient Israel. These are described in the Book of Leviticus. See also *U.J.E.,* s.v. "Sacrifice."

to his visitors, "For what purpose did you come here?" They replied, "We were sent here to ask that you pray for rain." And he replied, "Praised be the Lord, that He spared you the need to seek Abba Helkiya's favor [since rain is already beginning to fall]."

They then said, "We know that this rain has come only because of your prayers; however, we would like to know the reason for several odd bits of action on your part. Why, when we first greeted you, did you not turn to face us?" To this, he replied, "Because I had hired myself out by the day, and thought I must not waste any time."[1] "Why did you carry the wood on one shoulder and your cloak on the other [and not under the wood for padding]?" they asked. "Because I borrowed the cloak to wear, and not to use as a pad for wood," he replied.

"Why did you go barefooted all the way home, and put on your shoes only when you came to water?" they inquired. And he answered, "Because I can normally see what I am stepping on, but in water I can not." "Why did you raise your garment when walking on a thorny path?" they asked. "Because if my flesh should receive a scratch, it could heal; but if the garment got torn, it could not easily be mended," was his response.

"Why, when you approached your home, did your wife come to greet you, dressed in fine apparel?" "In order that I might not be tempted to look at another woman." "Why did she enter the house first, then you, and we last of all?" "Because you were unknown to me, and I could not judge your intentions." [He would not leave his wife unprotected.] "When you sat down to eat, why did you not invite us to join you?" "Because there was not sufficient food for all, and I did not wish to invite you only to be thanked for naught."

"Why did you give the older child a single piece of bread and the younger child two pieces?" "Because the older one was at home all day and probably helped himself, while the younger was at school all day and was hungrier." "Why did the raincloud first appear from your wife's corner of the room [where you prayed for rain]?" "Because my wife is always at home, being useful and doing good in many ways, while whatever good I do is indirect [such as contributing to charity]. Thus her actions are more worthy than my own." [Immediate and direct aid is more meritorious than impersonal assistance. While his

---

[1] The rabbis insist that an employee must be fair to his employer as well as an employer to the employee. See item 214.

wife gave bread that she had baked to the needy, he supplied only funds with which to buy bread.] *Taanith, 23a*

Nakdimon's prayers are answered

646. It once happened when all Israel came up [on one of the Jewish festivals] for a pilgrimage to Jerusalem that there was no water available for drinking. Nakdimon b. Gurion therefore approached a certain [non-Jewish] lord and said to him, "Provide me with twelve wells of water for the pilgrims, and I will repay you that amount. If I do not, then I will instead give you twelve talents of silver," and he set a time limit for repayment. When that day came and no rain had fallen, the nobleman sent a message to him in the morning [saying], "Return to me either the water or the money that you owe me." But Nakdimon replied, "I still have time; I have the whole day."

At noon the nobleman [again] sent Nakdimon a request for the water or the money. Nakdimon replied, "I still have time." In the afternoon he [once more] sent such a request, and Nakdimon answered, "I still have time." Then the nobleman said to him sneeringly, "Since it has not rained all year, will it rain now?" and he went cheerfully to the baths. Nakdimon, on his part, went to the Temple depressed. Wrapping himself in his cloak, he stood in prayer, saying, "Master of the Universe! It is known unto Thee that I have not done this for my own honor, nor for the honor of my father's house, but for Thine honor have I done this, so that water might be available for the pilgrims."

Immediately the sky became cloudy and rain began to fall, until the twelve wells were filled with water, and there was even much more. Just as the nobleman came out of the baths, Nakdimon came out of the Temple court and the two of them met. Nakdimon said to the lord, "Pay me for the extra water you have received." The latter replied, "I know that the Holy One disturbed the order of nature only on your account, yet my claim against you for the money is still good, for the sun has already set, and the rain fell on my time."

Nakdimon thereupon reentered the Temple precincts, once again wrapped himself in his cloak, and stood in prayer. He prayed, "Master of the Universe! Make it known that Thou hast beloved ones in Thy world." Suddenly the clouds dispersed and the sun broke through. Thereupon the nobleman said to him, "If the sun had not broken through [prolonging the day], I would still have had a claim against you for the money."

It has been said that his name was not Nakdimon but Boni, and that
he was called Nakdimon because the sun had broken through
[*nikdera*] on his behalf. *Taanith, 19b*

The mission of Rabbi Nahum of Gamzu

647. At one time the Jews desired to send a gift to the emperor.
They agreed that R. Nahum of Gamzu should deliver it because he
had experienced many miracles [and the journey was fraught with
danger]. They sent with him a bag full of precious stones and pearls.

On the way, he spent a night at an inn, and during the night
someone at the inn arose and emptied the bag, filling it with earth.
The following morning, when he discovered what had happened, he
exclaimed, "This too is for the best!" When he arrived at his destina-
tion and opened the bag, the king wanted to put all the Jews to death,
declaring, "The Jews are mocking me." And Nahum said, "This too
is for the best."

Thereupon Elijah the prophet appeared in the guise of a Roman and
remarked, "Perhaps this is some of the earth used by their father
Abraham, for when he threw earth [at the enemy] it turned into
swords, and when he threw stubble it changed into arrows; for Scripture states: (Isa. 41:2) *His sword maketh them as dust, His bow as the driven
stubble.*" [An association is made between earth and a sword, stubble
and a bow: the dust turns into swords, the stubble into bows].

The emperor then put this to the test. There was one province
which he had not heretofore been able to conquer, but when he tried
some of this earth [against it] he was able to do so. Then Nahum was
taken to the royal treasury and his bag was filled with precious stones
and pearls. Afterward he was sent home with great honor.

On his return journey, he again spent the night at the inn where he
had slept before. He was asked [by the innkeeper], "What did you
take to the king that caused him to treat you with such honor?" He
replied, "I brought him that which I had taken from here." The
innkeeper thereupon razed the inn to the ground and took some of
the earth to the king saying, "The earth that was brought to you
belonged to me."

They [the Romans] thereupon tested it, and it was not found to be
effective [in warfare], and the innkeeper was put to death.[1]

Taanith, 21a

---

[1] For another account of Nahum of Gamzu, see item 834.

The miracle of bread for the Sabbath

648. On the eve of each Sabbath the wife of R. Hanina used to make a fire in her oven and throw twigs into the stove [as if preparing food for the Sabbath] to avoid the disgrace of being exposed in her poverty.[1] However, she had a bad neighbor who once said to herself, "I know that they have nothing to cook for the Sabbath. What is the meaning of all this smoke? I shall go and find out."

When she knocked on the door, R. Hanina's wife withdrew to her bedroom in great embarrassment. When her neighbor entered the house, a miracle took place. The oven was filled with bread and the kneading-trough with dough. The neighbor saw the bread in the oven and called out to Hanina's wife, "Bring the bread-shovel quickly, or the bread will be burned!" Whereupon R. Hanina's wife called back to her, "I've just gone to get it."

We are told in a *baraitha* that Hanina's wife really did go into the other room for a bread-shovel because she was accustomed to having miracles happen for her. *Taanith, 24b*

Oil for the Sabbath lamp

649. One Sabbath eve Hanina noticed that his daughter was in a troubled mood. When he asked her what the problem was, she replied, "I mistook the two vessels containing oil and vinegar, and I poured the vinegar into the Sabbath lamp." To this he replied, "My daughter, He Who has ordained that oil should burn can ordain that vinegar will also burn."

We are told [in a *baraitha*] that the vinegar in the lamp burned all night and all of the next day, so that it could be used to kindle the *havdalah* light [at the close of the Sabbath]. *Taanith, 25a*

The miracle of the golden table leg

650. One day R. Hanina's wife said to her husband, "How long shall we be troubled for want of our daily bread?" To this he replied, "What can I do?" "Pray to God that He may supply some provision," said she. As he began to pray, an arm appeared, holding out to him a golden table leg.

Later his wife had a dream[2] that in the World to Come all of the

---

[1] Hanina was reputed to have been quite poor.
[2] Or R. Hanina had a dream. The text is not clear.

righteous would eat at golden tables with three legs, while her husband's table would have only two. She then said to Hanina, "Would you like it if all of the righteous ate at a perfect table [in the World to Come] while we should eat at an imperfect table? Pray to God that the golden table leg may be taken back." He prayed accordingly, and the table leg was taken back.[1]

We are told in a *baraitha* that the miracle of the withdrawal of the gift was even greater than the miracle whereby it was presented; for it is customary for heaven to bestow gifts but not to reclaim them.

Taanith, 25a

Miracles cannot serve to prove one's point

651. R. Eliezer used every possible argument [during a discussion] to bolster his view, but his opinion was not accepted. So he exclaimed, "Let this carob tree prove that the Halachah [law] is as I say!" The carob tree was miraculously transported to a distance of one hundred ells. But his colleagues merely said, "The carob tree proves nothing." He then said, "Let this stream of water prove that the Halachah prevails according to my view!" Thereupon the stream reversed its direction and flowed backwards. But the Sages declared that this too proved nothing.

R. Eliezer then said, "Let the walls of this house of study prove that I am right!" At this, the walls shook, and seemed about to fall. R. Joshua, however, rebuked the walls, saying, "If scholars are discussing a matter of law, why should you interfere?" Out of respect for R. Joshua, the walls did not collapse; nor did they become straight again, out of deference for R. Eliezer. Then R. Eliezer said, "Let it be announced by heaven that the Halachah is in accordance with my view!"

Thereupon a heavenly voice declared, "Why do you quarrel with R. Eliezer, whose opinion should prevail?" But R. Joshua arose defiantly and said [to the heavenly voice], "Scripture states: (Deut. 30:12) *The law is not in the heavens!*"

What did R. Joshua mean by this? R. Jeremiah explained it to mean that the Torah was given to us long ago at Mount Sinai, and we do not need a heavenly voice to tell us what to do; for the Torah itself

---

[1] This story serves to illustrate the widespread belief that one could not have the best of both worlds, i.e., this world and the next. See also item 652.

tells us (Exod. 23:2) *to incline after the majority* [i.e., the majority view must prevail].[1]

[Some time later] R. Nathan met Elijah the prophet and asked him, "How did the Holy One react when R. Joshua expressed defiance of the heavenly voice?" Elijah replied, "He laughed and said, 'My children have overruled Me! My children have overruled Me!' "[2] [See fns. to items 87 and 104.] *Baba Metzia, 59b*

One must not rely upon miracles

652. R. Huna had stored wine in a dilapidated house, the walls of which could collapse at any moment. He wished to remove the wine but was afraid to enter. He therefore asked R. Ada b. Ahaba to enter the house with him, and engaged him there in discussing a matter of law until he had time to remove the wine. After they left, the walls collapsed.

When R. Ada b. Ahaba learned how he had been used, he became upset for he agreed with the dictum of R. Jannai who declared, "A man should never expose himself to danger, expecting that a miracle will be wrought for him; for it may be that a miracle will not take place. And even if a miracle is wrought for him, it will be deducted from the rewards due him for his merits [in the Hereafter]."[3]

Taanith, 20b

653. Where danger seems certain, one must not rely upon a miracle; for Scripture states: (1 Sam. 16:2) *And Samuel said, 'How can I go? If Saul should hear it, he will kill me.'* [Samuel did not depend upon divine intervention in his behalf, even though his mission was at God's command.] *Kiddushin, 39b*

Some miracles can be rationally explained

654. (Mishnah) (Exod. 17:11) *And it came to pass, when Moses held up his hand, Israel prevailed.* Did then the hands of Moses cause war

---

[1] Rashi points out that Exod. 23:2 actually reads, *Thou art not to incline after the majority to do evil,* encouraging minority dissent when evil is being contemplated. Implicit here is the idea that to follow the majority is otherwise commendable, a rabbinic contribution to Jewish thought. See item 971.

[2] Here the majority not only overrules but also reminds the heavenly voice that the Torah itself indicates (indirectly) that the majority view should prevail, and God is represented as being pleased that they themselves had been able to discover this principle in His Torah.

[3] See also item 650 and fn.

to be waged or to cease? This passage really intends to teach us that when the people of Israel looked upward and pledged their hearts to their Father in heaven, they prevailed, but that when they ceased to do so, they failed.

We find a similar instance in the passage (Num. 21:8) *Make unto thee a fiery serpent and set it on a pole, and every one that is bitten, when he looketh upon it, shall live.* Could the image of a serpent kill a person or heal him?[1] This passage is intended to teach us that when the Israelites looked upward for aid, and pledged their hearts to their Father in heaven, they were healed, but that when they did not, they perished.

Rosh Hashanah, 29a

Man's wishes do not alter the laws of nature

655. R. Phineas b. Jair once set out on a mission to ransom captives. As he approached the rivulet Ginnay, he said to it, "Divide your waters for me so that I may be able to cross over." But the Ginnay replied, "You are on your way to do the will of your Creator, but I am already performing the will of my Creator. Whether or not you will be able to accomplish your mission is uncertain. But I am surely fulfilling my mission [since by divine command all rivers flow to the sea]. Hence I cannot stop performing my duty for your sake."

Hullin, 7a

---

[1] The association of the serpent with healing, of ancient origin, is continued in the physician's emblem to this day. The rabbis here repudiate the serpent's healing power.

12

SIN AND REPENTANCE

F̌OR the rabbis of the Talmud, sin consists of a departure from God's will as defined in Scripture. They are primarily concerned with the sins specified in the Ten Commandments: idolatry, taking God's name in vain, failure to observe the Sabbath, disrespect for parents, murder, adultery, stealing, bearing false witness and covetousness. Idolatry, adultery and murder are considered the three cardinal sins.

While fully aware that all but the most saintly are prone to sin to some degree, the rabbis do not conceive of humankind as born in sin. They recognize that people are neither wholly good nor irretrievably wicked, and that the inclination to good and evil are often in conflict. However, they reject the Zoroastrian notion that the conflict is that of two separate deities striving for mastery of human conduct.

The rabbis tell us that evil influences may lead us to sin, that minor transgressions may lead to greater offenses and that the repetition of a misdeed may render such action habitual. For them, the remedy for sinfulness is the avoidance of conditions conducive to sinful acts and the conscious exercise of self-restraint. If one has sinned, there is still hope: one can win God's pardon and find favor in His sight through genuine repentance and the performance of good deeds. Indeed, the rabbis declare that God is not only forgiving, but that He also is particularly compassionate toward the sincere penitent and eagerly awaits his return to righteous living.

A. TRANSGRESSION

Man's ambivalent nature

656. R. Nahman b. R. Hisda asked, in comment on the verse (Gen. 2:7) *Then the Lord God formed man,* etc., "Why is *vayyitzer* ['and He formed'] spelled with a double 'y' [i.e., with two *yods*]?" And he

answered, "[To show that] God created man with two impulses, one good and the other evil."[1] *Berachoth, 61a*

657. R. Jose the Galilean said, "The good impulse is dominant in the righteous person; as Scripture states: (Ps. 109:22) *My heart is wounded within me.* [2] The evil impulse controls the wicked; as Scripture states: (Ps. 36:1) *Transgression speaketh to the wicked, methinks—There is no fear of God before his eyes.* Both impulses are operative in average persons." *Berachoth, 61b*

When does the evil impulse first assert itself?

658. Antoninus[3] asked R. Judah, "At what moment [during gestation] does the evil inclination start to function? Is it during the formation of the embryo, or when the child emerges from the womb?" And R. Judah answered him, saying, "From the time when it begins to form." To this Antoninus replied, "In that case, it would kick about in the body of its mother and emerge prematurely of its own volition! Surely it must therefore be from the time of its emergence from the womb!"

R. Judah then said, "Antoninus has taught me something. His view is corroborated by the Scriptural verse (Gen. 4:7) *Sin croucheth at the door* [i.e., where the child emerges]."[4] *Sanhedrin, 91b*

We are free to choose between good and evil

659. R. Hanina b. Papa said, "The angel charged with overseeing conception is called Lailah. He takes a seminal drop, sets it before the Holy One, and asks, 'Sovereign of the Universe! What is to become of this drop? Is it to develop into a person strong or weak, wise or foolish, rich or poor?' No mention is made of its becoming a person who is wicked or righteous." *Niddah, 16b*

660. R. Eliezer said, "From the Torah, the Prophets and the Writings [Hagiographa] it may be shown that one is permitted to follow

---

[1] The Hebrew word for "impulse" or "inclination" is *yetzer*, here associated with *vayyitzer.* The doubling of the *yod* is taken to represent both the *yetzer tov* ("the good impulse") and the *yetzer ha-ra* ("the evil impulse"). Contrast Zoroastrian dualism in fn. to item 5.

[2] From the victorious struggle against the evil inclination.

[3] Antoninus or Marcus Aurelius (121–180) was unique among Roman rulers by virtue of his scholarship and mild character. He is best known for his *Meditations,* a compendium of moral precepts considered a fine example of Stoic philosophy.

[4] See also item 759.

the road he wishes to pursue [whether good or evil]."[1]

Makkoth, 10b

661. R. Hanina said, "Everything is in the hands of Heaven except the fear of Heaven; for Scripture states: (Deut. 10:12) *And now, Israel, what doth the Lord thy God require of thee, but* [only] *to fear* [revere] *the Lord thy God." Berachoth, 33b*

The three cardinal sins

662. R. Johanan said in the name of R. Simeon b. Jehozadak that it was resolved by a majority vote [in the Sanhedrin] that if a person is told to transgress [any law of the Torah] or be put to death, he may do so to save his life, with the exception of idolatry, adultery or bloodshed. [Rather than be guilty of these sins, he must forfeit his life.] *Sanhedrin, 74a*

663. Why was the first Temple destroyed [in 586 B.C.E.]? Because of three evil conditions: idolatry, adultery and bloodshed.

Yoma, 9b

The sin of idolatry

664. R. Abbahu cited R. Johanan as saying, "Whatever a prophet commands you to do which involves a transgression of the Torah, listen to him,[2] with the exception of idolatry. Even if he were to cause the sun to stand still in the heavens, you must not listen to him [if he requires that you worship idols]."[3] *Sanhedrin, 90a*

Taking the life of another

665. A man once came before Raba and said to him, "The ruler of my city has ordered me to kill a certain man, saying that if I refuse he will have me put to death. [What shall I do?]" Raba told him, "Die yourself, but do not kill another. Do you think that your blood is redder than his? His blood may be redder than

---

[1] It is interesting that John Spenkelink, the first person involuntarily executed (for murder) in the United States since 1967, stated before his death (May 25, 1979), "Man is what he chooses to be. He chooses that for himself" (*Time*, "At Issue: Crime and Punishment," June 4, 1979, p. 14). See fn. to item 15.

[2] As in the case of Elijah, who ordered that sacrifices, which were normally permitted only on the Temple Mount, should be offered on Mount Carmel. See 1 Kings 18.

[3] The commandment against idolatry is the first prohibition of the Ten Commandments. Its abrogation is therefore viewed as a repudiation of all the rest. See also item 674.

your own." [The life of the other may be more valuable.]

Pesahim, 25b

Justifiable homicide

666. Raba declared, "The Torah teaches that if someone tries to kill you, you may stop him from doing so by killing him."[1]

Sanhedrin, 72a

Wanton hatred is the root of much evil

667. Wanton hatred is equivalent to the transgressions of idolatry, adultery and bloodshed combined, and was the cause of the destruction of the second Temple. [See also item 227.] *Yoma, 9b*

The power of the evil inclination

668. The evil inclination of man is so strong that it is noted by the Creator. Scripture states: (Gen. 8:21) *For the imagination* [inclination] *of man's heart is evil from his youth.* R. Isaac declared, "The evil inclination renews its struggle against man every day; for Scripture states: (Gen. 6:5) *And that every imagination* [inclination] *of the thoughts of his heart was evil continually." Kiddushin, 30b*

669. R. Samuel b. Nahmani quoted R. Johanan as saying, "The evil impulse leads a man astray in this world and testifies against him in the Hereafter [i.e., on the Day of Judgment]." [See chapter 13.]

Sukkah, 52b

Evil is progressive in its hold upon us

670. Simeon b. Pazzi said, "What does the verse (Ps. 1:1) *Happy is the man who hath not walked in the counsel of the wicked, nor stood in the way of sinners, nor sat in the seat of scorners* [*letzim*][2] mean? If one has not walked [among the wicked], how could he stand [among them]? And if he did not stand, how could he sit [with them]? If he did not sit [with them], how could he scorn? The intent of the verse is this: if one [as much as] walks with the wicked, he will later stand with them; and if he stands with them, he will eventually sit and scorn [i.e., spend more time in bad company].

---

[1] In this case, differing from his judgment in item 665, Raba ignores the question of "redder blood," presumably because the problem is more directly one of self-defense.

[2] *Letzim* denotes scorners of what is good and right; those who engage in gossip and slander, or use foul language; frivolous persons.

In further comment, R. Simeon also said that the words *who hath not walked in the counsel of the wicked* refer to the person who does not walk to the theaters and circuses of the heathens; *nor stood in the way of sinners* refers to one who does not stand as a spectator at the bestial contests [of the Romans]; and *nor sat in the seat of scorners* refers to an individual who never sits in bad company. *Abodah Zarah, 18b*

Transgression and transgressor: common types

671. Scripture states: (Lev. 19:18) *Thou shalt not take revenge nor bear any grudge.* This applies to matters of money or possessions, as we are taught in the following *baraitha*:

How can we distinguish between revenge and bearing a grudge? Revenge is involved when one comes to another and says, "Lend me your spade," and the other says, "No." Later, the second man comes to the first and asks to borrow that man's axe. He answers, "I won't lend it to you since you did not lend me your spade."

Bearing a grudge is involved when one comes to another and says, "Lend me your sickle," and the other replies, "No." Thereafter the second man comes to the first and asks to borrow his spade. He answers, "I will lend it to you because I am not like you who recently refused to lend something to me." *Yoma, 23a*

672. There are four types of people who are insufferable: a poor man who is haughty; a rich man who engages in flattery; an old man who is lewd; and a leader who lords it over a community to no purpose. Some also add: he who has divorced his wife twice and marries her again. [See also item 25.]

Pesahim, 113b

Avoiding situations conducive to sin

673. R. Abbahu said in the name of R. Huna who quoted Rab, "A man must not stand and gaze at his neighbor's field when the fruit is ripening because this may lead to [the sin of envy, or] an evil eye."[1] *Baba Metzia, 107a*

674. Our rabbis taught that if one pays money to a woman, count-

---

[1] The term "evil eye" generally meant "envy" but was sometimes also used for "lust." Both involve a desire for that which is not one's own. In Jewish folklore, as in that of other cultures, the evil eye could also cause injury to the person or object viewed, in this case the ripening fruit of the field.

ing it from his hand into hers in order to gaze at her, even if he abounds in Torah and good deeds like Moses our Teacher, he will not escape the punishment of Gehinnom.[1]

R. Johanan said, "A man should walk behind a lion rather than behind a woman [for doing so may engender lascivious thoughts]. But he should rather walk behind a woman than follow an idol [in a procession, for idolatry is the greater sin]." *Berachoth, 61a*

675. Our rabbis taught that there are three things that cause a man to disregard his better judgment and the will of his Creator [and act sinfully]: idolatry, an evil spirit [*ruah raah*][2] and the stress of poverty. Why did they tell us this? So that we might pray for deliverance from these [causes of wrongdoing]. *Erubin, 41b*

Minor transgressions may lead to greater sins

676. R. Simeon b. Eleazar said in the name of R. Hilpha b. Agra who quoted R. Johanan b. Nuri, "He who tears his garments or throws away his money in great anger [thereby displaying a lack of self-control,] should be regarded as one who worships idols. For such is the treacherous way of the evil inclination that one day it says to someone, 'Do this,' and the next day it will tell him to do something else, until it tells him to worship idols and the person obeys."

R. Abin asked, "What is the Scriptural verse that proves this to be so?" [And he answered,] "It is (Ps. 81:10) *There shall be no strange god in thee;* [3] *nor shalt thou worship any foreign god.* What is the *strange god* within a man [that leads him to idolatry]? The evil inclination."

Sabbath, 105b

Evading victimization from the sins of others

677. The [sinful] people of Sodom[4] had a special bed for any visiting stranger. If a person was too tall for the bed, they made him shorter [by chopping off his feet]. If he was short, they stretched him to fit the bed.[5] When Eliezer was there, he was asked to sleep in the

---

[1] See chapter 13, on reward and punishment. In this item, the rabbis go beyond adultery to deplore actions and thoughts that could lead to adultery.

[2] *Ruah raah* is an overpowering feeling or temporary insanity.

[3] *In thee* refers to the collective Jewish community but is here applied to the individual. Abin's comment is based on the seeming redundancy in this verse.

[4] The story of Sodom is told in Genesis, chapters 13–20.

[5] Cf. the bed of Procrustes ("the Stretcher"), a robber in Greek legend who tortured his victims by cutting or stretching them to fit the bed.

bed, but he replied, "Ever since my mother died, I have vowed not to sleep in a bed." *Sanhedrin, 109b*

Causing others to sin is unpardonable

678. R. Shesheth said, "In connection with trees, which cannot eat or drink or smell, the Torah commands that those which have been employed for idolatrous worship are to be burned,[1] because through them men have been led to stumble [into evil]. How much more deserving of extermination is a person who causes his fellowmen to depart from the paths of life to pursue the paths of [spiritual] death!"

Sanhedrin, 55a

679. If one induces a community to do good, no sin will [ever] come about through his actions. But if one leads others to act sinfully, no opportunity will be given him for repentance [i.e., his penitence will be of no avail]. *Yoma, 87a*

680. R. Johanan overheard a young woman pray, "Thou hast created both Paradise and Gehinnom, both the wicked and the righteous. May it be Thy will that no man may be led to transgress because of me [through sexual arousal]." *Sotah, 22a*

The evil inclination can be resisted

681. R. Katina said, "Even at the time of Jerusalem's moral decline, virtuous persons could still be found there." *Hagigah, 14a*

682. R. Joshua b. Levi said, "Happy is the man who conquers his evil inclinations. He is a true hero." *Abodah Zarah, 19a*

One must set his own standards of behavior

683. R. Kapara said, "Where there is no [righteous] man, try to be one yourself."[2] *Berachoth, 63a*

Guarding against repeated transgression

684. R. Huna said, "When a man commits the same offense twice, it becomes for him an allowable action."

Kiddushin, 40a; Sotah, 22a

685. R. Assi said, "At first the evil inclination is as fragile as a

---

[1] Deut. 12:3 reads *And ye shall break down their altars, and dash in pieces their pillars, and burn their Asherim with fire.* The word *Asherim* refers to the sacred groves where men often worshipped in ancient times. So too does the word *pillars* refer to sacred pillars used for worship. It has been suggested that the latter were phallic symbols.

[2] The same advice was offered by Hillel before the time of Kapara (Mishnah Aboth, 2:5).

spider's web, but in time it becomes as strong as a wagon rope [and holds us in its grip]."[1] *Sanhedrin, 99b*

One should not persist in sinning

686. R. Ulla asked, "What does the verse (Eccles. 7:17) *Be not wicked overmuch* mean? Does this mean that it is acceptable for one to be slightly wicked? Not at all! This means that one should not persist in evil. For example, if one has eaten garlic and has a bad breath, he should not eat still more of it and cause an even worse odor to emanate from him."[2] *Sabbath, 31b*

Cultivating the inclination to do good

687. R. Levi b. Hama said in the name of R. Simeon b. Lakish, "At all times must one rouse his inclination toward good against his evil inclination." *Berachoth, 5a*

Acting as if every deed makes a difference

688. A man should always behave as if his merits and misdeeds are equally balanced. If he fulfills a *mitzvah* ["good deed"], he may rejoice, for that will serve to tip the scale toward the side of virtue. If he commits an offense, he should be unhappy, for it will tip the scale toward the side of guilt; as Scripture states: (Eccles. 9:18) *But one sinner* [sin] *causeth much to be lost.* This means that a single sin committed by an individual may cancel out much goodness on his part.

Kiddushin, 40b

Contrasts between the righteous and the wicked

689. R. Eleazar said, "The righteous man, even if he lives with two wicked persons, does not acquire their bad habits. But the wicked man, even if he lives with two righteous persons, will not emulate their good deeds." [Good habits keep us from evil, while bad habits are not easily broken.] *Yoma, 38b*

690. Seven pits [of temptation] may confront the righteous person, yet he escapes them all. Only one may present itself to the evil-doer, yet he falls into it. Samuel said to R. Judah, "This is attested by the

---

[1] Cf. "Oh, what a tangled web we weave, when first we practice to deceive!" (Sir Walter Scott, "Lochinvar," *Marmion,* Canto 6, Stanza 15.)

[2] For another view of garlic, see item 274.

verse (Prov. 24:16) *For a righteous man falleth seven times yet riseth up again, but the wicked man stumbles under adversity."* Sanhedrin, 7a

691. In the Hereafter, the Holy One will bring forth the evil impulse and destroy it in the presence of the righteous and the wicked.[1] To the righteous, it will appear to be like a high mountain, and to the wicked, like a single hair. Each of them will weep at the sight of it. The righteous will weep and exclaim, "How were we able to conquer so lofty a mountain!" The wicked will weep and say, "How were we unable to conquer a single hair like this!" *Sukkah, 52a*

How God determines the severity of our sins

692. (Isa. 3:10) *Say ye of the righteous that he is good.*[2] Raba said that R. Idi expounded this verse as follows: Can there be a righteous person who is good and one who is not good? The verse means that one who is good toward heaven [i.e., pious] and also toward his fellowmen is a righteous man who is indeed good. But one who is good toward God yet evil toward men is a [self-] righteous man who is not [really] good.

So too with the verse (Isa. 3:11) *Woe unto the wicked who is evil.* Is there a wicked person who is evil and one who is not evil? He who is wicked toward God [ignoring prayer, etc.] and wicked also toward his fellowmen is a wicked man who is truly evil. But one who is wicked toward God but good to men is a wicked person who is not evil.

Kiddushin, 40a

Summary thoughts on good and evil

693. R. Hidka said, "Good things are brought about through the agency of good men, and bad things are brought about through the agency of bad men." [They do not happen by themselves but result from human actions.] *Baba Bathra, 119b*

694. Since those who claim that evil is good and good evil have grown numerous, troubles have increased in the world.[3] *Sotah, 47b*

---

[1] This would seem to suggest a single universal Day of Judgment. For further comment on the subject, see chapter 13b.

[2] The 1917 J.P.S. translation reads, *that it shall be well with him*, which would destroy the point made here. In the next paragraph, instead of *who is evil*, it offers *it shall be ill with him*, which is equally inappropriate in this context.

[3] Cf. our modern problems in defining right and wrong in debates over nuclear fission, abortion, sex changes, cloning, etc.

Psalm 41

B. ATONEMENT

The greatness of repentance

695. R. Samuel b. Nahmani said in the name of R. Jonathan, "Great is repentance, for it prolongs the years of a man's life. Scripture states: (Ezek. 33:19) *And when the wicked turneth from his wickedness*[1] *. . . he shall live thereby.*" *Yoma, 86a*

696. Resh Lakish said, "Penitence is great indeed, since it reduces intentional transgressions to inadvertent acts; for Scripture states: (Hos. 14:2) *For thou hast stumbled in thine iniquity.* Note that iniquity is intentional, yet it is here referred to as [merely] stumbling, which is not." *Yoma, 86b*

God smooths the way for the penitent

697. Resh Lakish asked, "What does the verse (Prov. 3:34) *If it concerneth the scorners* [i.e., the wicked] *He scorneth them, but to the humble* [i.e., the contrite] *He giveth grace* mean?" [And he answered,] "This means that if someone wishes to defile himself with sin, the door is left open for him to do so. But if one seeks to purify himself, he is actively assisted."

The school of Ishmael taught that this is comparable to a merchant who sells both naphtha and perfume. When a customer buys naphtha, the merchant says to him, "Measure out the quantity you need." But when someone buys perfume, the merchant says to him, "We will both measure it out, so that I too may inhale its fragrance."

Sabbath, 104a; Yoma, 38b

God accepts repentance from a contrite heart

698. R. Joshua b. Levi said, "When the Temple existed, if one brought a burnt-offering, he received the reward only for a burnt-offering. If he brought a meal-offering, he was rewarded only for that. But if one is truly contrite, God regards him as one who has offered all kinds of sacrifices; for Scripture states: (Ps. 51:19) *The* [most acceptable] *sacrifices of God are a broken spirit.* His prayers are never rejected; for the passage continues, *A broken and a contrite heart, O God, Thou wilt not despise.*" *Sanhedrin, 43b*

---

[1] The word for "repentance" (*teshubah*) is from the same root as the word for "return" (*shub*). In repentance, one turns away from evil and returns to God. Repentance is regarded as being so important that it is declared to be one of the seven things created before the creation of the world itself. See item 792.

He pardons those who themselves forgive transgression

699. Raba said that if one refrains from retaliation, all of his transgressions will be pardoned; for Scripture states: (Mic. 7:18) *He pardoneth iniquity and* [him who] *forgiveth transgression.* Whose iniquity does God pardon? That of the person who forgives transgression [against himself].[1] *Rosh Hashanah, 17a; Yoma, 23a*

[handwritten: ✳ Psalm 4/ +2/]

Repentance must be sincere

700. Raba b. Hinena the Elder said in the name of Rab, "Whoever commits a transgression and is overcome with remorse will have all of his sins forgiven." *Berachoth, 12b*

701. R. Johanan said in the name of R. Jose, "A single self-reproach in one's heart is more effective than punishment by many stripes of the lash." *Berachoth, 7a*

Repentance must be verified by changed behavior

702. R. Adda b. Ahaba said, "If one is guilty of a transgression and confesses, but does not change his ways, what is he like? He is like a person holding a defiling reptile in his hand.[2] Even if that person were to immerse his body in all the waters of the world, his immersion will not serve to cleanse him [while he holds the reptile; i.e., persists in sinning]. But if he casts the reptile away and immerses himself in as little as forty *seah* of water, he will be [ritually] clean;[3] for Scripture states: (Prov. 28:13) *Whoever confesseth* [his sins] *and forsaketh them shall obtain mercy.*"

Taanith, 16a

One good deed outweighs many bad ones

703. Our rabbis taught that repentance and good deeds are one's intercessors [at divine judgment], and that even if nine hundred and ninety-nine [bad deeds] plead against him and only one [good deed] speaks in his defense, he is considered guiltless.

Sabbath, 32a

---

[1] Cf. "It is in pardoning that we are pardoned" (Prayer of Saint Francis).

[2] Touching the carcass of a reptile is forbidden by Scripture as a defiling act, rendering one ritually unclean (Lev. 11:30).

[3] A *seah* is a liquid measure. Forty *seah* is the required minimum capacity of the ritual bath (*mikveh*) mandated by Biblical law after sexual emissions, contact with the dead or after menstruation. Scripture states that the defiled individual must "bathe his flesh in running water" to be cleansed from his impurity (Lev. 15:13). See *U.J.E.*, s.v. "Mikveh."

When one should repent

704. R. Eliezer said, "Repent one day before your death."[1] His disciples then asked him, "Does a man know when he will die?" R. Eliezer replied, "This means one must repent today, lest he die [unrepentant] tomorrow. If he follows this practice, he will repent every day of his life. Solomon in his wisdom declared, (Eccles. 9:8) *At all times let thy garments be white* [in penitence], *and let oil not be wanting on thy head."*

R. Johanan b. Zakkai said, "This may be compared to an invitation, extended by a king, to attend a banquet at the palace without indicating the hour. The invitation is sent to all of his attendants, but they do not all react the same way. The wise ones dress properly and stand ready before the palace, knowing that in a king's palace nothing is lacking [and a banquet can be arranged quickly]. The fools go about their business thinking, 'Can a banquet be held without lengthy preparation?'

"Without further notice, the king calls in all of his attendants. The wise enter, attractively attired, but the fools come in wearing their daily garments. The king, pleased with the wise but displeased with the fools, declares, 'Those who are properly attired may sit down to eat and drink. Those who are not appropriately dressed shall merely stand by and look on.' " *Sabbath, 153a*

It is never too late to repent

705. R. Simeon b. Johai said, "If one has been utterly wicked all his life yet repents at the end, his wickedness will not be remembered against him [by God]." *Kiddushin, 40b*

The mark of the true penitent

706. How does one prove he is a repentant sinner? R. Judah said, "One is a true penitent when the temptation to sin comes to him a first and then a second time, yet he resists it." *Yoma, 86b*

Limitations of repentance on the Day of Atonement

707. (Mishnah) He who says to himself, "I will sin and repent, then sin and repent again," will not be exculpated [since he never experienced remorse]. If one thinks, "I will sin and the Day of Atonement will release me from guilt," the Day of Atonement will not do

---

[1] The statement appears in the Book of Ben Sirah (Ecclus.) 5:8.

so. Moreover, sins involving the relationship between man and God can be expiated on the Day of Atonement, but sins which involve the relationship between two individuals are not vitiated on the Day of Atonement unless one first appeases his fellowman [by asking him for forgiveness].

(Gemara) R. Eleazar b. Azariah expounded in a similar vein on the verse (Lev. 16:30) *From all your sins before the Lord shall ye be cleansed.* He declared that sins involving the relationship between man and God [*before the Lord*] can be expiated on the Day of Atonement, but that sins involving matters between one person and another [i.e., before man, rather than *before the Lord*] will not be exculpated on the Day of Atonement until one's fellowman has been placated.[1]

Yoma, 85b

Should a sin be confessed more than once?

708. Our rabbis taught that the sins which one has confessed on the Day of Atonement need not be confessed again on the following Day of Atonement. This is so if one has not repeated the sin. If the sin has been repeated, he should repeat the confession also. However, if he confesses again without having sinned again, then to him applies the verse (Prov. 26:11) *As a dog returneth to his vomit, so doth a fool repeat* [mention of] *his folly.*

R. Eliezer b. R. Jacob disagreed. He said, "On the contrary; he is rather to be praised all the more; for Scripture states: (Ps. 51:5) *For of my transgressions I have full knowledge, and my sin is before me constantly.*" *Yoma, 86b*

God wants sin to be destroyed, not the sinner

709. There were some highwaymen in R. Meir's neighborhood who annoyed him so much that he once prayed that they should die. But his wife Beruriah[2] said to him, "How do you justify such prayer? Is it based on the verse (Ps. 104:35) *Let sins* [*hattaim*] *be consumed*

---

[1] The reference to one's sins *before the Lord* is taken to exclude sins against man, which are not as readily forgiven. This verse from Leviticus appears in the synagogue service for the Day of Atonement. It is common practice for one to seek forgiveness for any offense against another person before that service takes place. A novel by Sholom Asch deals with the impact of this tradition on a businessman whose guilt drives him to locate and attempt to make amends to a man who does not even realize he was cheated by him years earlier. (Sholom Asch, *A Passage in the Night,* trans. Maurice Samuel [New York: G. P. Putnam's Sons, 1953].)

[2] "Beruriah" is equivalent to "Valeria." Through the centuries Jews have adopted, often in Hebraized form, names in common use.

[which you take to mean that the wicked should be destroyed]? The verse does not refer to sinners [*hotim*] but rather to sins! The passage continues *and the wicked shall be no more.* The way to achieve this is to pray that sinners may be led to repent; then it will come to pass that *the wicked shall be no more* [no longer wicked]!"[1] R. Meir prayed for them, and they ultimately did repent. *Berachoth, 10a*

The virtue of inspiring others to repent

710. There were some insolent fellows in the neighborhood of R. Zera. He nonetheless associated with them and showed them respect, hoping that they might repent. The rabbis were displeased with his display of leniency. However, when R. Zera died, these insolent fellows said, "Up until now, there was the little man who prayed in our behalf, but who will do so now that he is gone?" They thereupon repented and became righteous. *Sanhedrin, 37a*

---

[1] See also item 976.

13

THE END OF LIFE

IN their effort to formulate a Jewish view of death and the Hereafter, the rabbis seek Scriptural support. In the early Biblical material,
however, death seems to be accepted as natural and final, with little
if any reference to a future existence. Abraham, Scripture tells us, died
"an old man, full of years, and was gathered to his people" (Gen.
25:8). Whether there is a veiled allusion here to an afterlife is doubtful.

The Bible also speaks of the dead as descending into *sheol,* a word
often translated as "the pit." Whether it means more than "the grave"
and implies a Hereafter is questionable. In Daniel, a late book of the
Bible, and elsewhere as well, eschatological references may be found,
but their meaning is often unclear. There are intimations in Scripture
that reward and punishment for good and evil take place in this world,
as in the commandment, "Honor thy father and thy mother, that thy
days may be long upon the land which the Lord thy God giveth thee"
(Exod. 20:12), and this view is sometimes expressed by the rabbis.

However, they recognize that virtue is not always rewarded here
on earth; that the righteous may endure personal misfortune while the
wicked often prosper. Some of the rabbis seek to explain such undeserved suffering as "chastisements of love," by which God reproves
the faithful, but this principle is not universally accepted. More dominant is the belief that reward and punishment are not of this world,
but take place in the Hereafter. Thus the rabbis speak of Paradise
(Gan Eden) and the Netherworld (Gehinnom) as otherworldly scenes
of recompense and retribution.

These concepts are by their very nature not easily defined, and are
variously perceived by the rabbis. Their meaning may also have un-
dergone change during the Talmudic era and is often further ob-
scured by the use of hyperbolic language. As a result, there is neither
complete clarity nor genuine consistency in rabbinic employment of

these terms. Nonetheless, the wrestling of the rabbis with the profound mysteries of good and evil serves as a tribute to their faith in God and their passion for justice.

Like Abraham, the first Jew, they ask, "Shall not the Judge of all the world act justly?" (Gen. 18:25). Though their answers may not be universally accepted, the question is still raised by many.

A. DEATH

Rabbi Ammi relates suffering and death to sin

711. R. Ammi said, "There is no death without sin [i.e., one's sins cause one to die]; and there is no suffering without [previous] iniquity. That there is no death without sin is attested by the verse (Ezek. 18:20) *The soul that sinneth, it shall die.* [1] That there is no suffering without iniquity is indicated by the verse (Ps. 89:33) *Then will I visit their transgression with the rod, and their iniquity with stripes* [of the lash]."

[In support of his view] R. Ammi quoted R. Simeon b. Eleazar as saying, "Even Moses and Aaron died because of their sins; for Scripture states: (Num. 20:12) *Because ye had no confidence in Me,* etc. If they had possessed faith [in God], their time to depart from this world would not have come." *Sabbath, 55a,b*

But the rabbis disagree with Rabbi Ammi

712. Though R. Simeon b. Eleazar held that Moses and Aaron did not die without sin, he nevertheless believed that death is [theoretically] possible without sin. We therefore infer that, just as there can be death without sin, so can there also be affliction without sin. This is a refutation of R. Ammi. [2] *Sabbath, 55b*

Longevity does not depend on virtue

713. Raba said, "Longevity, sexual fertility and earning a livelihood depend not on virtue but rather on chance [*mazal*]." [3]

Moed Katan, 28a

---

[1] The verse continues, *the son shall not bear the iniquity of the father,* reflecting a quite different intent.

[2] The Book of Job is of course the classic refutation of Ammi's view of the relationship between sin and suffering or death.

[3] See item 609 and fn.

God affirms that all must die

714. The ministering angels asked the Lord, "Sovereign of the Universe! Why didst Thou impose the penalty of death upon Adam?" God replied, "I gave a simple command, yet he disobeyed it." "But Moses and Aaron fulfilled the whole Torah," they continued, "yet they too died!" To this God replied, (Eccles. 9:2) *"There is one event to the righteous and to the wicked."*

Sabbath, 55b

Scripture regards death as natural

715. Seventy is called an old age; eighty an age of uncommon vigor. Scripture states: (Ps. 90:10) *Our years are three score years and ten, or even by reason of strength, four score years. Moed Katan, 28a*

Death teaches us wisdom for living

716. R. Meir said, "What does the passage (Eccles. 7:2) *It is better to go to the house of mourning than to go to the house of feasting; for that is the end of all men, and the living will lay it to his heart* mean? What do the words *and the living will lay it to his heart* teach us?

"This refers to matters connected with death. He who mourns the death of others will [lay the lesson of human mortality to heart, and live in such a fashion as to] be mourned by others. He who raises his voice in lamentation on the death of another will [so conduct his life that he will] in turn be lamented by others. And he who carries [the bier of] others will be carried with honor by others."

Kethuboth, 72a

The death of the righteous

717. R. Eleazar said in the name of R. Hanina, "When the righteous man dies, it is really a loss to that generation. This may be compared to losing a pearl. Wherever it may be, it nonetheless exists. The loss is that of its owner." *Megillah, 15a*

When news of a death should be withheld

718. If one who is ill sustains a bereavement, they should not inform him thereof lest he become depressed. *Moed Katan, 26b*

Rending one's garment when a death occurs

719. Our rabbis taught that these are the *kerioth* ["rends"] that must not be mended: clothes that are torn [in mourning] for one's

father, his mother, one's teacher, or for a Nasi or Ab Beth Din ["Chief Justice"]¹

How far [down] should one rend his garment? To the region of the navel. Some say, only to the [region of the] heart. Although there is no proof of this, there is a Scriptural allusion to it; for Scripture states: (Joel 2:13) *And rend* [to] *your hearts and not your* [total] *garments.* [The verse actually suggests a disparagement of the practice where atonement is intended.] *Moed Katan, 26a,b*

Bringing food to those who are in mourning

720. Our rabbis taught that formerly it was the custom to bring food to the house of mourning, the rich bringing it in silver and gold baskets and the poor in wicker baskets, with the result that the poor felt embarrassed. They therefore decreed that all should use wicker baskets out of consideration for the poor. *Moed Katan, 27a*

The length of the period of mourning

721. (Jer. 22:10) *Weep ye not for the dead, neither bemoan him.* The first words mean *Weep ye not for the dead* too much. And the words *neither bemoan him* mean that we are not to mourn longer than the usual period of time. How long should that be? Three days for weeping, seven days for eulogy and thirty days for abstaining from wearing fine garments and having the hair cut.² After that [one should cease active mourning for], the Holy One says, "You need not grieve over him more than I do."

R. Judah said in the name of Rab, "Whoever mourns too much over a death will as a consequence have to mourn over still another [to justify the excessive mourning]." *Moed Katan, 27b*

722. Rab said, "The memory of the deceased is not dimmed in the heart until twelve months have elapsed;³ for Scripture states: (Ps. 31:13) *I am forgotten like a dead man out of sight; I am like a lost vessel*

---

¹ Rending one's garments as a sign of mourning goes back to early Biblical times. See 2 Sam. 1:11,12. The practice may derive from an even earlier custom of cutting one's flesh in expiation of sins committed against the dead. Cutting a black ribbon attached to the clothing is now often substituted.

² These successive periods of diminished mourning are still observed as periods of prayer and limited activity. The first three days are *shloshah*, the week *shivah* and the month *shloshim*. *Shivah* may be derived from (Gen. 50:10) *And he made for his father a mourning of seven days.* See also item 761.

³ The anniversary of the death is observed each year thereafter as *Jahrzeit*, with recitation of the *Kaddish* prayer.

[which is considered lost after twelve months have passed]."[1]

How Rabban Gamaliel changed funeral practice

723. We are taught in a *baraitha* that in early times, burial expenditures were so great that they sometimes affected the survivors more than did the death of their loved ones. The mourners often found the cost so burdensome that Rabban Gamaliel instructed that he be buried in a plain linen shroud. Following his example, people began to bury their dead in linen shrouds [even if they were rich, to spare the feelings of the poor].[2] *Kethuboth, 8b*

Words of eulogy spoken for a rabbi

724. When Rabina [Rabbi Abina] died, these words were spoken:

"Bend, O ye majestic palms, in grief sincere
O'er one who, like a palm, has flourished here;
Nor cease your mourning when the moon's soft ray
Changes to shadowy night the brilliant day.
For the moon's broad glare had oft to midnight waned
Ere sleep upon his studious eyelids reigned."[3]

Moed Katan, 25b

How to take leave of the deceased

725. R. Levi b. Hitha said, "He who takes leave of the deceased after burial should not say [to the dead] 'Go with peace,' but rather 'Go *in* peace.' Conversely, when one takes leave of his living friends, he should not say, 'Go *in* peace,' but rather 'Go *with* peace.' " [Whence do we derive this?]

R. Levi explained, "When one takes leave of the dead, he should say, 'Go in peace'; for Scripture states at the death of Abraham: (Gen. 15:15) *But thou shalt come to thy fathers in peace* [*b'shalom*]. When one

---

[1] See also item 762.
[2] Besides the plain shroud, Jewish tradition dictates a simple pine coffin. Today, Jews are in varying degrees influenced in such matters by the norms of society at large. Interestingly enough, recent books critical of modern funeral practices have made Jews more aware of their own traditions of simple burial.
[3] Adapted from one of several eulogies translated into English by Sekles in *Poetry of the Talmud*, and quoted by S. H. Glick in *En Jacob: Legends of the Talmud*, 5 vols. (New York: Rosenberg Press, 1916-22), 2:283-285. For a different rendition of this eulogy, see the Soncino Talmud, Moed Katan, pp. 159-162.

takes leave of a living friend he should say, 'Go with peace'; for Jethro [the father-in-law of Moses] said to Moses: (Exod. 4:18) *'Go with peace* [*l'shalom*]'[1] and Moses was successful in his mission. David said to Absalom: (2 Sam. 15:9) *'Go in peace,'* and Absalom was hanged." [The son of King David, who had conspired against his father, was accidentally hanged by his long hair.] *Moed Katan, 29a*

A father's bequest to his sons

726. At the approach of death a man declared, "I bequeath a barrel full of earth to one son, a barrel full of bones to the second and a barrel full of stuffing to the third." His sons failed to understand this, and came to ask R. Bana'a what their father had intended. He asked if the family had any land, and they answered in the affirmative. Then he asked, "Do you have any cattle?" and they indicated that they did.

"Have you also any [stuffed] furniture?" he inquired. And again they replied in the affirmative. "If that is the case," said he, "these constitute your father's bequest to the three of you."

Baba Bathra, 58a

B. DIVINE JUDGMENT

Even minor misdeeds are taken into account

727. Rab said, "Even slight remarks passed between a husband and his wife are recorded against them in the hour of their death."

Hagigah, 5b

God also takes note of evil intentions

728. Resh Lakish said, "He who merely raises his hand with the intention of striking another is called wicked, even if he has not actually struck him; for Scripture states: (Exod. 2:13) *And he said to the wicked one, 'Wherefore smitest thou thy fellowman?'* This verse does not read: 'Why hast thou smitten?' but why *smitest thou?* Hence, one is called wicked if he merely raises his hand in order to strike another."

Sanhedrin, 58b

---

[1] The 1917 J.P.S. translation renders both passages as *'Go in peace,'* ignoring the difference in the Hebrew text, but the difference in the Hebrew must be recognized here.

But sinful thoughts are not equivalent to evil actions

729. The Holy One does not consider an evil thought to be equivalent to an evil act [for none would be guiltless]. *Hullin, 142a*

The kind man receives special consideration

730. The school of Hillel said, "He who abounds in kindness tips the scale [of judgment] toward the side of kindness [to himself]."

Rosh Hashanah, 17a

God takes into account one's good intentions

731. R. Ammi said, "If one intended to fulfill a *mitzvah* ['good deed'] but is accidentally prevented from doing so, Scripture credits him with having fulfilled it." *Sabbath, 63a*

732. The Holy One adds the merit of a good intention to that of the good deed [by rewarding both]. [See also item 162.]

Kiddushin, 40a

Questions to be asked at the time of judgment

733. Raba said, "When a man faces divine judgment, he will be asked, 'Have you dealt honestly with others? Have you set aside regular time for study? Have you married? Have you longed for salvation [i.e., the coming of God's Kingdom]? Have you searched after wisdom? Have you trained your mind to infer one thing from another?'

"Even if all of these questions are answered affirmatively, only if the words (Isa. 33:6) *the fear of the Lord is his treasure* may be applied to him will these answers avail him; otherwise they will not."[1]

Sabbath, 31a

Divine judgment takes place on the Day of Atonement

734. We are taught in a *baraitha* that R. Meir said, "All are called to account for their sins on New Year's Day [Rosh Hashanah], and on the Day of Atonement [Yom Kippur] their judgment is sealed."[2] *Rosh Hashanah, 16a*

---

[1] Ps. 111:10 reads: *The fear* [reverence] *of the Lord is the beginning of* [all] *wisdom.* Regard for God's will must govern men's actions.

[2] This tradition is preserved in the synagogue service for these two Holy Days. The Book of Life lies open before God on Rosh Hashanah and is closed on Yom Kippur, sealing men's destinies for the coming year. However, prayer, penitence and good deeds can alter the divine decree and win God's favor during the ten days that intervene. Beyond considerations of

Judgment is rendered twice yearly

735. Raba said, "Judgment is passed on men twice a year, at the time of sowing and at the time of reaping."[1] *Rosh Hashanah, 16a*

We are being judged constantly

736. R. Jose said, "Judgment is passed upon a person daily; for Scripture states: (Job 7:18) *Thou rememberest him every morning.*" But R. Nathan maintained that we are judged constantly; for Scripture states: (ibid.) *Thou triest him every moment.* Rosh Hashanah, 16a

Final judgment occurs at death

737. Our rabbis taught that at the time of a man's departure from this world, all his actions are detailed before him and he is told, "Such and such have you done in such a place on such a day." He agrees, and is then ordered to sign the record. He also admits the justice of the verdict and declares, "Rightly hast Thou judged me," so that the words of Scripture may be fulfilled (Ps. 51:6) *That Thou mayest be justified* [i.e., be declared to act justly] *when Thou speakest.*

Taanith, 11a

How men are classified in divine judgment

738. We are taught in a *baraitha* that the school of Shammai declared that there are three classes with respect to the Day of Judgment. These are the perfectly righteous, the totally wicked and those of average character. Those in the first category are immediately inscribed and sealed for eternal life. Those in the second group are forthwith inscribed and sealed for Gehinnom; as Scripture states: (Dan. 12:2) *Many of them that sleep in the dust shall awake, some to everlasting life and some to shame and everlasting contempt.*

The third class will descend to Gehinnom, cry out [from pain], and then ascend; for Scripture states: (Zech. 13:9) *I will bring the third part through fire, and will refine them as silver is refined, and I will try them as gold is tried; they shall call on My name and I will hear them.*

Rosh Hashanah, 16b

---

theology, this annual *heshbon hanefesh* ("accounting of the soul") is a remarkable expression of the human spirit.

[1] The symbolism of reaping what one has sown is suggested in this statement. See also N.T., Gal. 6:7, "Be not deceived; God is not mocked: for whatsoever a man soweth, that shall he also reap."

Divine judgment is inescapable

739. The Roman ruler Antoninus said to Rabbi, "On the day of judgment, the body and soul may seek to exculpate themselves. The body may say, 'The soul has sinned; for since her departure, I have lain inactive like a stone in the grave.' And the soul may say, 'The body has sinned; for since I have departed from it, I fly about [guiltless] like a bird.' [How then will punishment take place?]"

Rabbi replied, "I will answer you with a parable. A lord who had an excellent orchard, containing splendid fig trees, appointed two watchmen over his orchard. One of them was blind and the other crippled. The cripple said to the blind man, 'I see some very fine figs, but they are out of reach. Place me on your shoulders, so that I can reach them, and we will both eat them.' The blind man placed the cripple on his shoulders, the cripple picked the fruit, and both partook of it.

"When the owner of the orchard later asked them, 'What became of those fine figs?' the blind man answered, 'Do I have eyes to see [so that you suspect me]?' And the lame man said, 'Do I have feet capable of walking there?' What did the owner do? He put the lame man on the shoulders of the blind man and punished the two of them together. Thus Scripture states: (Ps. 50:4) *He will call to the heavens above and the earth beneath, to judge His people.* The words *to the heavens above* refer to the soul, and *to the earth beneath* refers to the body."

Sanhedrin, 91a

Rabbi Johanan contemplates his judgment

740. When R. Johanan b. Zakkai became ill, his disciples came to visit him. When he saw them, he burst into tears. "Rabbi," they said to him, "why are you weeping?" And R. Johanan replied, "Were I to be brought before a king of flesh and blood, who is here today and will be in his grave tomorrow; who may become angry with me, but whose anger would not be everlasting; who may imprison me, but whose imprisonment is not eternal; who may put me to death, but only in this world; and whom I might even be able to bribe—even then would I be fearful.

"Now, however, I am about to appear before the King of kings who lives through all eternity. If He is angry with me, His wrath can be unending; if He imprisons me, it can be forever; if He slays me, my death will be eternal; and I can neither appease Him with words nor bribe Him with money. Moreover, two paths now lie before me, one leading to Paradise and the other to Gehinnom, and I know not which I am destined to take. Should I then not weep?" *Berachoth, 28b*

The nations will also face judgment

741. The Holy One will question Edom [Rome] on the day of reckoning before all other nations. . . . He will ask, "What was your work in the world?" To this, the Romans will reply, "Sovereign of the Universe! We have established many markets, built many bathhouses and accumulated much gold and silver. All this have we done for the sake of Israel so that they might sit and study Torah."

The Holy One will reply, "It is foolish of you to say that all you have done was done only for the sake of Israel when, in fact, it was done only for yourselves. You built markets for the purpose of prostitution. You built bathhouses for your own bodily pleasure. And as to your accumulating gold and silver, these are Mine; as Scripture states: (Hag. 2:8) *Mine is the silver, and Mine the gold.* Are there any among you who have studied Torah?" Then they will depart in despair.

Abodah Zarah, 2a,b

742. Rome will be followed [at the time of judgment] by the Persians. The Holy One will ask, "With what have you occupied yourselves?" The people of Persia will answer, "Lord of the Universe! We have built many bridges and conquered many cities. Many wars have we waged. And we did all this for the sake of Israel so that the people of Israel might devote themselves to the study of Torah."

Then the Holy One will reply, "All that you did was for your own benefit. You built bridges in order to collect tolls from those who used them. You conquered cities in order to force their inhabitants to labor for you. And as for wars, it is I who wage them; as Scripture states: (Exod. 15:3) *The Lord is a man of war.* Are there any among you who have studied Torah?" And they will leave in despair.

Abodah Zarah, 2b

C. CHASTISEMENTS OF LOVE

The concept of "chastisements of love"

743. Raba—others say it was R. Hisda—declared, "If troubles beset a man, he should examine his actions; for Scripture states: (Lam. 3:40) *Let us search and examine our ways and let us return unto the Lord.* If one has examined his ways and finds nothing wrong [in his conduct], he should attribute his difficulties to his neglect of Torah study;

for Scripture tells us: (Ps. 94:12) *Happy is the man whom Thou admonish-est, O Lord, and teachest out of Thy Torah* [i.e., God afflicts a man in order to induce him to study Torah].

"But if he does examine his actions and finds that he has not neglected study of the Torah, then he may be certain that his suffering is due to God's love for him; for Scripture states: (Prov. 3:12) *Because whomsoever the Lord loveth He admonisheth.*"[1] *Berachoth, 5a*

744. R. Eleazar b. Zadok said, "The Holy One brings suffering upon the righteous in this world in order that they may have a place in the Hereafter; as Scripture states: (Job 8:7) *Though thy beginning was small, yet thy latter end shall greatly increase.* Similarly, the Holy One grants happiness to the wicked in this world in order to banish them to the lowest depths; as Scripture states: (Prov. 14:12) *There is a way which seemeth right to a man, but the end thereof are the ways of death.*"

Kiddushin, 40b

The principle is questioned

745. R. Hiyya b. Abba fell ill and R. Johanan went to see him. R. Johanan asked him, "Are your afflictions welcome to you?" To this R. Hiyya replied, "Neither they nor their [reputed] reward." R. Johanan then said to him, "Give me your hand." R. Hiyya extended his hand, and he [R. Johanan] raised him [i.e., cured him].[2]

Berachoth, 5b

746. R. Johanan once took sick, and R. Hanina came to see him. R. Hanina said to him, "Are your sufferings welcome to you?" Replied R. Johanan, "Neither they nor their reward." Then R. Hanina said to him, "Give me your hand." R. Johanan gave him his hand, and R. Hanina raised him [i.e., made him well].

Why could not R. Johanan raise [heal] himself since he was able to heal R. Hiyya [above]? Just as the prisoner is not able to free himself from prison, so cannot the patient heal himself. *Berachoth, 5b*

R. Meir rejects the doctrine

747. R. Meir declared, "When God said: (Exod. 33:19) *I will be gracious to whom I will be gracious,* He meant even though one may not be deserving. And when He added: *and I will show mercy on whom I*

---

[1] Cf. N.T., Heb. 12:6, "For whom the Lord loveth, He chasteneth."

[2] For similar instances of healing by taking the hand of the sick individual, see also N.T., Matt. 8:15, 9:25.

will show mercy, He likewise meant this to apply even if one is not deserving [i.e., reward and punishment are not of this world]."

Reward and punishment take place only in the Hereafter

748. We are told in a *baraitha* that R. Jacob said, "There is no commandment in the Torah which mentions a reward for its fulfillment yet [which] is not dependent on a life hereafter for the attainment of that reward. In connection with honoring parents, Scripture states: (Deut. 5:16) *That thy days may be prolonged, and that it may be well with thee.* And in connection with the commandment to release the mother bird [while removing young birds from a nest] Scripture states: (Deut. 22:7) *That it may be well with thee, and that thou mayest prolong thy days.*

"Now let us suppose we have a person whose father has told him to climb to the top of a tower and bring down to him the young pigeons which are nesting there. He climbs up the tower [thereby fulfilling the commandment to honor one's parents] and sets the mother bird free while taking the young from the nest [as is commanded in the Torah]. However, on his descent he falls and dies. Where is the well-being or the prolongation of the days of this individual [who has simultaneously fulfilled two divine commandments]? The answer is that in these commandments, the words *that it may be well with thee* refer to that world where all is good, and the words *that thou mayest prolong thy days* similarly refer to the world of endless days."[1] *Kiddushin, 39b*

D. REWARD AND PUNISHMENT

Paradise: the Garden of Eden

749. R. Samuel b. Nahmani said, "What does the verse (Isa. 64:3) *Men have not heard, nor perceived by the ear, neither hath the eye seen, a God beside Thee, Who worketh for him that waiteth for Him* mean? This refers to the Garden of Eden, upon which no human eye has ever gazed.

"But one may ask, 'Where then did Adam [who saw it with a human eye] dwell?' The answer is, 'In a garden.' One may then say, 'The Garden of Eden [in the Hereafter] is the same as that in which Adam

---

[1] Such an incident was said to have shattered the faith of Elisha ben Abuyah, thereafter known as Aher ("Another"). See also item 35 and fn.

lived!' This is contradicted by the verse (Gen. 2:10) *And a river went out of Eden* [to another place] *to water the garden* [which was elsewhere]. Thus the garden of Adam and the Garden of Eden are two different places."[1] *Berachoth, 34b*

It will be a place of great joy

750. R. Helbo said, "In the future, the Holy One will arrange a dance for the righteous in the Garden of Eden. He will sit in their midst, and each of them will point to Him and declare: (Isa. 25:9) *'Lo, this is our God, for Whom we have waited, that He might save us; this is the Lord, for Whom we have waited, and we will be glad and rejoice in His salvation.'* " *Taanith, 31a*

The righteous will be amply rewarded

751. Rabbi was preparing for the wedding of R. Simeon, his son, and failed to invite Bar Kappara. The latter thereupon wrote on the wall of the house where the marriage was to take place, "Twenty-four thousand *denars* is the cost of this wedding, yet Bar Kappara was not invited." And he said to his attendants, "If so much is granted [in this world] to those who act contrary to God's will, how much more will be given to those who perform God's will!"

When Rabbi heard about this, he invited Bar Kappara to attend the wedding. Then Bar Kappara said, "If so much is given in this world to those who do God's will, how much more will be given to them in the Hereafter!" *Nedarim, 50b*

752. Rabban Gamaliel, R. Eleazar b. Azariah, R. Joshua and R. Akiba were once travelling on the road together when they heard from a distance joyous sounds coming from the streets of Rome.[2] All began to weep, but R. Akiba smiled. When they asked, "Why are you smiling?" he answered, "Why are you weeping?"

They said to him, "Those idolators who bow down before images and burn frankincense to idols are at peace, while we are beset by trouble. Even our sacred Temple has been destroyed by fire. Should we then not weep?"

---

[1] While a seemingly non-terrestrial Garden of Eden is here envisioned, it is unclear whether or how the Garden of Eden differs from the World to Come (chapter 14b). The happy circumstances ascribed to Gan Eden are much like those expected in the World to Come, perhaps indicating that the pleasures of Gan Eden would be enjoyed in the World to Come.

[2] The Soncino translation suggests that this may have been on the occasion of their journey to Rome in the year 95 C.E.

But R. Akiba replied, "It is for this very reason that I smile. If such is the reward [in this world] of those who act against His will, how much greater will be the reward [in the future] of those who act in accordance with His will!" *Makkoth, 24a*

Scripture refers to Gehinnom indirectly

753. R. Samuel b. Nahmani, commenting on the words (Song of Songs 3:8) *because of the terror of the night*, stated that R. Johanan said, "This refers to Gehinnom, which is as dark as the night."

Yebamoth, 109b

754. R. Joshua b. Levi said, "Scripture refers to Gehinnom by several names. These are: (Jon. 2:3) *sheol*, (Ps. 88:12) *abbadon*, (Ps. 16:10) *beor shahas*, (Ps. 40:3) *tet yaven* and (Ps. 107:10) *tzalmaveth*. [1] The designation *eretz tachtith* is a traditional usage [i.e., non-Biblical]."[2]

What then of the name *Ge Hinnom?* This is applied [in Scripture] only to a valley as deep as Gehinnom to which people went in order to practice abominations. There is, however, another name [in Scripture] for Gehinnom. That is *topheth* ["a hearth"]; for Scripture states: (Isa. 30:33) *For a hearth is ordered of old . . . deep and large; the pile thereof is fire and much wood.* He who is dominated by his evil inclination will fall into it. *Erubin, 19a*

How long the sinful will remain in Gehinnom

755. R. Akiba said, "The judgment of the generation of the flood lasted for twelve months, of Job for twelve months, of the Egyptians for twelve months, of Gog and Magog in the Hereafter for twelve months, and will last for the wicked in Gehinnom for a similar period."

R. Johanan b. Nuri said, "It will last for the wicked only for the space of time between Passover and Shabuoth [i.e., seven weeks]."

Eduyoth, 2:10

---

[1] In the 1917 J.P.S. translation, these words are rendered respectively: "grave," "destruction," "the pit," "miry clay" and "shadow of death." Rabbi Joshua states that these are allusions to Gehinnom; they convey the meaning of deep distress or complete abandonment.

[2] The term *eretz tachtith* ("subterranean world") is here admitted to be non-Biblical; so too with the term *Gehinnom*, in the next paragraph, used in reference to a life hereafter. Isaiah's use of *topheth* ("a hearth") is ambiguous.

Those who will not behold Gehinnom

756. Three classes of individuals will not behold Gehinnom: those who have suffered the afflictions of poverty, disease of the bowels and the tyranny of Roman rule. *Erubin, 41b*

Rabbi Simeon denies the existence of Gehinnom

757. R. Simeon b. Lakish said, "There is no Gehinnom in the Hereafter. Instead, the Holy One will bring forth the sun from its sheath so that it is fierce. By its rays, the wicked will be punished and the righteous will be healed.

"The wicked will be punished by it; for Scripture states: (Mal. 3:19) *For behold, the day cometh, it burneth as a furnace; and all the proud, and all that work wickedness, shall be stubble; and the day that cometh shall set them ablaze, saith the Lord of Hosts; that it shall leave them neither root nor branch.* The word *root* refers to this world and the word *branch* refers to the next world [i.e., they will find no place in this world or the Hereafter].

"The righteous will be healed by it [the sun]; for Scripture states: (Mal. 3:20) *But unto you that fear My name shall the sun of righteousness arise with healing on its wings.*" *Abodah Zarah, 3b; Nedarim, 8b*

14
THE FUTURE LIFE

THE relatedness of the concepts of divine judgment, Paradise (Gan Eden) and the Netherworld (Gehinnom) is of course obvious. However, the unfoldment of each of these doctrines and the intricacies of their relationship are difficult to trace; so too with the belief in a World to Come (Olam ha-Ba) and in the advent of a Messiah, two additional components of the cluster of beliefs embraced in rabbinic eschatology.

In its earliest usage, the term Olam ha-Ba appears to have been linked with the hope for a national rebirth in the Holy Land. With the frustration of that hope, there seems to have been a broadening of the concept to signify a new world order and a non-terrestrial, spiritual World to Come. In some of the excerpts cited here, it is uncertain whether a national restoration or a universal new order is envisioned. It is at times equally unclear whether that new order is to be of this world or another.

A somewhat similar development appears to have taken place with the concept of the Messiah, closely allied to the belief in a World to Come. The term means "an anointed one" and originally designated the kings of Israel, who were ritually anointed as rulers. However, with the loss of sovereignty, it came to signify an awaited descendant of King David who would reestablish the Davidic dynasty. As this prospect faded, the image of the longed-for successor to David's throne was transmuted into that of a supernatural being, more capable of achieving the awaited redemption of his people.

The convergence of the concepts of a non-terrestrial World to Come and of a superhuman Messiah brought into sharper focus a belief which was latent but hitherto not fully articulated in Judaism. That was the doctrine of personal immortality, which was to have a marked impact on the subsequent development of the Jewish faith and on the rise of Christianity. This offered the prospect of a life hereafter, and the promise of reward for the righteous in a totally spiritualized World to Come.

The hope for a renewal of Jewish autonomy in the Holy Land, long associated with the expected advent of the Messiah and with the belief in a World to Come, has been fulfilled in our time. The doctrine of personal immortality, however it may be construed, remains a basic tenet of Judaism. And the messianic idea, with its confidence in the future and conviction that "the best is yet to be," still impels men to strive for a nobler society, inspired by a vision of the kingdom of God here on earth.[1]

A. THE SOUL AND RESURRECTION

The soul exists before the person is born

758. Resh Lakish said, "Araboth [heaven][2] is the dwelling-place of righteousness, justice, grace, the treasures of life and of blessing, the souls [neshamoth] of the righteous and the spirits [ruhoth] and souls of those who are yet to be born." [See item 801.]

Hagigah, 12b

When the soul enters the body

759. Antoninus asked Rabbi, "When does the soul enter the body, at the moment of conception or when the fetus is [already] formed?" Rabbi replied, "When the fetus is already formed." Antoninus then said to him, "Is it then possible that a bit of [non-living] flesh can keep for more than three days without being salted and not begin to smell?"

Thereupon Rabbi answered, "It must therefore be at the time of conception." And he added, "Now I have learned something from Antoninus." [See item 658.] *Sanhedrin, 91b*

---

1 Even non-religious societies rejecting messianic theology are moved by the messianic impulse and claim a messianic goal. Father Vladimir Shtepa, of the Byzantine Church of the Resurrection in Oster, U.S.S.R., has stated, "The main principle of Christianity and Marxism is the same. Believers try to enter the kingdom of God, and Marxists strive for true Communism. The bright future for man and the kingdom of God—aren't they the same?" (*Time,* "Religion," December 3, 1979, pp. 102–103).

2 Araboth is the highest, or seventh, heaven. See Ps. 68:5. The 1917 J.P.S. Bible renders this as "upon the skies."

The soul returns to God Who gave it

760. Our rabbis taught that (Eccles. 12:7) *And the spirit returns to God Who gave it* means that one must return the soul to God just as He gave it. He gave it to us pure; we must return it pure. This may be compared to a human king who distributed new clothes to all of his attendants. The wise among them folded the garments and placed them in a box. The foolish ones put them on and did their daily work in them.

One day the king demanded the return of these clothes, and the wise returned the clothing clean and pressed, but the foolish returned theirs in a dirty and torn condition. The king was pleased with the action of the wise, but angry at the others. He thereupon ordered that the clothing of the wise be stored and that they were to depart in peace. And he ordered that the clothes of the foolish were to be laundered and that they themselves were to be sent to prison.

Sabbath, 152b

The soul of the deceased mourns his passing

761. R. Hisda said, "The soul of a person mourns for him during the first seven days after his death. Scripture states: (Job 14:22) *And his soul shall mourn for him*; and Scripture also states: (Gen. 50:10) *And he made for his father a mourning for seven days.*"[1] *Sabbath, 152a*

For twelve months the soul revisits the body

762. For twelve months [after death] the body still exists, and the soul descends [to rejoin the body] and ascends again.[2] After twelve months the body ceases to exist and the soul ascends without again descending. *Sabbath, 152b*

Job's denial of the resurrection of the dead

763. The Book of Job states: (Job 7:9) *As the cloud is consumed and vanisheth away, so he that goeth down to the grave [sheol] shall come up no*

---

[1] See item 721 and fn. regarding the successive, diminishing periods of mourning for the dead. Here, the observance of *Shivah* is given added theological support in that the soul itself is said to mourn seven days for the departed.

[2] See item 722. There the loss of an individual is compared to the loss of an object which is not given up as lost until a year has passed. The selection offered here may provide a theological basis for the full year of mourning. Since the soul is not fully at rest during that period, mourning and prayer may serve to intercede with heaven for the soul's welfare. After a year has passed, and the soul is permanently with God, mourning ceases, but the anniversary of the death is observed thereafter.

more. [In comment on this verse,] Raba said, "From this we learn that Job denied the resurrection of the dead [*tehiath methim*]."

Baba Bathra, 16a

Others question resurrection

764. A *min* ["heretic" or "dissenter"] once said to R. Ammi, "You believe that the dead will be revived. But they turn to dust. Is it possible for dust to come alive?"[1] R. Ammi replied, "I will offer you a parable as an answer. The matter is comparable to the case of a human ruler who ordered his servants to build him a palace at a site where there was no water available and no soil [suitable for making bricks]. They managed to build it, but it soon collapsed.

"He then ordered them to build one at a site where water and suitable earth could be found. But they said, 'We cannot do this.' Thereupon the king became angry and said, 'If you were able to build a palace at a site where there was neither water nor suitable earth, surely you can do so where these are readily available!' "[2]

Sanhedrin, 91a

765. There once was a *min* who said to G'bihah b. P'sisah, "You claim that the dead will be restored to life. But if even the living are destined to die, how can the dead come back to life?" And G'bihah answered, "Woe unto you, Wicked One, who say that the dead cannot come back to life. If one who has never lived can come to life, should not those who have lived be able to do so?"

The *min* replied, "You call me wicked. But if I were really wicked, I would kick you so hard as to level the hump on your back."[3] And G'bihah answered, "If you could do that, you would be a remarkable physician and command large fees." *Sanhedrin, 91a*

Resurrection is derived from Scripture

766. There is a *baraitha* in which R. Meir is quoted as having said, "Whence do we learn that the resurrection of the dead is mentioned in the Torah? This can be found in the verse (Exod. 15:1) *Then Moses*

---

[1] While the Sadducees rejected the belief in resurrection, this doubter could not have been a Sadducee because they no longer existed in Ammi's time (third to fourth centuries C.E.).

[2] The intent here is that if God can create men without prior ingredients, surely He can do so from their dust.

[3] G'bihah was hunchbacked.

and the children of Israel sang [*yashir*; literally, 'will sing'] this song.[1] The text does not read *shar* ['sang'], but rather *yashir.* This is an intimation of the resurrection in the Torah. The same is the case in (Josh. 8:30) *Then Joshua built an altar.* The text does not read *banah* ['built'] but rather *yivneh* [literally, 'will build']. Here we have another intimation in the Torah of the resurrection." *Sanhedrin, 91b*

767. Our rabbis taught that (Deut. 32:39) *I make one die, and I make one live* does not mean that God causes one person to die and another person to live; for immediately thereafter the text reads: (ibid.) *I wound and I heal.* Just as wounding and healing [obviously] apply to the same person, so too do death and life apply to the same person. [Thus God brings the dead back to life.] This is in answer to those who say that the resurrection is not mentioned in the Torah [and in refutation of the Sadducees]. *Sanhedrin, 91b*

768. It has been taught that R. Simlai said, "Whence do we learn that resurrection is derived from the Torah? From the verse (Exod. 6:4) *And I also have established my covenant with them* [the Patriarchs], *to give them the land of Canaan.* The passage does not read 'to give you' but rather *to give them* [personally] *the land of Canaan.* Thus resurrection is proved from the Torah [for the promise could be literally fulfilled only by the resurrection of the Patriarchs]."

Sanhedrin, 90b

The resurrection may be deduced from glassware

769. The school of R. Ishmael taught that it [the resurrection of the dead] can be deduced from glassware. If glassware, which is made by the breath of human beings,[2] can be repaired when broken [by being melted down again], then how much more so can man, who is created by the breath of the Holy One! *Sanhedrin, 91a*

. . . from pottery

770. The emperor said to Rabban Gamaliel, "You maintain that the dead will revive. But they turn to dust, and can dust come to life?" R. Gamaliel's daughter said to her father, "Let me answer him."

---

[1] Hebrew usage requires *yashir,* the future form of the verb, after *az* ("then"), instead of the past tense *shar,* which is the usual word for "sang." However, this rule of Hebrew grammar is bypassed by R. Meir, in the statement here attributed to him, in order to make his point. So too with the Biblical use of *az yivneh* for "then he built" instead of the past tense *banah* in the next verse cited.

[2] This is a reference to the blowing of glass.

And she said, "In our town there are two potters. One fashions [his products] from water, and the other from clay. Who is the most praiseworthy?" The ruler replied, "He who fashions them from water [a much more difficult task]." Then she said, "If the Holy One can fashion man from water [semen], then surely He can do so from clay [i.e., the dust of the dead]!"

Sanhedrin, 90b

Those who will not be resurrected

771. R. Akiba said, "Resurrection will be denied him who reads the books of the *hitzonim* ['separatists']¹ and to him who engages in mumbling [incantations] over a wound, reciting the verse (Exod. 15:26) *I will put none of those diseases upon thee which I have brought upon the Egyptians, for I the Lord am thy physician.*" [See also item 322 regarding use of incantations for healing.]

Abba Saul said, "Also those who pronounce the divine name [JHVH] as it is written, using its letters."² *Sanhedrin, 90a*

772. R. Eleazar said, "Those who are ignorant of the Torah will not be resurrected; [of them] Scripture states: (Isa. 26:14) *They are dead, they shall not live.* Whoever makes use of the light of the Torah will be revived; and whoever does not make use of the light of the Torah will not be revived." *Kethuboth, 111b*

773. R. Eleazar said, "The haughty will not be resurrected; for Scripture states: (Isa. 26:19) *Awake and sing, ye that dwell in the dust.* Scripture does not say, 'lie in the dust,' but rather *dwell in the dust.* This means one who has dwelt in the dust [acted humbly] during his lifetime." *Sotah, 5a*

Resurrection will take place in the Holy Land

774. R. Eleazar said, "Those who die outside the Holy Land will not live again; for Scripture states: (Ezek. 26:20) *I will set delight in the land of the living.* That is, those who die in the land of God's delight will live again, but those who do not die there will not live again."

---

¹ *Hitzonim* is from the word *hitzah* ("partition"), meaning "outer" or "external"; thus those who set themselves apart. "Those who follow their own interpretation of the Law, irrespective of public usages" (*Dictionary of the Talmud,* s.v. "hitzah"). The "books of the *hitzonim*" are the extra-canonical books.

² It is forbidden to pronounce God's name. The Tetragrammaton is usually read as *Adonoi.* Orthodox Jews substitute *ha-Shem* ("the Name") to avoid even that locution. See *U.J.E.,* s.v. "Tetragrammaton." See also fn. 4 to item 4.

But is this really so? R. Illai said, "They too will revive, but they will have to roll underground [tunnelling their way] for resurrection in the Holy Land."[1] [See also item 597.] *Kethuboth, 111a*

775. R. Abbahu said, "Even a Canaanite maid-servant in the land of Israel is sure of inheriting eternal life." *Kethuboth, 111a*

It will be of endless duration

776. The righteous whom the Holy One will restore to life will never return to their dust. *Sanhedrin, 92a*

B. THE WORLD TO COME

Those who will enter the World to Come

777. The question was sent from the land of Israel to the rabbis in Babylonia, "Who will be privileged to enter the World to Come?" The answer came back, "He who is meek and humble, who walks with a lowly demeanor, studies the Torah constantly and seeks no distinction for himself." *Sanhedrin, 88b*

778. R. Eleazar said, "The leader of a congregation[2] who leads them humbly will be permitted to lead them also in the World to Come; for Scripture states: (Isa. 49:10) *For He* [he] *that hath mercy on them will lead them; even by springs of water will He* [he] *guide them* [in the Hereafter]."[3] *Sanhedrin, 92a*

779. R. Joshua b. Levi said, "He who has recited praises to his Creator in this world will be rewarded by the privilege of reciting His praise in the World to Come; for Scripture states: (Ps. 84:3) *Blessed are they who dwell in Thy* [heavenly] *house; they shall ever praise Thee."*

Sanhedrin, 91b

780. R. Eleazar b. Abina said, "Whoever recites thrice daily Psalm 145 [acknowledging thrice daily his dependence on God] will be eligible for the World to Come. The reason is that this Psalm contains the verse [verse 16] *Thou openest Thy hand and satisfiest every living thing with favor." Berachoth, 4b*

---

[1] This may be the origin of the custom of buying the dead with the head toward Jerusalem. The image is that of a screw, the slenderest part of which leads the way as it penetrates the wood.

[2] See fn. to item 25.

[3] In Hebrew, "He will lead them" is expressed in the single word *y'nahagem,* from the root *nahag,* meaning "to lead." Since there are no capital letters in Hebrew, the word *y'nahagem* may be read as "He will lead them," signifying God, or "he will lead them," suggesting a human leader.

781. R. Hiyya b. Ammi said, "Scripture speaks of him who is content to enjoy the fruit of his labor when it states: (Ps. 128:2) *When thou eatest of the labor of thy hands, happy shalt thou be, and it shall be well with thee.* The words *happy shalt thou be* refer to this world, but the words *and it shall be well with thee* refer to the World to Come."

Berachoth, 8a

Some who will not be admitted

782. (Mishnah) All Israelites have a share in the World to Come; for Scripture states: (Isa. 60:21) *And all thy people shall be righteous; they shall inherit the land forever.* [1] Nonetheless, the following will have no share in the World to Come: he who says that the resurrection of the dead is not indicated in the Torah;[2] he who says that the Torah was not given by the Almighty; and the Apikorsim [i.e., Epicureans, or unbelievers].[3] *Sanhedrin, 90a*

783. He who exposes his fellowman to shame in public will have no share in the World to Come. [See also items 172–175.]

Sanhedrin, 107a

Each person will have his own eternal place

784. In comment on (Eccles. 12:5) *Because man goeth to his eternal home,* R. Isaac said, "This [the word *his*] teaches us that, to every righteous man, a place is assigned in the World to Come, according to his merits. This is comparable to a human king who enters a city with his retinue of servants. On entering the city all pass through the same gate. But as night approaches each is assigned a berth according to his rank." *Sabbath, 152a*

785. R. Zera—others say R. Joseph—taught that there will be no upright person who will not have a place in the World to Come commensurate with the honor due him.[4] *Baba Metzia, 83b*

---

1 The World to Come here appears to be an earthly one.

2 Among the Jews, these were the Sadducees and the Samaritans, as previously noted. Josephus states: "But the doctrine of the Sadducees is this: that souls die with the bodies" (*Antiquities,* Bk. 18:1, 4). See also N.T., Acts 23:8.

3 Epicurus, the Greek philosopher (fourth century B.C.E.), taught that true happiness could be achieved only through virtue but denied the survival of the soul. Cultured Romans equated Epicureanism with hedonism. The rabbis frequently use the term *Apikorsim* for freethinkers, whether Jewish or non-Jewish.

4 The Tosefta, a collection of teachings and traditions of the Tannaim supplementary to the Mishnah, extends the principle to non-Jews as well as Jews, declaring, "The righteous among the non-Jews have a share in the World to Come" (Tosefta Sanhedrin, 13:2).

A special place is reserved for the penitent

786. R. Abbahu said, "The place which the penitent will occupy, [even] the perfectly righteous will be unable to occupy."[1]

Berachoth, 34b

Scholars will continue to study there

787. The disciples of the wise have rest neither in this world nor in the World to Come; for Scripture states: (Ps. 84:7) *They go from strength to strength* [in study] *every one of them* [who] *appeareth before God in Zion* [i.e., in the Hereafter].[2] *Berachoth, 64a*

God's mysteries will be revealed to them

788. R. Nahman b. Isaac said, "To the disciples of the wise, who wrinkle their foreheads with study of the Torah in this world, God will reveal its mysteries in the World to Come." *Hagigah, 14a*

How to achieve eternal life

789. When R. Eliezer became ill, his disciples came to visit him. "Rabbi," they said, "teach us the [proper] way of life so that we may achieve eternity in the World to Come." He replied, "Be careful to honor your associates; know before Whom you pray; restrain your children from frivolous thoughts and set them before learned men. By these means, you will deserve eternal life in the World to Come."

Berachoth, 28b

A celestial World to Come is envisioned

790. Rab used to say, "Not like this world is the World to Come; for in the World to Come, there is neither eating nor drinking; no begetting of children or business dealings;[3] no envy or hatred or rivalry. The righteous sit on thrones, crowns on their heads, enjoying the brilliance of the *Shechinah;* as Scripture states: (Exod. 24:11) *And they beheld God, and did eat and drink* [i.e., God's presence was their food and drink]." *Berachoth, 17a*

---

[1] The penitent is preferred over the perfectly righteous person. See Sanhedrin 99a and N.T., Luke 15:7; also fn. to item 695.

[2] A heavenly Jerusalem (Zion) is here referred to (see item 604). On scholars continuing their studies in heaven, see also items 238 and 477.

[3] Cf. N.T., Matt. 22:30, "For in the future they will neither marry nor be given in marriage, but will be as the angels of God in heaven."

A glimpse of the other world

791. Joseph, the son of R. Joshua b. Levi, was once in a state of catalepsy. When he recovered, his father asked him, "What did you see in the other world?" And Joseph answered, "I saw a reversed world, in which the man who would normally be honored in this world is held in poor esteem and vice versa." His father then said, "It is not a reversed world that you saw but a rational world."

Baba Bathra, 10b; Pesahim, 50a

C. THE MESSIAH

The coming of the Messiah is part of the plan of creation

792. Our rabbis taught that seven things were created before the world itself: the Torah, repentance, the Garden of Eden [Paradise], Gehinnom, the Throne of Glory, the Temple and the name of the Messiah.[1] *Nedarim, 39b*

The terrible conditions that will precede his advent

793. R. Isaac said in the name of R. Johanan, "In the generation in which the son of David will come, scholarly men will be few in number, and the eyes of the people will protrude from sighing and sorrow. Many afflictions and many evil government decrees will be imposed upon them; one will not have passed when another will come."[2] *Sanhedrin, 97a*

794. R. Nehorai said, "The Messiah, son of David, will appear when the young will expose the old to shame in public, and the old will rise up in respect before the young; a daughter will rebel against her mother, a daughter-in-law against her mother-in-law. The leaders of that generation will be like dogs, and a son will feel no shame when reproached by his father."

Sanhedrin, 97a

795. We are told in a *baraitha* that R. Nehemiah said, "The Messiah will come when insolence will increase and respect will be missing; the vine will give forth its fruit abundantly, yet wine will be costly [i.e., all will be drunkards and wine, therefore, scarce]. All govern-

---

[1] The belief in the Messiah's preexistence is also found in Pesahim, 54b. On the development of the belief in a Messiah, see *U.J.E.,* s.v. "Messiah."

[2] Rabbinic literature speaks of the "birth pangs" of the Messiah.

ments will turn to *minuth* ['godlessness']¹ and no admonitions will be of any avail." *Sanhedrin, 97a*

796. R. Hanina said, "The son of David will not come until a fish is sought [as food] for an invalid and cannot be secured." [Total disregard of human values is indicated.] *Sanhedrin, 98a*

797. Rab said, "The son of David will not come until the [Roman] power encompasses all Israel for nine months." [The comparison is with a woman in gestation. See also fn. to item 793.]

Sanhedrin, 98b

798. R. Johanan said, "The son of David will appear in a generation in which all will be righteous, or in a generation in which all will be wicked." *Sanhedrin, 98a*

Attempts at dating the Messiah's arrival

799. R. Hanina said, "Four hundred years after the destruction of the [second] Temple and onwards [i.e., from 470 C.E.], if someone says to you, 'Buy a field that is worth one thousand *denars* for one *denar,*' do not buy it." [Property will have no value when the Messiah comes.]

In a *baraitha,* it is taught that beginning with the year 4231 since the creation of the world [this equals 470 C.E.],² if someone says to you, "Buy a field that is worth one thousand *denars* for one *denar,*" do not buy it. *Abodah Zarah, 9b*

800. R. Elijah said to R. Judah, the brother of R. Sala the Pious, "The world will endure for at least eighty-five jubilee periods [i.e., 4,250 years], and in the last jubilee period, the son of David will come."³ He was asked, "Will he come at the beginning of that period or at its end?" He answered, "I do not know." *Sanhedrin, 97b*

801. R. Assi said, "The son of David will not come until all the souls in the *guph* ['heavenly storehouse'] will come to an end [i.e., they will have been incarnated]." [See item 758.] *Yebamoth, 62a*

---

¹ Literally, *minuth* means "heresy." R. Nehemiah (150 C.E.) refers here to the Roman Empire, perhaps implying its ultimate conversion to Christianity. (See fn. on this in Soncino Talmud, Sanhedrin, 97a.)

² The Hebrew calendar dates time from the creation *(anno mundi).* The allusion to the Era of the World is the earliest on record and the only one in the Talmud. See Soncino Talmud, Abodah Zarah, fn. p. 47. The dating from creation is still used for the Jewish calendar and in religious observance. See *U.J.E.,* s.v. "Calendar."

³ Every fifty years was a jubilee period when property was to be returned to its original owner and indentured servants were to be set free. See Lev. 25:10. Eighty-five jubilee periods yield a date between 440 and 490 C.E. See fn. to item 799.

The season of his arrival

802. R. Joshua said, "Our ancestors were redeemed [from Egyptian bondage] in Nissan [April], and in Nissan will we be redeemed in the future." *Rosh Hashanah, 11a*

Resistance to such speculation

803. R. Samuel b. Nahmani said in the name of R. Jonathan, "May despair come upon those who sit and calculate the time of the coming of the Messiah; for when the expected time comes and he does not appear, they say that he will not come at all. Just wait for him; as Scripture states: (Hab. 2:3) *Though it* [the Messiah's arrival] *tarry, wait for it."* *Sanhedrin, 97b*

How conditions will change at his advent

804. R. Giddel said in the name of Rab, "In the future [*athidin*],[1] Israel will enjoy the abundance which the messianic time will bring." And R. Joseph retorted, "Isn't this self-evident? Who else should enjoy it? Hilek and Bilek [Harry and Barry]?" *Sanhedrin, 98b*

805. R. Hiyya b. Joseph said, "In the future [*athidin*], the land of Israel will produce baked loaves made of the finest flour and garments of the finest wool. The soil will bring forth corn, the ears of which will be the size of the two kidneys of a large ox." *Kethuboth, 111b*

806. R. Gamaliel said, "In the future [*athidin*], women will bear children daily, and trees will produce fruit daily." *Sabbath, 30b*

807. The present world is not like the World to Come [Olam ha-Ba].[2] In this world, much effort is required to gather the grapes and press them, but in the next world, one grape will be delivered in a wagon or a ship, from which an entire household will partake, and its stem will serve as firewood for cooking. *Kethuboth, 111b*

808. Rabbah said in the name of R. Johanan, "In the future [*athidin*], God will prepare a banquet for the righteous from the flesh of Leviathan, and the remainder will be divided and sold in the streets of Jerusalem." *Baba Bathra, 75a*

---

[1] The word *athidin*, from *athid* ("future"), means "the time ahead" and not necessarily the World to Come. The views quoted here and in items 805–809 seem to refer to an earthly messianic era as a transition to the World to Come. Note the references to child-bearing and other mundane activities. Rab excludes these from his vision of the World to Come in item 790.

[2] While the term *Olam ha-Ba* is used here, reference to delivery of grapes, eating and cooking suggests an earthly messianic era.

Things may not really be much different

809. Samuel said, "There will be no difference between this world and the days of the Messiah except [freedom from] the servitude of heathen rulers; as Scripture states: (Deut. 15:11) *For the poor shall never cease out of the land.*"

Berachoth, 34b; Pesahim, 68a

R. Hiyya rejects speculation about the World to Come

810. R. Hiyya b. Abba said in the name of R. Johanan, "The prophets prophesied only with regard to the messianic era, but concerning the World to Come Scripture states: (Isa. 63:3) *No eye hath seen, O God, besides Thee.*"[1] *Sanhedrin, 99a*

Mixed reactions to the coming of the Messiah

811. R. Ulla said, "May the Messiah come soon, but I do not wish to see him." R. Joseph said, "I pray that he may come in my time so that I may be privileged to sit in the shadow of his ass."

Sanhedrin, 98b

The duration of the messianic era

812. It was taught in the school of R. Elijah that the world will endure six thousand years: two thousand years in chaos [i.e., from the creation to the revelation at Sinai], two thousand years with the Torah [as man's guide] and two thousand years in the period of the Messiah.

Sanhedrin, 97a

813. R. Abimi b. Abbahu said, "Seven thousand years [will be the reign of the Messiah]." But R. Judah said in the name of Rab, "As long as the world has already lasted." And R. Nahman b. Isaac said, "As long as from the days of Noah to the present."

Sanhedrin, 99a

814. R. Eliezer taught that the period of the Messiah's reign will be forty years; for Scripture states: (Ps. 99:15) *Make us glad according to the days Thou hast afflicted us.* [As the people of Israel suffered forty years in the desert, so would they rejoice forty years under the rule of the Messiah.] But R. Eleazar [b. Azariah] said, "Seventy years," and R. Judah HaNasi said, "Three generations."

Sanhedrin, 99a

---

[1] Hiyya asserts that the messianic era is not identical with the World to Come, merely preliminary to it.

The identity of the Messiah

815. R. Nahman asked R. Isaac, "Have you heard when Bar Naphle ['son of the fallen'] will come?" And R. Isaac said, "Who is Bar Naphle?" He answered, "The Messiah." Then R. Isaac asked, "Do you call the Messiah [by the name of] Bar Naphle?" And R. Nahman replied, "I do, because Scripture states: (Amos 9:11) *In that day will I raise up the tabernacle of David that is fallen.*" [He takes this to mean that David, and not the tabernacle, is *the fallen.*] *Sanhedrin, 96b*

816. R. Nahman said, "If he is among those living today, he [the Messiah] could be one like myself;[1] for Scripture states: (Jer. 30:21) *And their nobles shall be of themselves, and their governors shall proceed from the midst of them.*" *Sanhedrin, 98b*

817. Rab said, "If he is one of those living today, it would be our holy Master [Judah HaNasi, known as Rabbi]. If he is of those who are dead, it would be Daniel [of the Bible]." *Sanhedrin, 98b*

The Messiah will be descended from King David

818. R. Papa said to Abaye, "Is not (Ezek. 37:25) *David, my servant, shall be prince over them forever* written in Scripture? This is the custom [in dynastic succession]. There is a ruler, and also a prince to succeed him [i.e., a descendant of King David]." *Sanhedrin, 98b*

819. R. Judah said in the name of Rab, "In the future, the Holy One will produce for Israel another David; as Scripture states: (Jer. 30:9) *And David their king, whom I will raise up unto them.* The verse does not read 'I raised' but rather *I will raise* [in the future]."

Sanhedrin, 98b

R. Johanan speaks of Hezekiah as the Messiah

820. R. Johanan b. Zakkai on his deathbed said to his disciples, "Prepare a seat for Hezekiah, King of Judah, who is coming."[2]

Berachoth, 28b

Hillel II also claims Hezekiah was the Messiah

821. Hillel II[3] said, "Israel can expect no Messiah, for we have

---

1 He had prestige as the son-in-law of the Exilarch.

2 R. Johanan, who witnessed the destruction of Jerusalem, lived in the first century C.E. He refers here to the King of Judah, who reigned from about 720–692 B.C.E. At a time of external threat from Assyria and internal spiritual decline, Hezekiah secured Judah's independence and purified its worship. See 2 Kings 18:1–16.

3 Hillel II lived in the fourth century C.E., long after Johanan.

already enjoyed him in the days of King Hezekiah."

Sanhedrin, 98b

The identity of the Messiah is God's secret

822. R. Tanhum said in the name of Bar Kappara, "The Holy One wanted to make King Hezekiah the Messiah and use Sennacherib [ruler of Syria] as Gog and Magog,[1] but the Attribute of Justice said, 'Sovereign of the Universe! David, King of Israel, who composed so many songs of praise in Thine honor, hast Thou not made the Messiah. Wilt Thou make Hezekiah the Messiah, for whom Thou didst perform so many miracles though he did not compose a single song for Thee?' Then a heavenly voice was heard saying, 'It is My secret; it is My secret.' " *Sanhedrin, 94a*

We ourselves can hasten the Messiah's advent

823. Rab said, "All the predicted dates [for the Messiah's arrival] have passed, and the matter now depends solely on repentance and good deeds." *Sanhedrin, 97b*

824. R. Simeon b. Johai said, "If Israel were to keep just two Sabbaths according to the Law we would be redeemed forthwith."

Sabbath, 118b

825. R. Joshua b. Levi pointed out a [seeming] contradiction in the verse (Isa. 60:22) *I the Lord will hasten it in its time.*[2] He said that this means "If you are worthy, I will hasten it; if you are not worthy, it will be *in its time.*" *Sanhedrin, 98a*

826. R. Joshua b. Levi met Elijah the Prophet standing at the entrance to the cave of R. Simeon b. Johai, and asked him, "When will the Messiah come?"[3] "Go and ask him yourself," came the reply. "Where can I find him?" "At the city gates." "By what sign shall I recognize him?" "He will be sitting among the poor lepers, bandaging their wounds," Elijah answered.

R. Joshua b. Levi then went to the city gates and found the Messiah

---

[1] The Messiah's advent was to be preceded by the wars of Gog and Magog. See Ezek. 38–39:11; also N.T., Rev. 20:8.

[2] The seeming contradiction lies in the question, how can the Messiah's advent be hastened if it has a fixed time?

[3] R. Simeon, a Tanna, was condemned to death for criticizing the Roman government. He is said to have lived in a cave for thirteen years, and is the reputed author of the Zohar. The life of R. Joshua, an Amora, is surrounded by legends. Elijah was regarded as the precursor of the Messiah.

bandaging the lepers' wounds. "Peace upon you, Master and Teacher," said R. Joshua. "Peace upon you," came the reply. "When will you come?" R. Joshua asked the Messiah. "Today," was the answer.

When R. Joshua b. Levi saw Elijah the Prophet again, Elijah asked what had happened. "He made a fool of me," replied R. Joshua, "for he told me that he would come today!" Thereupon Elijah said, "What he really told you was this: (Ps. 95:7) *Today, if ye would but hearken to His voice* [and obey the will of God]." *Sanhedrin, 98a*

God too awaits the messianic age

827. In comment on the verse (Ps. 2:4) *He that sitteth in heaven laugheth* [*yishak*], R. Isaac said, "The Lord does not smile [or laugh].[1] He will only do so on the coming of the Messiah."

R. Judah disagreed. He quoted Rab as having said, "There are twelve hours in a day. The first three hours the Lord is occupied with the Torah. For another three hours He sits in judgment on the world. Seeing that the world may merit destruction, He arises from the chair of justice and sits on the chair of mercy. The next three hours he spends providing the whole world with sustenance, from the largest creatures to the smallest. The last three hours He amuses Himself with the Leviathan; as Scripture states: (Ps. 104:26) *Leviathan, whom Thou hast made to sport* [*l'sahek*] *therewith.*"

Said R. Nahman, the son of R. Isaac, "*With* His creatures He smiles; but *upon* them He will smile only at the advent of the Messiah." *Abodah Zarah, 3b*

---

[1] The root verb *sahak* may mean "to laugh," "to smile," "to engage in amusement" or, as in Ps. 104 in the following paragraph, "to sport."

15

TALES AND LEGENDS

A number of tales and legends appear in the preceding pages. These are usually cast in the form of parables or allegories and serve a didactic purpose, illustrating and supporting rabbinic comments on the subject under discussion. But the rabbis' fondness for embellishing their discourse is not limited by such considerations; many stories in the Aggadah cannot readily be classified under the previous chapter headings.

The tales cited here vary widely in character, and the line between reality and fantasy is often blurred. There are several which deal with historical personalities, such as those which recount the experiences of Rabbi Joshua ben Hanania, while a few are obviously fictional. Some of the selections, like "It takes a thief to catch a thief," deal with universal themes; others, as seen in "Joseph, observer of the Sabbath," focus on specifically Jewish motifs. Some combine both the universal and the particular, as in the case of "Honi, the Jewish Rip Van Winkle"; still others, like "King Solomon's encounter with Asmodai," involve demonology and the supernatural.

Despite their variety, it should not be surprising that the tales which follow are often homiletical in tone, extolling wisdom and virtue, the values most cherished by the rabbis.

The wisdom of Rabbi Shesheth

828. R. Shesheth was blind, yet when the whole community turned out to greet the ruler, he went along with the others. He was met by a *min* who taunted him, saying, "All the earthen pitchers are going to the stream to draw water; where do the broken vessels go?" [Why would a blind man go to see the king?] R. Shesheth replied, "I will show you that I know what I am doing."

When the first contingent of troops passed, a shout arose from the crowd. Said the *min*, "The king must be coming." But R. Shesheth

238

answered, "Not yet." A second company of troops passed, and again a shout arose. The *min* said, "Now the king is coming." R. Shesheth responded, "The king is not yet coming." A third troop passed, and again a shout arose, but the ruler did not appear. After that there was complete silence, and R. Shesheth said, "Now indeed the king is coming." And so it came to pass.

The *min* then asked R. Shesheth, "How did you know that this would be as you stated?" And he replied, "Because the earthly kingdom reflects the kingdom of Heaven; and Scripture tells us: (1 Kings 19:11f) *a great and strong wind rent the mountains, and broke in pieces the rocks before the Lord; but the Lord was not in the wind. And after that an earthquake; and after the earthquake a fire, but the Lord was not in the fire; and after the fire a still, small voice.*"[1] *Berachoth, 58a*

Rabbi Tanhum is saved from the lions

829. The ruler said to R. Tanhum, "Let us unite and become one people, of one and the same faith." R. Tanhum answered, "Very well. But we who are circumcised cannot be like your people. You, however, are able to be like us if you will be circumcised." To this the ruler replied, "You are right. But we have a tradition that he who prevails over the ruler must be thrown to the beasts." Thereupon R. Tanhum was thrown into the lion pit, but he was not harmed.

"Do you know why the animals did not devour him?" a *min* remarked to the ruler; "it is because they were not hungry." So the *min* was thrown into the pit, and he was devoured. *Sanhedrin 39a*

Rabbi Joshua teaches the ruler a lesson

830. The ruler [Hadrian] said to R. Joshua b. Hanania,[2] "Your God is likened to a lion; for Scripture states: (Amos 3:8) *The lion hath roared, who will not fear?* But what is remarkable about a lion? Does not a hunter kill a lion?" R. Joshua replied, "He is not compared to an ordinary lion, but rather to the lion of the forest of Ilai."

"If so," said the ruler, "I would like to see that lion." "You cannot see it," R. Joshua replied. "But I must see it," insisted the ruler.

---

[1] It is in the *still, small voice* that the prophet Elijah hears God speak. Similarly, the arrival of a human ruler would be acknowledged not with clamor but with awed silence.

[2] Rabbi Joshua lived in the first century C.E. under the reign of Hadrian. He visited Rome and Alexandria several times, together with Gamaliel and others, on behalf of his people. It appears that he was favored by Gentile scholars and engaged in discussion with them. See Gershom Bader, *The Jewish Spiritual Heroes*, 1:226ff.

Thereupon R. Joshua prayed and caused the lion of the forest of Ilai to leave its place.

When the lion reached a distance of four hundred *parsahs*[1] from Rome, it let out a roar which caused pregnant women to miscarry and the walls of Rome to tremble. When it was three hundred *parsahs* from Rome, it roared again and caused people's teeth to fall out and the Caesar to fall from his throne. He then said to R. Joshua, "I beg of you, pray for mercy and have it return to its place." R. Joshua then prayed and the lion returned to its abode. *Hullin 59b*

Rabbi Joshua and the princess

831. The daughter of the Caesar [Hadrian] once said to R. Joshua b. Hanania, "How unbecoming it is that such an ugly vessel [as you are] should contain such glorious wisdom!" To this he replied, "My daughter, in what does your father, the ruler, keep his finest wine?" "In earthen vessels," came her response. Then he said to her, "But the common people keep their wine in earthen vessels! Should your father, the ruler, also keep his in earthen vessels?"

"How then should it be kept?" she inquired. "You, who are wealthy," said R. Joshua, "should keep it in vessels of silver and gold." When she told this to her father, he ordered that his wine be placed in silver and golden vessels. Subsequently the wine became sour,[2] and when the ruler was informed of this he asked his daughter, "Who told you that our wine should be placed in vessels of silver and gold?" And she replied, "It was R. Joshua b. Hanania."

The ruler sent for R. Joshua and asked him, "Why did you advise her to do this?" "It was only in answer to a direct question asked by the princess,"[3] R. Joshua explained, and he indicated how this had come about. Then the Caesar asked him, "Are there not scholarly men who are also handsome?" R. Joshua replied, "Yes, but if they were ugly they would be even greater scholars [devoting more time to their studies]!" *Nedarim 50b; Taanith 7a*

---

[1] A *parsah* is a *parsang,* a Roman mile, equivalent to about 4,000 yards or 2.8 English miles (Soncino Talmud, fn. on this passage). Jastrow defines it as a Persian mile (*Dictionary of the Talmud,* s.v. "parsah").

[2] While the Romans knew enough to avoid souring their wine, they were unaware that the lead linings of their earthenware casks could cause poisoning. Such poisoning has been blamed for reducing female reproductive capacity in the first and second centuries B.C.E. and for contributing to the fall of the Roman Empire. See S. C. Gilfillan, "Lead Poisoning and the Fall of Rome," *Journal of Occupational Medicine* (1965), 7:53–60.

[3] One could not volunteer advice to a princess. See also item 841.

Rabbi Joshua ransoms a young captive

832. When R. Joshua b. Hanania went to the great city of Rome, he was told about a Jewish boy of fine appearance, with bright eyes and curly locks, who was being held for ransom. He went to the gate of the prison and quoted the words of the prophet: (Isa. 42:24) *Who gave Jacob for a spoil, and Israel over to plunderers?* When he heard these words the lad replied, (ibid.) *Was it not the Lord, He whom we have sinned against? For they would not walk in His way, neither did they hearken unto His Law.*

R. Joshua then thought, "Surely this lad will in the future become a rabbi. I shall not leave here until I succeed in liberating him at whatever price it may require!" And it is said that he did not return home until he had ransomed the lad for a large sum of money. The youth later became a rabbi, and his name was R. Ishmael b. Elisha.[1] [See also item 643.] *Gittin 58a*

How Rabbi Joshua learned from others

833. R. Joshua b. Hanania said, "During my lifetime, I was put down once by a woman, once by a little girl and once by a young boy. What was the incident involving the woman? It happened when I lived at a house where I also took my meals. The woman of the house set before me a plate of beans, and I ate the entire portion, leaving nothing on the plate. The next time she served beans I again ate all of it and left nothing. But the third time it was too salty, and after tasting it I left it uneaten.

"When she said to me, 'Rabbi, why have you not eaten?' I replied [trying to offer an excuse], 'I have already eaten during the day.' 'You should then have eaten less bread,' she answered. Then she added, 'Rabbi, I suspect that you are not eating now because you did not leave any *peah*[2] on your plate the two previous times I served beans. Have not the Sages declared that *peah* should not be left in the pot [by the cook] but on the plate, after the food has been served? [You must therefore have left all of it on the plate now to suffice for all three occasions.]' In this [gentle] fashion did she reprimand me for not leaving *peah* [without embarrassing me].

---

[1] A Tanna of the third generation in the Holy Land.

[2] Literally, *peah* is "a corner." Scripture states that the corner of a field must not be harvested, and that a portion of its produce must be left for the poor (Lev. 19:9f). Leaving *peah* on the plate is a symbolic thanks-offering.

"What was the incident involving the little girl? I was once walking near an open field and, spotting a trodden path which ran across the field, I took that path. A little girl standing nearby said to me, 'Rabbi, are you not crossing an open field?' To this I replied, 'Is there not a trodden path across the field?' Thereupon she declared, 'Yes, that is so. But it is only because law-breakers like yourself have made it a trodden path!'

"Finally, what was the incident involving the young boy? I was out walking and I noticed a lad sitting near a crossroad. I asked him, 'Which of these roads leads to the city?' And he replied, 'They both do. However, one of these roads is a long one, yet short. The other is a short road, yet long.' I took the road that was short, yet long, and followed it. As I came near the city, I discovered that the approach to town was so completely surrounded by gardens and orchards that I had to return to the crossroad from which I had come.

"I said to the lad sitting there, 'My son, did you not tell me that this road is the short one?' And he answered, 'Rabbi, did I not also tell you that it was nonetheless a long one?' I thereupon kissed him on the forehead and said, 'Blessed are you, O Israel, that all of your children are wise, whether they are young or old.' "

Erubin 53b

The trials of Rabbi Nahum of Gamzu

834. R. Nahum, the man of Gamzu, was blind in both eyes and crippled in both hands, his two legs crushed and his body covered with sores. He lived in a tottering house and lay in a bed, the legs of which stood in buckets of water to prevent worms from reaching his body. It is said that when his disciples wanted to remove his bed from the house and then his furniture, he said to them, "My children, first take everything else, and then remove my bed; for you can be sure that as long as I am in this house it cannot collapse." They did as he suggested and after they removed his bed the house collapsed.

His disciples then said to him, "Rabbi, since you are such a righteous man, why are you so terribly afflicted?" "My children," he replied, "I myself am responsible for that. I was once on my way to the home of my father-in-law, and had with me three asses. One was laden with food, another with drink, and the third with various delicacies. In the course of my journey a poor man approached me and said,

'Rabbi, give me some food,' and I answered, 'Wait until I can unload my asses.' But before I had finished doing so, the poor man expired. So I said, 'May my eyes, which had no consideration for your eyes, be blind! May my hands, which had no mercy upon your hands, be crippled! May my feet, which had no pity on your feet, be crushed!' And I could not achieve full expiation until I had said, 'May my whole body be covered with sores!' "

His disciples then said to him, "Woe unto us that we must see you in such a condition!" But he replied, "Woe would have been unto me if you had not seen me in this condition [for I would otherwise be punished in the Hereafter]!"[1]

Why was he called Nahum, the man of Gamzu? Because whenever any adversity befell him he would say, *"Gam zu l'tovah"* ["This also is for good."] [See also item 18.] *Taanith, 21a*

How Rabbi Johanan rebuked his disciples

835. R. Hiyya b. Abba and R. Assi were once seated with R. Johanan when R. Johanan dozed off. Hiyya then asked R. Assi, "Why are the fowl of Babylonia so fat [i.e., fatter than those in the land of Israel]?" R. Assi replied, "Why? Go to the desert of Aza [in Palestine], and there you will find still fatter ones." R. Hiyya b. Abba then asked, "Why are the Babylonians so joyous during their festivals?" "Because," he answered, "they are poor [and need occasions to rejoice]."

"Why are our scholars in Babylonia so well dressed?" asked R. Hiyya. "Because," said R. Assi, "they are not as well versed in the Torah as our own scholars [and thus dress well to command respect]." "Why are the Babylonian people so filthy?" continued R. Hiyya. "Because," replied R. Assi, "they eat abominable and filthy things."[2]

At that moment, R. Johanan awoke and said to them, "Youngsters! Have I not warned you to keep in mind the words (Prov. 7:4) *Say unto wisdom, thou art my sister*? This means that if a thing is as certain to you as the fact that you cannot marry your sister, only then may you say it. Otherwise, you should not." [See also item 549.]

Sabbath, 145b

---

[1] Regarding punishment in the Hereafter, see chapter 13d. For another account of Nahum of Gamzu, see item 647.

[2] Ritually unclean foods, forbidden to Jews. See Lev. 11.

R. Johanan assures the survival of Jewish learning

836. Abba Sikra, the leader of the *biryoni* [the Zealot rebels against Rome][1] in Jerusalem, was the nephew of R. Johanan b. Zakkai. R. Johanan sent word to him, saying, "Come to me in secrecy." When he arrived, R. Johanan said to him, "How long are you going to continue these rebellious acts [which have caused the siege of Jerusalem] and bring only death [by starvation] to our people?"

His nephew answered, "What can I do? If I say a word against the actions of the rebels they will kill me." "Find a way," said R. Johanan, "for me to leave Jerusalem to visit the enemy camp. Perhaps there can be some relief from the siege." His nephew then said, "Pretend you are ill and let people come to visit you as a sick person. Then let the rabbis announce that you have died. Your disciples will then enter the house to carry you off [for burial], but no one else shall be permitted to enter [to help carry the coffin], so that no one will notice that you are light in weight and discover that you are alive, for a living person weighs less than a dead one."

R. Johanan acted accordingly, and R. Eleazar and R. Joshua carried him out of the house. When they came to the city gate to take the body outside of Jerusalem for burial, the [Jewish] watchmen wanted to thrust their spears into the body to make sure R. Johanan was dead. But Abba Sikra said to them, "The Romans will say, 'Their own rabbi have they pierced with their spears.'" The watchmen then wanted to throw the casket over the gate, and Abba Sikra said to them, "The Romans will say, 'Their own rabbi have they thrown over the gate.'" Consequently, they opened the gate for the body to pass through and R. Johanan's disciples left.

R. Johanan then appeared before Vespasian [the Roman general] and said to him, "Peace unto you, O king; peace unto the king!" Vespasian said to him, "You deserve to be put to death on two counts. First, because I am not an emperor, and you called me by that title. Second, if it were true that I am the emperor, you should have come to me before now." R. Johanan then said to him, "As to your statement that you are not the ruler, I claim that you are; for were you not a king, Jerusalem would not have fallen into your hands. As to your question asking why I did not come to you before now, the answer

---

[1] Of the four discernible factions (Zealots, Pharisees, Sadducees and Essenes), the Zealots were the most militant in their resistance to Rome at the siege of Jerusalem in 70 C.E. and the Essenes were the most withdrawn from the struggle.

is that the Zealots among us prevented me from doing so. . . ."

While they were talking, a courier arrived from Rome and said to Vespasian, "Arise, for the Caesar is dead and the nobles have placed you at their head. . . ." Vespasian [amazed that Johanan had foreseen his elevation] then said to R. Johanan, "I will leave here and send another in my stead. Neverthless, ask some favor of me and I shall try to grant it." R. Johanan thereupon said to him, "Spare the city of Jabneh with its sages and the entire noble family of Rabban Gamaliel for the founding of an academy—and provide doctors to cure R. Zadok from his illness." [Vespasian assured him that this would be done.]

Upon his return to Rome, Vespasian dispatched Titus the Wicked to Jerusalem in his place. . . . At sea, a storm arose and threatened to sink the ship, and Titus said, "It seems that the God of the Hebrews has no power anywhere except at sea. He drowned the forces of Pharaoh and now He wants to drown me also. If indeed He is mighty, let Him go ashore and wage war with me there." Then a heavenly voice declared, "O thou wicked one, son of a wicked one, go ashore. I have an insignificant creature in My world called a gnat. Go and do battle with it."

As soon as Titus landed, a gnat flew up into one of his nostrils. It gnawed at his brain for a period of seven years. One day he happened to pass a blacksmith's shop, and he found that the noise of the hammer soothed the gnawing at his brain. "Aha!" said Titus, "I have found a remedy at last." He ordered that a blacksmith should hammer constantly before him. A Gentile blacksmith was paid four *zuzim* a day, but a Jewish blacksmith he paid nothing, saying, "It is enough for you that you see your enemy suffer so painfully." *Gittin, 56a*

Why Jerusalem was destroyed

837. R. Judah said in the name of Rab, "What does the passage: (Mic. 2:2) *Thus they oppress a man and his household, the master and his heritage* mean? It once happened that a carpenter fell in love with his employer's wife. When his employer was in need of a loan the carpenter said to him, 'Send your wife over to me, and I will send back with her the money you need.' The master sent his wife to the carpenter's home and the carpenter detained her for three days.

"The employer then came to see the carpenter and said to him, 'Where is my wife, whom I sent to you?' The carpenter answered, 'I sent her home immediately after she came; but I heard that ruffians accosted her on her way back.' The employer then said, 'What shall I do now?' and the carpenter replied, 'If you would take my advice, you would divorce her.' 'But how can I do that,' said the employer, 'since her dowry amounts to a large sum of money [and I cannot repay it]?'

"Thereupon the carpenter said, 'I will lend you the money to repay her.' The master then divorced her, and the carpenter forthwith married her. When the time to repay the loan arrived and the master was unable to repay it, the carpenter said to him, 'You will have to repay me by working for me.' And so it came to pass.

"While the carpenter and his new wife were seated at the table eating and drinking, with her former husband waiting on them, tears dropped from his eyes and fell into the wineglass of the carpenter who was now his master. At this very moment a heavenly decree was issued that Jerusalem should be destroyed."[1] *Gittin, 58a*

The special power of Rabbi Isaac

838. R. Mani, a frequent visitor of R. Isaac b. Eliashib, told the latter that the rich members of his father-in-law's family were giving him much trouble. Said R. Isaac, "May they become poor!" And they did indeed become poor. R. Mani later came and complained that his relatives, now poor, required that he should support them. R. Isaac then said, "May they become rich again!" And they did.

Some time afterward R. Mani complained to R. Isaac that his wife was very ill-favored. "What is her name?" asked R. Isaac. R. Mani replied, "Hannah." R. Isaac then said, "May Hannah become beautiful!" And so it came to pass. Then R. Mani came back again. He now complained that since his wife had become attractive she had made life miserable for him by her vanity. R. Isaac then said, "May Hannah become ugly again!" And so it happened.

Some time later two disciples of R. Isaac b. Eliashib said to him, "Let the Master pray to the Lord for us that we may grow wiser and more competent in study." Whereupon he said to them, "I once had the power to do such things, but I have abandoned that practice."

Taanith, 23b

---

[1] The rabbis perceive God as acting in history, and historic events as an expression of His will, a view embraced by the prophets. The destruction of Jerusalem is regarded as punishment for the sins of Israel.

What Rabbi Nahman learned from Rabbi Isaac

839. R. Nahman and R. Isaac were dining together, and R. Nahman said to R. Isaac, "Will the Master say something?" R. Isaac replied, "Thus said R. Johanan: 'While eating, one should not talk lest the food enter the windpipe and cause danger.' "

After they had finished their meal, R. Isaac said, "R. Johanan b. Zakkai once declared that Jacob the Patriarch never died." "Why then," asked R. Nahman, "did the mourners mourn him, the embalmers embalm him, and the undertaker bury him?" "I can prove R. Johanan's statement with Scripture," was R. Isaac's reply, "for Scripture states: (Jer. 30:10) *Therefore fear thou not, O Jacob, My servant, saith the Lord. Neither be thou dismayed, O Israel; for lo, I will save thee from afar, and thy seed from the land of their captivity; and Jacob shall again return, and be quiet and at ease, and none shall make him afraid.* Now, can Jacob really return? [This is impossible!] This teaches us that as long as his children [descendants] still live, he is still alive."

When they were about to part R. Nahman said to R. Isaac, "Bless me." And R. Isaac answered, "Instead of blessing you I shall tell you a parable. To what may your request for a blessing be compared? To the experience of a man in the desert. When he became hungry, thirsty and tired, he found a tree bearing delicious fruit and offering much shade, with a spring of water beside it. He drank of the water, ate of the fruit of the tree and rested in its shade.

"When he was ready to leave, he turned to the tree and said, 'O tree, wherewith can I bless you? That your fruit may be sweet? That is already the case. That a spring may be near you? This too you have. That you should provide plentiful shade? Even this you already have. The only thing left that I can wish for you is that all trees planted from your seed may be as fruitful as you are!'

"So it is with you, R. Nahman. Shall I bless you with knowledge? This you already have. Shall I bless you with honor? This too you have. Shall I bless you with riches? You also have that. Shall I bless you with children? Even children you do not lack. Hence all I can say to you is, 'May it be His will that your children be as well endowed as you are!' " *Taanith, 5b*

King Solomon's encounter with Asmodai

840. Before he undertook the building of the Temple, Solomon asked, "How can I accomplish this task without using tools made of

iron?"[1] He was told, "There is a *shamir* stone ['flint']² which Moses used in cutting the precious stones of the *ephod* [a priestly garment]."³ "Where can it be found?" he inquired. And he was told, "Summon forth a male demon and a female demon, and coerce them both [to tell you where it is]. Perhaps they know, and they will tell you."

He then conjured into his presence a male and a female demon and tortured them. But in vain, for they said, "We do not know its whereabouts. Perhaps Asmodai, king of the demons, knows where the *shamir* is located." "But where can Asmodai be found?" Solomon asked. And they answered, "On yonder mount is his dwelling. There he has a pit filled with water, covered with a rock and sealed with his own seal. He ascends to heaven daily, and studies in the heavenly academy [*yeshivah shel ma'alah*]. Then he comes down and studies for a while down here.[4] After that, he goes to his pit and examines the seal, then opens it. After quenching his thirst from its waters, he covers it again, seals it and leaves."

Solomon then sent Benayahu, the son of Yehoyadu, to the mountain, providing him with a chain and a ring, upon each of which the name of God was engraved. He also provided him with a fleece of wool and several skins of wine. Arriving at the mountain, Benayahu dug a pit below that of Asmodai, drained the water down into it, and plugged the duct between the two pits with the fleece. Then he dug another hole, higher up, leading into the emptied pit of Asmodai. Through this opening he filled the pit of Asmodai with the wine which he had brought along. He then smoothed the ground [to avoid suspicion] and climbed a nearby tree to see what would happen.

Before long Asmodai came and examined the seal on the opening of his pit. Seeing that all was in order, he raised the stone, but to his surprise he found wine in the pit. He muttered to himself, "Scripture states: (Prov. 20:1) *Wine is a mocker; strong drink is riotous, and whoever reeleth thereby is not wise.* I shall therefore not drink of it." But when he became unbearably thirsty, he could no longer resist the temptation.

Asmodai proceeded to drink the wine, became intoxicated, and lay down to sleep. Then Benayahu came out of hiding and fastened the

---

[1] It was forbidden to use tools made of iron in the building of the Temple because iron was used in the forging of weapons of war. See 1 Kings 6:7.

² Possibly the *shamir* referred to was a diamond. See *Dictionary of the Talmud,* s.v. "shamir."

³ See fn. to item 408.

4 Note that even the demons were presumed to study the Torah!

chain [bearing the name of God] around the neck of the sleeper. When Asmodai awoke he began to fret and fume, and tried to tear off the chain that bound him. But Benayahu said to him, "The name of the Lord is upon you [and you cannot escape]."

As they journeyed along on the way back to King Solomon, they came to a palm tree and Asmodai rubbed his back against it until he had uprooted it. In the same fashion he knocked down a house. When they approached a small hut, the poor widow who lived in it came out and entreated Asmodai to refrain from rubbing against it. As he suddenly turned to avoid doing so, he snapped a bone in his body and he remarked, "This is in keeping with the passage (Prov. 25:15) *And a soft tongue breaks the bones.*"

Seeing a blind man straying from the path, Asmodai directed him properly. He also did this for a man who was overcome by wine, helping him find his way. Later, at the sight of a wedding party passing merrily by, he wept. And he burst into laughter when, at a shoe-maker's shop, he heard a man order a pair of shoes that would last him seven years. When he passed a magician performing his craft, he broke forth with words of derision and scorn.

After arriving at the royal city [Jerusalem], three days elapsed before he was presented to King Solomon. . . . When he was brought before the king, he took a stick and with it measured off four cubits [six feet] on the floor, then threw the stick before the king, saying, "When you die, you will not possess more than four cubits of earth. Yet now, having conquered the world, you are not satisfied unless you subdue me also!"

To this the king replied, "I want nothing of you for myself; but I wish to build a Temple and have need of the *shamir.*" Asmodai answered, "The *shamir* is not entrusted to my care, but to the Prince of the Sea, who has placed it with a wild cock, upon an oath that he hold it in safekeeping and return it on demand." "What does the bird do with the *shamir?*" asked Solomon. Asmodai replied, "He takes it to a barren, rocky mountain, and by means of it he cleaves the mountain asunder. Into the cleft of it, formed into a valley, he drops the seeds of trees, and thus the place becomes fit for habitation."

Solomon then ordered a search for the nest of the wild bird which Benayahu succeeded in finding. It contained a young brood, and Benayahu covered the nest with a sheet of glass. When the father bird came and saw the nest covered over, he flew off to fetch the *shamir.* As the bird applied it to the glass in order to cut it, Benayahu gave a startling shout which frightened the bird so that it dropped the *shamir*. Benayahu seized it and made off with it [thus enabling the Temple to be built without the use of iron tools].

[On the journey back to Jerusalem,] Benayahu asked Asmodai why it was that when he saw a blind man straying from his path, he promptly intervened to help him. "Because," said Asmodai, "it was proclaimed in heaven that he is perfectly righteous, and that whoever did some good for him in this world would be rewarded with a place for himself in the World to Come."

"And when you saw the man overcome by wine staggering on his way, why did you help him?" asked Benayahu. And Asmodai answered, "Because it was announced in heaven that he was exceedingly wicked, and I have done him a good service so that, through my act of kindness, he might be rewarded in this world for whatever good he may have done [since he will have no reward in the next world]."

Then Benayahu asked him, "Why did you weep when you saw the merry wedding party?" He replied, "Because the bridegroom is destined to die within thirty days, and the bride will then have to wait thirteen years to marry his brother, who is now but a lad."[1]

"Why did you laugh when the man ordered a pair of shoes that would last him seven years?" "Because the man himself could not be sure of living seven days." "Why did you jeer at the conjuror doing his tricks?" "Because," said Asmodai, "he was at that very moment sitting on a princely treasure and he did not, with all his pretensions, know that it was under him."

King Solomon decided to detain Asmodai until the building of the Temple was completed. One day, when he was alone with Asmodai, Solomon asked him, . . . "In what way are you superior to me?" Asmodai replied, "If you will remove the chain from around my neck and give me your signet ring I will show you." No sooner did Solomon comply with the request than Asmodai, snatching him up, swallowed him whole. Then, stretching his wings—one touching the heavens, the other the earth—he took flight. He vomited Solomon out again at a distance of four hundred *parsahs*. . . . [Asmodai in the guise of Solomon then assumed the throne.]

Finding himself in an unfamiliar place, Solomon went from door to

---

[1] A widow who had no children by her husband was to marry his brother in order to raise up children who might enjoy her deceased husband's inheritance and perpetuate his family. See Deut. 25:5ff.

door begging, and wherever he came, he recited the passage (Eccles. 1:12) *I, Koheleth, was king over Israel in Jerusalem.* When, in his wanderings, he came before the Sanhedrin, they reasoned, "If he were insane, he would not simply keep saying this particular verse over and over again [but would show it in other ways as well]."

They asked Benayahu, "Does the king ever invite you into his presence?" "No," came the reply. They then inquired whether the king ever visited his harem, and the response was, "Yes, he does." Then the Sages sent word that at the harem they should examine the king's feet [for the feet of a demon are like those of a bird]. But they were told, "He comes to us in his stockings."

Upon receiving this information, the Sages escorted Solomon to the palace, and restored to him the chain and the ring, on each of which the name of God was inscribed. Equipped with these, Solomon entered the throne room [where Asmodai sat enthroned]. When Asmodai saw Solomon enter, he became frightened, spread his wings, and flew away. *Gittin, 68a*

The friendship of Rabbi and Antoninus

841. Antoninus once said to Rabbi, "I would like to have Asverus,[1] my son, reign after me, and also that the city of Tiberias be made a free city. However, if I ask my people to fulfill one request, they may not grant me the other."

Rabbi [instead of replying directly] took two men, put one upon the shoulders of the other and gave the man on top a dove. He then said to the man below, "Tell the man on your shoulders to set the dove free." Antoninus thereby understood that Rabbi intended to tell him that he should first ask [the Senate] to proclaim his son king after him, and instruct his son to declare Tiberias a free city.

Once Antoninus said to Rabbi, "The officers of Rome irritate me." Rabbi led him to the royal gardens and [in his presence] plucked out the largest radishes one by one, planting a smaller one in the place of each. Antoninus understood from his actions that Rabbi suggested replacing the old officers [with officers loyal to himself] one by one, but not all at once in order to prevent a revolt.

---

[1] Presumably Asverus is Alexander Severus, Roman emperor from 222–235, who restored to the Jews the privileges granted to them by Julius Caesar. Rabbinic literature apparently refers to Alexander Severus in certain passages which relate the acts of "Severus, the son of Antoninus."

Why did not Rabbi answer him directly [instead of going through these motions]? He thought the officers at Rome might hear about this and plot revenge. Then why did he not speak to Antoninus about this privately? He hesitated to do so; for Scripture states: (Eccles. 10:20) *For a bird of the air shall carry the voice.* [1]

Antoninus had a daughter named Gilla and it once happened that she sinned. He sent to Rabbi some white mustard [called *gargilla* in Aramaic]. And Rabbi understood him to be saying that something untoward had happened to Gilla. [*Gar Gilla* means "Gilla has gone astray" in Aramaic.] Rabbi then sent Antoninus a coriander seed. [This is called *husbartha* in Aramaic, and when read as *hus bartha* means "remove the daughter."]

Antoninus next sent him some garlic [called *karthi* in Aramaic, meaning also "cut off"], and Rabbi understood him to be asking, "Shall I cut off my child?" In response, Rabbi sent him some lettuce [called *hassa* in Aramaic, meaning also "have mercy"]. Antoninus understood the message [and showed mercy to his daughter]. [2]

Abodah Zarah, 10a

"It takes a thief to catch a thief"

842. R. Huna had four hundred jars of wine which turned into vinegar. On hearing of this, R. Judah, the brother of R. Sala the Pious —or as some say, R. Ada b. Ahabah—came to visit him, accompanied by other sages. They said, "Let the Master look into his affairs." [3]

"What!" said he. "Do you accuse me of some wrongdoing?" And they replied, "Shall we then suspect the Holy One of being unjust?" R. Huna then said, "If you have heard anything against me do not hide it from me, but tell it to me."

They said to him, "We have heard that the Master allows his tenant to share in the vintage." "Yes," said R. Huna, "and my tenant has been stealing the produce of my vineyard and left nothing for me." "There is a maxim," they replied, "that whoever steals from a thief is also a thief." And R. Huna [abashed] declared, "I promise hence-

---

1 Rabbi offers his counsel by indirection because the ruler could not seek direct advice from a commoner. See also item 831.

2 The Gemara of the Talmud is in Aramaic. It is assumed throughout that Antoninus knew this language, commonly used by Jews in the Roman period. Aramaic is still spoken (but not written) in the valley of Maakoula in Syria (Bernd Debusoman, "Aramic, Language of Christ, Survives," *Los Angles Times*, January 20, 1980, Part 1, p. 5/1).

3 It is here assumed that this was a sign of divine disfavor.

forth to give him his proper share" [thus admitting that he underpaid his tenant-farmer].

Thereupon, according to some, the vinegar turned to wine again. But according to others, the price of vinegar rose to the price of wine.

Berachoth, 5b

Joseph, observer of the Sabbath

843. Joseph, who was a faithful observer of the Sabbath, had a very rich neighbor. The neighbor was told by the Chaldeans that all of his wealth would eventually belong to Joseph.[1] The neighbor therefore sold his estate and bought a large diamond, which he concealed in his turban.

One day while he was crossing a bridge, a sudden gust of wind blew his turban into the water, and a large fish swallowed the diamond. The fish was later caught and it was brought to the market on a Friday. "Who wants to buy this fish?" the fisherman called out. He was told to go to Joseph who honored the Sabbath and usually bought fish for the Friday evening meal.

The fish was brought to Joseph, and he bought it. When it was opened, Joseph found the diamond, and he sold it for thirteen purses of gold *denars.* When the man who had directed the fisherman to Joseph learned of this, he said to Joseph, "He who lends to the Sabbath [by incurring additional expense to honor it], the Sabbath will repay." *Sabbath 119a*

Honi, the Jewish Rip Van Winkle

844. R. Johanan said that, throughout his life, Honi the Righteous thought about the interpretation of the passage (Ps. 126:1) *When the Lord brought back the captives to Zion, then were we like unto dreamers.*[2] He kept asking himself, "How can a man sleep, or be like a dreamer, for a period of seventy years?"

Once he was walking along the road and he noticed a man planting a carob tree. He asked the man how many years it would take for the tree to bear fruit. "Seventy years," the man replied. Said Honi, "Are you sure that you will live another seventy years?" And the man

---

[1] The Chaldeans (Babylonians) engaged in astrological speculation. Cf. N.T., Matt. 2:1, 2.

[2] See Jer. 25:11 and 29:10, where the collapse of the Babylonian empire after a rule of seventy years, and the return of the Jews to their land, is predicted. The Psalmist portrays the exiles in Babylonia as sleepers during their captivity. When Cyrus the Persian conquered Babylonia (539 B.C.E.), he permitted the Jews to return to Palestine. See also Ezra 1:2,3.

answered, "I found carob trees in existence when I came into the world, which my ancestors must have planted. Why should I not plant them for those who will come after me?"

Honi became hungry, and sat down to eat [near the newly planted trees]. After eating, he fell into a sound and prolonged sleep. He slept for seventy years, and as he slept a grotto formed around him. When he awoke, he saw a man gathering fruit from the carob trees. "Are you the man who planted these trees?" he asked. "I am his grandson," came the reply. Honi then said to himself, "Surely, I must have slept for seventy years!"

He noticed that several generations of offspring had been born to his ass. He then made his way toward his home, and asked whether the son of Honi was still living. He was told that Honi's son was no longer alive, but that his grandson was living. Then he said, "I am Honi Hamagel," but no one would believe him.

He went to the house of study, and there he heard one of the rabbis say, "This Halachah [legal passage] is as clear as in the days of Honi Hamagel who, upon entering the house of study, would render a clear decision on any questions put before him by the rabbis." Hearing this, he said to them, "I am Honi." But they did not believe him nor would they accord him proper respect. This disheartened him, whereupon he prayed that he might die, and so it came to pass.

Raba said, "This serves to illustrate the saying, 'Give me honor, or give me death.' "[1] *Taanith, 23a*

The captives who taught their captor wisdom

845. It once happened that two Jews were taken captive on Mount Carmel. As their captor walked behind them, one of the captives said to the other, "The camel which has preceded us on this road is blind in one eye and is carrying two pouches, one filled with wine and the other containing oil. As for the men leading the camel, one of them is an Israelite while the other is a heathen."

Their captor, overhearing this, said to them, "Stiff-necked people, whence do you know this?" And he was told, "From the grass, which is close-cropped on only one side of the road; from the side on which the camel is able to see, he ate, while the other side has been left untouched. It is also clear that the camel is carrying two saddlebags,

---

[1] On the importance of self-esteem beyond life itself, see Mark Twain, "What is Man?" (Charles Neider, *The Complete Essays of Mark Twain* [New York: Doubleday, 1963], p. 342ff.).

one filled with wine and the other with oil; for drops of wine are absorbed [into the earth], while drops of oil remain on the surface of the road and can be seen. It is also certain that one of the men leading the camel is an Israelite and the other is not; for an Israelite leaves the road to perform his natural functions while others do not."

Their captor continued to follow them, and when they overtook the camel ahead of them he found that it was indeed as they had said. He kissed them on their heads, brought them to his home, prepared a meal for them and waited upon them, saying, "Blessed be He Who chose the descendants of Abraham and gave them of His wisdom. Wherever they go, they become the masters of their masters!" He then set them free, and they returned in peace to their homes.

Sanhedrin, 104a

Minor matters may produce major consequences

846. "On account of Kamtza and Bar Kamtza [literally, 'locust' and 'son of locust'], Jerusalem was destroyed; because of a hen and a rooster, Tura Malka [literally, 'Mountain of the King'] was destroyed; because of a wheel on a carriage, Bethar was destroyed." [What is the basis for this popular saying?]

The first part of this statement is about a man who had a friend named Kamtza and an enemy named Bar Kamtza. He once held a banquet and ordered his servant to bring his friend Kamtza. The servant went and instead brought his enemy Bar Kamtza. When the host found the man he disliked seated at the banquet table he said, "You fabricate tales about me. What are you doing here?" and ordered him to leave.

However, Bar Kamtza said to him, "Since I am already here, allow me to stay and I will pay for whatever I eat and drink." "No," said the host. "I will pay you one-half the cost of the banquet [to avoid embarrassment]," pleaded Bar Kamtza. But the host refused. Instead, he seized him by the arm and put him out.

Bar Kamtza then said to himself, "Since many people were present and observed my disgrace without protest, I take it that they assent to the way I have been treated. I shall therefore go to the [Roman] ruler and inform against them." He then went to the ruler and said to him, "The Judeans have rebelled against you."

The ruler asked, "How can I be sure?" And Bar Kamtza replied, "Send them [an animal for] an offering, and see whether they will accept it [for the altar]." The ruler then sent with Bar Kamtza a fine calf. But on the way, Bar Kamtza made a blemish on its upper lip, and the animal was not used as an offering [since blemished animals could not be used for that purpose]. This led to the destruction of Jerusalem. . . .

"Because of a hen and a rooster, Tura Malka was destroyed" can be similarly explained. There was a custom that when a bride and groom were escorted to a wedding, people would greet them with a hen and a rooster, the idea being that they should multiply like fowl.

On one occasion, during a wedding procession, a troop of [Roman] soldiers passed by and took away the hen and the rooster. This caused the crowd to fall upon the soldiers and beat them. As a consequence, the troop sent word to the Caesar, saying, "The Judeans have rebelled against you." Then he attacked Tura Malka. . . .

How can we explain "Because of the wheel on a carriage, Bethar was destroyed"? It was the custom in Bethar[1] that, when a child was born, the parents would plant a cedar tree if it was a boy and a pine tree for a girl. At the time of the child's marriage, the tree would be cut down to make a marriage canopy out of it.

It happened that the ruler's daughter was passing through that city one day when the shaft of her litter broke, and her attendants cut down a young cedar tree to use it as a replacement for the broken shaft. The man who had planted that tree attacked the attendants of the princess and beat them severely. Thereupon the attendants told the ruler that the Judeans had revolted against him, and he sent a large force to subdue them. *Gittin, 55b*

Should bequests be left to unworthy children?

847. (Mishnah) If one bequeaths his estate to strangers and leaves nothing for his children, while such an act is legally valid, the Sages do not approve of his action. However, R. Simeon b. Gamaliel declared, "If his children were undeserving, he will be remembered for blessing [for this will serve as a warning to wicked offspring]."

(Gemara) Joseph b. Joezer had a son of bad habits. He also possessed a great number of *denars*. He therefore contributed the money to the Temple treasurer [withholding it from his son]. The son later married the daughter of Gadil, the master of the crowns for King Janai. When his wife bore him a child, he bought

---

[1] Bethar, in southern Palestine, was the center of the final revolt against Rome under Hadrian, who ruled from 132–135 C.E. The revolt was led unsuccessfully by Bar Kochba.

a fish for the occasion, and in it he found a large pearl.

His wife said to him, "Do not take it to the king's court for assessment of its value. It will be appraised cheaply and you will get little for it. Take it rather to the Temple treasurer. But make no mention of its worth; for there is a rule that a figure spoken to the Temple treasurer is regarded as a pledge of that amount to the Temple treasury, which cannot be reduced."

He did as she suggested, and the Temple treasurer appraised the pearl at thirteen measures of *denars.* The treasurer then said to him, "We now have in the Temple treasury only seven measures of *denars,* not enough to cover the value of the pearl." And the son of Joseph b. Joezer replied, "Let six measures be consecrated to the Lord, and I will accept the seven measures which you have."

Then the Temple treasurer recorded in his book, "Joseph b. Joezer contributed to the Temple treasury one measure of *denars,* but his son contributed six measures." *Baba Bathra, 133b*

The story of Onkelos the convert

848. Onkelos ben Klonikos[1] embraced the Jewish faith, and the Caesar sent soldiers to arrest him. However, he dissuaded them from taking him, and they also became proselytes to Judaism. The Caesar then sent others, warning them that they should not converse with Onkelos.

When they apprehended him, and were about to leave with him, he said to them, "Let me ask you something. Usually the torchbearer carries the light in front of the royal litter; the chief *lecticarius* [walking behind the litter, carries the light] for the *dux*; the *dux* carries it for the *hegemon*; the *hegemon* for the *comes.* Does the *comes* then carry the light before the people?" They answered, "No."

Then he said, "But the Holy One, blessed be He, Himself provides the light before the entire people of Israel; for Scripture states: (Exod. 13:21) *And the Lord went before them by day in a pillar of cloud; and by night in a pillar of fire, to give them light.*" Then they too became proselytes.

The Caesar sent still others to seize him, telling them to be sure not

---

[1] Onkelos, a Tanna of the first century C.E., was the reputed translator of the Torah into Aramaic. The translation is usually called Targum Onkelos. Talmud Jerushalmi speaks of the convert Aquila (Akylos) of the second century, who translated the Bible into Greek. The two are sometimes confused in rabbinic literature; tales depicting Onkelos as a member of the Roman imperial family who was converted to Judaism probably refer to Aquila.

to talk to him. But when they took him, they noticed a *mezuzah*[1] on the doorpost of his house, and he said to them, "Do you know what this is?" They answered, "No, but you may tell us." He then said, "When a human king is in his palace, it is customary for his servants to guard him from without. With the Holy One of Israel the opposite is true. When His servants are in their homes, He guards them from without; as Scripture states: (Ps. 121:8) *The Lord will guard thy going out and thy coming in.*" These men also became proselytes, and the Caesar did not send any others to seize him. *Abodah Zarah, 11a*

Why Rabbi Judah's face was ruddy

849. R. Judah [ben Baba] was sitting with R. Tarphon, when the latter remarked to him, "You appear radiant today." R. Judah replied, "Yesterday your disciples [including myself] went out into the field, and we brought back a certain kind of beet which we ate unsalted. Had we eaten it with salt, our faces would be even brighter."

A certain matron[2] once said to R. Judah, "You are a teacher and yet you are a drunkard [i.e., red-faced]!" Thereupon he said to her, "I have not touched any wine, except for *kiddush* and *havdalah* [at the start and close of the Sabbath] and the four traditional cups on Passover eve; and my head ached from Passover until the Feast of Shabuoth [a period of seven weeks]. The reason for the brightness of my countenance is found in the verse (Eccles. 8:1) *A man's wisdom maketh his face to shine.*"

A *min* ["dissenter"] once said to him, "Your countenance is like that of a usurer or of one who raises pigs." To this he replied, "Among Israelites, both pursuits are prohibited. My face is so ruddy because I take good care of myself." *Nedarim, 49b*

---

[1] The *mezuzah*, an elongated little box of wood or metal, is attached to the doorpost of Jewish homes to this day, in fulfillment of the injunction to *write them upon the doorposts of thy house* (Deut. 6:9). It contains two passages from the Torah: Deut. 6:4–9 and Deut. 11:13–21. The literal meaning of the word *mezuzah* is "doorpost."

[2] "Matron" was a term applied to Roman ladies of noble birth.

16

PROVERBS AND MAXIMS

Proverbs and maxims have been produced in many lands and in numerous languages as an expression of folk-wisdom, presenting simple truths with special charm. Some of the aphorisms offered here have their parallels in the proverbs of other peoples, for they emerge from common human experiences; moreover, the Jews came in contact with a variety of cultures, influencing and being influenced by their folklore.

Jewish proverbs, like those of other cultures, are often couched in metaphor, at times ascribing human traits to animals. They sometimes rhyme or play on words. In addition, the proverbs of the Aggadah frequently contain Biblical allusions or refer to events in Jewish history without diminishing their universal appeal.

The oldest collection of Jewish proverbs is of course the Book of Proverbs in the Bible. A later compilation which is sometimes quoted in the Talmud is the Book of Ben Sirah, also known as Ecclesiasticus. Originally in Greek, this is one of the books of the Apocrypha. The making of proverbs has been an ongoing process, and an abundance of such material has emerged in the Yiddish language, reflecting the East European origin and the immigrant-American experience of the masses of Jews who found refuge in the new world.

Some popular sayings appear in preceding pages in diverse contexts. The selections which follow are arranged by subject.

Advice
850. R. Kahana said in the name of R. Akiba, "Be careful of him who counsels you and has something to gain thereby." [His advice may be biased.] *Sanhedrin, 76a*

851. A pregnant woman once came to a house to do some baking and the owner's dog barked at her, causing her fetus to be loosened.

"Don't be afraid," said the home-owner, "for his teeth and his claws have been extracted." The woman replied, "Take your good advice and throw it over the hedge; the embryo is already loosened." ["The embryo is already loosened" became a reproach for advice that comes too late.] *Sabbath, 63b*

Affection

852. R. Johanan said, "There are three special kinds of affection: the fondness of its inhabitants for their own community; the fondness of a husband for his wife; and the fondness of a buyer for the object he has purchased." *Sotah, 47a*

Anxiety

853. Let not anxiety enter thy heart for it has slain many a person.
Sanhedrin, 100a

Beards

854. A thin-bearded person is shrewd and a thick-bearded person is a fool. . . . If the beard of a man is divided, the whole world will not overrule him [i.e., he is stubborn]. *Sanhedrin, 100b*

Character

855. If a peasant becomes a king, he will not take his basket off his shoulders. ["You can't make a silk purse out of a sow's ear."]
Megillah, 7b

856. R. Abba remarked, "People say, 'A myrtle, even if it stands among reeds, is still a myrtle, and is identified as such.'" [The context here is that, even if Israel has sinned, it is still called by the honorable name of Israel.] *Sanhedrin, 44a*

Compassion

857. People say, "To him who has had a hanging in the family, do not even speak of hanging up a fish." [See also item 986.]
Baba Metzia, 59b

Coping

858. R. Papa said, "There is a popular saying, 'If the ox falls while performing his task, a horse is placed in its stall.'" [The horse, though not as strong, replaces it.] *Sanhedrin, 98b*

859. R. Benjamin b. Japhet said in the name of R. Eleazar, "When

the fox has his day, bow to him." [Submit to the inevitable.]

Megillah, 16b

860. People say, "Not everyone has the merit of two tables." ["You can't have the best of both worlds."] *Berachoth, 5b*

Cunning

861. Rab said to Rabba b. Mari, "Whence can we derive the popular saying, 'Though a duck keeps its head down while walking, its eyes look ahead?' " He replied, "Scripture states: (1 Sam. 25:31) *And when the Lord shall have dealt well with my master, then remember thy handmaid.*" [This was spoken by Abigail to David, implying that she wanted to be his wife.] *Baba Kamma, 92b*

862. There is a saying, "While a woman talks, she spins." [Abigail, while speaking to David about Nabal, her husband, hinted that David should marry her if Nabal should die.] *Megillah, 14b*

863. R. Hisda said, "He who picks up a moist log [useless for burning] wants to place a press on that spot." [Men often act with ulterior motives.] *Erubin, 40b*

864. A proverb says, "As a stylus cuts through the stone, so does one cunning mind penetrate the other." [This is applied to business dealings.] *Abodah Zarah, 22b*

Curses

865. There is a tradition that the curse of a sage, even if undeserved, comes to pass. [It could be self-fulfilling.][1] *Berachoth, 56a*

866. Even the curse of an ordinary person should not be treated lightly. *Baba Kamma, 93a*

Destiny

867. Change of name and change of place [or residence] are acts which avert the divine decree. [Making a fresh start.]

Rosh Hashanah, 16b

Elders

868. We are taught in a *baraitha* that R. Simeon b. Eleazar said, "If your elders tell you to tear down, and the young tell you to build, rather destroy according to the advice of the elders and do not build;

---

[1] On the power of the spoken word, see item 63. In Jewish folklore the curse could cause great harm.

for [even] destruction by the elders is constructive, while the construction of the young is destructive." [Wisdom comes with age. Rheoboam refused the advice of his elders and his kingdom was split. See 1 Kings 12.] *Nedarim, 40a*

869. At the time of the Exodus from Egypt, Moses and Aaron walked ahead, followed by Nadab and Abihu [sons of Aaron], who in turn were followed by the multitude. Nadab turned to Abihu and said, "When will the two old men die so that you and I can become the leaders of Israel?" Thereupon the Holy One said, "Time will show who will bury whom." [Nadab and Abihu died young. See Lev. 10:1–3.]

R. Papa remarked, "This is an illustration of the popular saying, 'Many an old camel is laden with the hides of younger ones.' " [Older men may outlast or out-perform younger men. "The race is not always to the swift."] *Sanhedrin, 52a*

870. People say, "When we were young we were treated as men; now that we have grown old we are treated as infants."

Baba Kamma, 92b

Enemies

871. R. Papa said that people say, "When you pass by the door of your enemy make your presence known [so that he will not think you plot his harm]." *Sanhedrin, 95b*

872. There is a proverb, "From the very forest itself comes the [handle of the] axe [that fells it]." [David, a descendant of Ruth the Moabite, attacked the Moabites. See 2 Sam. 8:2.]

Sanhedrin, 39b

873. People say, "The man on whom I depended has raised his club against me." Samuel said to R. Judah, "This is found also in the passage (Ps. 41:10) *Yea, even the man who should have sought my welfare, in whom I trusted, who hath eaten of my bread, hath lifted up his heel against me.*" *Sanhedrin, 7b*

874. R. Samuel b. Nahmani said in the name of R. Jonaan, "What does the verse (Prov. 27:6) *Faithful are the wounds of a friend; but the kisses of an enemy are deceitful* mean? Better is the curse wherewith Ahijah the Shilonite cursed Israel than the blessing with which the wicked Balaam blessed them."[1]

Sanhedrin, 105b

---

[1] See 1 Kings 14:1ff and Num. 23:5ff.

Environmental influence

875. People say, "If there are two dry pieces of wood and a green piece is placed between them, the green piece will burn with the dry ones." [Environment influences one's behavior.] *Sanhedrin, 93a*

Fools

876. A fool never feels trouble as dead fish do not feel the pain of the knife. [He is insensitive.] *Sabbath, 13b*

877. People say, "You can do nothing with a fool. Weep before him or laugh with him, it will make no difference." [He can't respond to reason.] *Sanhedrin, 103a*

Friends

878. Rabbi said, "A man should not acquire too many [close] friends; for Scripture states: (Prov. 18:24) *There are friends that one hath to his own hurt.*" [Friends may betray us.] *Sanhedrin, 100b*

879. R. Papa said, "In doing business, one has many friends, but in disgrace he has no friends." ["A friend in need is a friend indeed."]
Sabbath, 32a

The Golden Rule in practice

880. R. Nathan said, "Do not reproach your neighbor with a fault which is also your own." [Cf. "And why beholdest thou the mote which is in thy brother's eye, but considerest not the beam that is in thine own eye?" in N.T., Matt. 7:3.] *Baba Metzia, 59b*

881. Resh Lakish said, "Correct yourself first, then others." [Cf. "Thou hypocrite, first cast out the beam out of thine own eye; and then thou shalt see clearly to cast out the mote out of thy brother's eye," in N.T., Matt. 7:5.] *Baba Metzia, 107b*

882. If there is a matter of reproach in you, be the first to tell of it. *Baba Kamma, 92b*

883. R. Meir said, "The same measure with which one measures others will be used in measuring him." [Cf. "For with what judgment ye judge, ye shall be judged; and with what measure ye measure, it shall be measured to you again," in N.T., Matt. 7:2.]
Sanhedrin, 100a

Gratitude

884. Though the wine belongs to the owner, thanks are nonetheless due to the waiter. *Baba Kamma, 92b*

885. If one says, "With what shall I eat the bread?" take the bread away from him. [He should be grateful for the bread.]

Sanhedrin, 100b

886. He who blows the foam from his cup shows that he is not thirsty. *Sanhedrin, 100b*

887. Do not throw clods into the well from which you drank water.

Baba Kamma, 92b

Greed

888. If you grasp a lot, you cannot hold it; but if you grasp a little, you can. *Rosh Hashanah, 4b*

Happiness

889. Three things refresh a man's spirit: a lovely melody, beautiful scenery and fragrant odors. Three things expand a man's soul: a fine home, a pretty wife and nice furniture. *Berachoth, 57b*

Laziness

890. There is a saying, "When a woman slumbers, her basket falls." [Laziness begets loss.] Samuel said to R. Judah, "This may also be found in the Scriptural passage (Eccles. 10:18) *Through slothful hands the rafters will fall." Sanhedrin, 7b*

Like meets like

891. The bad palm will [even] travel to find an empty can. ["Birds of a feather flock together." This was applied to (Gen. 28:9) *So Esau went unto Ishmael.*] *Baba Kamma, 92b*

Love

892. People say, "When our love was strong, we could both sleep on the blade of a sword. Now that our love is gone, a bed sixty cubits [ninety feet] wide is not broad enough for us." [When love departs, proximity becomes intolerable.] *Sanhedrin, 7b*

Mixed blessings

893. "We have here a fat tail with a thorn in it." ["A fly in the ointment." The reference involves a breed of long-tailed sheep, called Telaim, the tail of which was a delicacy. But since it trailed on the ground, it often picked up thorns. See item 228, final fn.]

Rosh Hashanah, 17a

894. In the land of Israel people say, "If the clouds are bright they contain little water; but if they are dark they contain much water." ["A blessing in disguise."] *Taanith, 10a*

Omens
895. If one sneezes during prayer it is a bad omen.[1]

Berachoth, 24b

896. If one awakens and a [Biblical] verse comes to his lips [spontaneously], it should be regarded as a minor prophecy. [See also item 791 and chapter 17b on dreams.] *Berachoth, 55b*

897. If a dog whines, it is a sign that the angel of death has entered the city [and someone will soon die]. *Baba Kamma, 60b*

898. R. Simeon b. Lakish said—and it was also taught in the name of R. Jose—that a man should never open his mouth for Satan [inviting misfortune by ominous words]. *Berachoth, 60a; Kethuboth, 8b*

Opportunity
899. R. Eleazar b. Azariah was asked whether he would be willing to serve as head of the academy. R. Eleazar replied, "I will consult my household," and he consulted his wife. "But they may later depose you and you will then be disgraced," said his wife. To this he replied, "There is a saying, 'Use your precious bowl while you have it, for it may be broken tomorrow.' " ["Seize the day."] *Berachoth, 28a*

900. R. Papa remarked, "There is a popular saying, 'If a decision is postponed overnight, its benefits may be lost.' " ["Opportunity knocks but once."] *Sanhedrin, 95a*

901. Raba said, "When the ox has already fallen, sharpen the knife for him." *Sabbath, 31b*

902. A small pumpkin [in hand] is better than a full-grown one in the field. ["A bird in the hand is worth two in the bush."]

Sukkah, 56b

Optimism
903. There is a saying, "Let him whose cloak [only] the court took away, sing a song and go on his way." [He has gotten off lightly; things could have been worse.] *Sanhedrin, 7a*

---

[1] In Jewish folklore and that of other cultures, a violent expulsion of the breath, which is essential to life and associated with the soul, could mean death. See Joshua Trachtenberg, *Jewish Magic and Superstition* (New York: Behrman, 1939).

Parents and children

904. A father's love is for his children; the children's love is for
their own children [and parents should not expect such affection from
them]. *Sotah, 49a*

Partnership

905. People say, "A pot that is shared by partners is neither hot nor
cold [since they disagree on how hot it should be]." *Erubin, 3a*

Poverty

906. R. Papa said, "There is a popular saying, 'When the barley is
gone from the kitchen, strife knocks and enters the house.' " [Poverty
produces problems.] *Baba Metzia 59a*

907. Raba asked Rabba b. Mari, "What is the origin of the popular
saying, 'Poverty pursues the poor' [i.e., the poor are always at a
disadvantage]?" He replied, "The answer is to be found in the Mishnah. There we are told that the rich bring an offering of the first fruits
[to the Temple] in golden or silver baskets [and take them back],
while the poor bring their offering in wicker baskets and the baskets
remain with the fruits for the priests."

"You find the explanation in the Mishnah," Raba said to him, "but
I find it in the words of Scripture, in the verse (Lev. 13:45) *and shall
cry, 'Unclean, Unclean.' "* [It is not enough that one is a leper, but he
himself is also compelled to announce it!] *Baba Kamma 92a*

908. Sixty pains reach the teeth of him who hears the sound of
another eating while he himself is hungry. *Baba Kamma 92b*

909. One who has bread in his basket is not like one whose basket
is empty. [This applies not only to poverty but also to our inability to
feel another's pain.] *Kethuboth 62b*

Punishment

910. A thief is not put to death for stealing, even if he steals more
than once. [The punishment should fit the crime.] *Sanhedrin, 7a*

911. Do not be dismayed if a thief goes uncaught for two or even
three thefts; he will be caught in the end. ["Murder will out." Ma-
lefactors are caught sooner or later.] *Sanhedrin, 7a*

912. Abaye said, "Let the maid continue to rebel; it will all go
under one rod." [She will get her comeuppance.] *Sabbath, 32a*

913. R. Hisda said, "Leave the drunkard alone; he will fall by
himself." [The punishment is built into the offense.] *Sabbath, 32a*

914. Together with the thornbush, the cabbage is smitten. [The good often suffer with the bad.] *Baba Kamma, 92a*

915. In Babylonia they would say, "Tobias sinned, but Ziggud [his servant] was punished." In the land of Israel they said, "Shechem wants to marry [Dinah], but Mabgai [the Shechemites, his subjects] must submit to circumcision." [This can be rendered, "Shechem got a wife, and Mabgai got the knife." See Gen. 34:15–25.]

Makkoth, 11a

916. Mar Ukba said, "The shepherd is lame, and the goats run swiftly away. When they appear at the gate of the fold, there are words; but in the stalls, where the flock is finally delivered, strict accounting takes place." [There will be a day of reckoning. See chapter 13b.] *Sabbath, 32a*

Reconciliation

917. Our rabbis taught, "Always let your left hand repel [the unworthy], but your right hand draw [them] closer." [Not like Elisha, who thrust Gehazi away with both hands. See 2 Kings 5:23–26.]

Sanhedrin, 107b

Relatives

918. Said Rabina, "People say, 'If your sister's son has been appointed a constable, look out that you do not pass before him on the street [for he knows your affairs and may try to blackmail you].' "

Yoma, 18a

Responsibility

919. In the academy of R. Ishmael it was taught that the load placed on a camel varies with the camel. [The greater the man, the greater his responsibilities.] *Sotah, 13b*

The righteous

920. R. Eleazar said, "The righteous promise little but do much; the wicked promise much and do nothing." *Baba Metzia, 87a*

Self-acceptance

921. Mar Zutra b. Tubia said in the name of Rab, "People say, 'A camel wanted to have horns, so his ears were cut off.' " [Be content with what you have. This refers to Balaam, who demanded a reward, and instead lost his life. See Num. 31:8.] *Sanhedrin, 106a*

922. If your neighbor calls you an ass, put a saddle on your back. [He may know your limitations better than you do.]

Baba Kamma, 92b

Similarities

923. Five things have in them a sixtieth part of five other things: fire is a sixtieth part of Gehinnom; honey a sixtieth part of manna [the food eaten by the Israelites in the desert]; the Sabbath a sixtieth part of the World to Come; sleep a sixtieth part of death; and dreams a sixtieth part of prophecy. *Berachoth, 57b*

Speech

924. Ulla said, "There is a popular saying, 'A single coin in an empty bottle makes a loud noise.' " [The empty-headed do the most talking.] *Baba Metzia, 85b*

925. R. Mari said, "He who is boastful is not favored even by his own household; for Scripture states: (Hab. 2:5) *A haughty man one abideth not at home*[1]—that is, even in his own home." *Sotah, 47b*

926. R. Jeremiah b. Eleazar said, "Only a portion of a man's praise should be spoken in his presence; his complete praise may be spoken only in his absence [lest he become arrogant]." *Erubin, 18b*

927. This is the punishment of liars: that even when they tell the truth nobody believes them. *Sanhedrin, 88b*

928. Silence is good for the wise; how much more so for the foolish! *Pesahim, 99a*

929. When R. Dimi came from the land of Israel [to Babylonia] he remarked, "In the West they say, 'A word is worth a *sela* [a small coin], but silence is worth two.' " *Megillah, 18a*

Successors

930. There is a saying, "Where the master of the house once hung up his armor, the shepherd now hangs up his pitcher." [An unworthy successor is here indicated; one who cannot match the prowess of his predecessor.] *Sanhedrin, 103a*

Sunshine

931. Abaye said, "There is a popular saying, 'When the sun begins to shine, the sick improve.' " *Baba Bathra, 16b*

---

[1] The J.P.S. 1917 translation of the Scriptures omits the words *at home*.

Trouble

932. A Jew and an idolator were once walking together, and the idolator could not keep pace with the Jew. He thereupon reminded the Israelite of the destruction of the Temple [to get him to slow down], and the Israelite breathed a low, anguished sigh. But his companion was still unable to keep up with his pace.

"Does not your tradition teach that sighing breaks half the body?" he asked. To this the Israelite replied, "That holds true only when one hears of something sad which is new; but the destruction of the Temple is already long past, and the mention of it does not have the same effect. As people say, 'A woman accustomed to miscarriages is no longer bewildered [when another takes place].' " [One gets used to trouble.] *Kethuboth, 62a*

Vengeance

933. R. Papa said, "There is a popular saying, 'He that wreaks vengeance [*kinayh*] destroys his own nest [*kiynay*].' " [This makes use of a play on words.] *Sanhedrin, 102b*

Virtue

934. When courage fails the thief, he becomes virtuous. [One who is deficient in other qualities may don a cloak of virtue to cover up his inadequacies, or "make a virtue out of necessity."]

Sanhedrin, 22a

Wealth

935. Behind a man of wealth, chips are dragged along. [The wealthy have followers who fawn upon them.] *Baba Kamma, 93a*

Wisdom

936. Although there may be many who wish you well, reveal your secrets to only one in a thousand. Be careful with your words, even with her who lies on your bosom. Do not worry excessively about tomorrow's trouble, for you do not know what today may bring. Perhaps when tomorrow comes you will not be alive, and thus would have worried about a world which is not yours. [Quoted from the Book of Ben Sirah in the Apocrypha.] *Sanhedrin, 100b*

937. If one humbles himself the Holy One will raise him up; and whoever exalts himself the Holy One will abase. Whoever pursues

greatness will find that it eludes him; but whoever flees from greatness will find that it will pursue him. Whoever forces time [being over-eager to succeed] will in return be forced back by time; but to him who gives way to time [yielding patiently to circumstances] time will ultimately give way. *Berachoth, 64a*

17

OTHER OBSERVATIONS

NOTHING human is alien to the rabbis, as may be seen in the fore-going chapters. Here they deal with subjects ranging "from cabbages to kings," discussing animals, dreams, etiquette, government, peace, prophecy, proselytes, the Sabbath and matters of scientific inquiry.

Rabbinic observations on animals at times display an uncanny awareness of the principle of biological adaptation. Views expressed on the meaning of dreams are no less diversified than those held in our own time. Perhaps of special interest are allusions to the appearance of Halley's comet and to an early use of the telescope.

A. ANIMALS

Animals provide models for human behavior

938. Had the Torah not been given to us for our guidance, we could have learned modesty from the cat, honesty from the ant, chastity from the dove and good conduct (*derech eretz*) from the cock.[1]

Erubin, 100b

Why dogs can tolerate hunger

939. R. Jonah raised the question, "What does the verse (Prov. 29:7) *The righteous considereth the cause of the needy* mean?" And he answered, "Its meaning can be discerned in the action of the Lord. He knows that a dog does not eat regularly, and therefore ordained that the food should remain in his stomach for three days."[2] *Sabbath,* 155b

---

[1] Literally, *derech eretz* means "the way of the world." The rooster rises early and "gets scratching." The term *derech eretz* is sometimes used for sexual intercourse.

[2] Dogs were not widely domesticated and often had to shift for themselves. Veterinarians know that dogs can go without food for as long as a week, that canine stomachs are more expandable than human stomachs and that dogs can more easily store food as fat, quickly converting it into energy when needed.

When dogs should be kept chained

940. No one should have a dog unless the dog is kept on a chain. In a town adjoining the frontier, however, this rule is modified. There dogs should be kept on a chain in the daytime, and left without a chain at night. *Baba Kamma, 83a*

Keeping mean dogs or having defective ladders

941. R. Nathan said, "Whence do we learn that one must not raise a mean dog nor have a defective ladder in his house? Scripture states: (Deut. 22:8) *That thou shalt not bring blood upon thy house* [by causing injury to someone]." *Baba Kamma, 15b*

Why cats have a poor memory

942. The disciples of R. Eleazar b. Zadok once asked him, "Why does the dog know his master while the cat does not?" He answered, " 'Anyone who eats food nibbled by a mouse is likely to have a poor memory.'¹ How much the more would this be true of a cat, which consumes the mouse itself!"²

Horayoth, 13a

Strong creatures often fear the weak

943. Our rabbis taught that there are five examples of fear of the weak by the strong. There is the fear of the *mafgia* by the lion;³ the elephant's fear of a mosquito [entering its trunk?]; the scorpion's fear of a spider [entering its ear?];⁴ the eagle's fear of a swallow;⁵ and the Leviathan's fear of the *kilbith* [perhaps a stickleback, a small fish with several free spines].

R. Judah said in the name of Rab, "The Biblical verse which alludes to this is (Amos 5:9) *That causeth destruction to flash upon the strong.*"

Sabbath, 77b

---

¹ This was a well-known folk-saying.
² In Yiddish, one who has a poor memory is said to have *a katz in kop* ("a cat in the head").
³ Rashi identifies the *mafgia* as a small creature which frightens a lion with its cry.
⁴ So rendered by the Soncino Talmud. Glick suggests that this is the ichneumon-fly. These terms are difficult to define.
⁵ Rashi explains that the swallow gets into the eagle's wings and keeps the eagle from spreading them.

Some creatures grow stronger with age

944. Our rabbis taught that there are three creatures which grow stronger as they grow older. These are the fish, the serpent and the pig. *Sabbath, 77b*

Questions and answers

945. R. Zeira once found R. Judah standing by the door of his father-in-law's house in a cheerful mood, disposed to answer questions. R. Zeira asked him, "Why is it that the goats take the lead of the flock, followed by the sheep?" "Because," answered R. Judah, "this is in accordance with the creation itself: at first there was darkness, then there was light." [Goats are darker in color.]

R. Zeira then asked him, "Why are goats not provided with tails like those of the sheep?" [Sheep have thick tails; goats have thin ones.] "Those who cover us [with wool]," replied R. Judah, "are themselves [fully] covered, and those who do not cover us are not." "Why has the camel a short tail?" "Because it feeds among thorns [and a long tail would become entangled among them]." "Why has the ox a long tail?" "Because it grazes in meadows, and must be able to beat off the gnats [with its tail]."

"Why are the feelers of the locust flexible?" "Because locusts swarm among willows. Were the feelers inflexible, the locusts would be blinded [by the breaking of their antennae] in knocking against the trees; for Samuel said, 'All that is needed to blind a locust is to remove its antennae.' " "Why do the eyelids of the chicken close upward [i.e., the lower eyelid overlapping the upper]?" "Because they ascend at night upon elevated perches. If their eyelids were to close downward, the least bit of smoke coming from below would blind their eyes." *Sabbath, 77b*

B. DREAMS

Dreams about animals

946. If one dreams about a white horse, whether standing still or running, it is a good sign for him; if it is a roan and standing still, it is a good sign, but if it is running, it is a bad sign. If one dreams of an elephant [*pil*], miracles [*pelaoth*] will be wrought for him. [A word association is involved here.] *Berachoth, 56b*

947. All kinds of animals are good signs in a dream except the

elephant, the monkey and the long-tailed ape. But has not a master said that if one sees an elephant in a dream, a miracle will be wrought for him? There is no contradiction. In the latter case it is saddled; in the former it is not. *Berachoth, 57b*

Good and bad dreams

948. To dream of any kind of fruit is a good sign, with the exception of unripe dates. To dream of any kind of vegetable is a good dream, with the exception of turnip heads. To dream of any kind of color is a good dream, with the exception of blue. To dream of any kind of bird is a good dream, with the exception of the owl, the horned owl and the bat. *Berachoth, 57b*

Certain special dreams

949. Our rabbis taught that there are three kings [who are important in dreams]. If one sees David in a dream, he may hope for piety; if Solomon, he may hope for wisdom; if Ahab, he should fear for punishment [since Ahab was punished for taking Naboth's vineyard; see 1 Kings 16:20ff.] *Berachoth, 57b*

R. Hisda on dreams

950. R. Hisda said, "Any dream is a good dream except that of fasting." He said further, "In the case of a bad dream, the anxiety it causes is sufficient in itself [as a reprimand, and no evil will follow]. In the case of a good dream, the pleasure of the dream is sufficient [and there is no need for it to be fulfilled]."

R. Hisda also said, "A bad dream is even preferable to a good dream [for it leads to self-examination and contrition]; neither a good dream nor a bad dream is entirely fulfilled; and a dream which is not interpreted is like a letter which is not read [and has no effect for good or evil]." *Berachoth, 55a*

Good dreams are not rewards for one's virtue

951. R. Huna said, "Bad dreams are experienced by good men [to make them reflect on their misdeeds], and good dreams are experienced by bad men [since they will be barred from the World to Come]."

We have a *baraitha* to the same effect. It states that during all the years of his life King David never dreamed a good dream; and during all the years of Ahitophel [who plotted against David] he never had a bad dream. [See 2 Sam. 15:12ff.] *Berachoth, 55b*

Some dreams are realized in time

952. R. Levi said, "One may look forward to the realization of a good dream even for as long as twenty-two years; for Scripture states: (Gen. 37:2) *These are the generations of Jacob: Joseph was seventeen years old* [when he had the dream of his rise to power]. It later states: (Gen. 41:46) *And Joseph was thirty years old when he stood before Pharaoh* [as viceroy].

"From seventeen to thirty constitutes a period of thirteen years. To this we must add the seven years of plenty [after Joseph's appointment as viceroy] and the two years of famine which followed, making a total of twenty-two years." [Joseph's dream was realized only when his brothers and father came to settle in Egypt, two years after the famine had begun. See Gen. 44.]

Berachoth, 55b

Types of dreams that are fulfilled

953. R. Johanan said, "Three types of dreams are fulfilled: a morning dream; a dream which one's friend has about one; and a dream interpreted in the midst of a dream." Some add: also a dream which is repeated. *Berachoth, 55b*

Some dreams are only partially fulfilled

954. R. Berehia said, "There are dreams which, though they may be partially fulfilled, are impossible of being entirely fulfilled. We find this in the story of Joseph; for Scripture states: (Gen. 37:9) *'The sun and the moon and the eleven stars bowed down to me'* [in Joseph's dream]. Then it states: (Gen. 37:10) *his father rebuked him and said unto him, 'What is this dream that thou hast dreamed? Shall we indeed come, I and thy mother and thy brothers, to bow down to thee?'* This was spoken at the time when Joseph's mother was already dead [yet she was included in the dream, as the moon]."

Berachoth, 55a

Dreams reflect men's waking thoughts

955. R. Samuel b. Nahmani said in the name of R. Johanan that one is shown [in a dream] only the thoughts of his mind. You may infer this from the fact that one is never shown a golden date palm or an

elephant entering the eye of a needle [since one never thinks of such things].[1] *Berachoth, 55b*

But dreams at times contain absurdities

956. (Jer. 23:28) *'The prophet that hath a dream, let him relate his dream; and he that hath received My word, let him speak My word faithfully.*[2] *What hath the straw to do with the wheat?' saith the Lord.*

Why does this passage speak of wheat and straw in the context of a dream? R. Johanan said in the name of R. Simeon b. Johai, "Just as it is impossible to have wheat without straw [stubble], so is it impossible for a dream to be without absurdities [i.e., truth must be separated from fantasy]." *Berachoth, 55a*

The interpretation of dreams may affect their consequences

957. R. Bizna b. Zabda related that he had heard that R. Banaah once said, "There were twenty-four interpreters of dreams in Jerusalem. I once had a dream and went to consult them all. Each gave me a different interpretation and all of their interpretations were fulfilled."

R. Eleazar declared, "All dreams are realized in accordance with their interpretation;[3] for Scripture states: (Gen. 41:13) *And it came to pass, as he interpreted to us, so it was.*"[4] *Berachoth, 55b*

Rabbi Meir discredits all dreams

958. R. Meir said, "Dreams are of no significance." [Literally, "Words of dreams neither bring up nor bring down."]

Horayoth, 13b

C. ETIQUETTE

Washing and dressing

959. When one puts on his shoes, he should first put on the right shoe and then the left. When he takes them off, he should first remove the left shoe and then the right. When one washes himself, he should

---

[1] A metaphor used to indicate the impossible. Cf. N.T., Matt. 19:24, on the difficulty of a rich man entering the Kingdom of God.

[2] Dreams are here associated with prophetic visions. See also item 982.

[3] The power of suggestion is here implied. In that sense, the interpretation of a dream may influence its outcome.

[4] Pharaoh's chief butler, who had been in prison with Joseph, here tells the ruler of Joseph's skill at interpreting dreams.

first wash the right hand and then the left. When he anoints himself [with oil] he should first anoint the right side and then the left. When one does the whole body, he should do the head first, for the head is the ruler over all the bodily organs. *Sabbath, 61a*

Dressing for the occasion
960. R. Aha b. Abba said in the name of R. Johanan, "Whence do we learn that the changing of clothes [for special occasions] is Biblical? Scripture states: (Lev. 6:4) *And he shall take off his garments, and put on other garments.* [1] It was said in the school of Ishmael that the Torah thereby teaches [indirectly] a lesson in good manners: that the garments worn while cooking for a master should not be worn while serving the master with wine at his table." *Sabbath, 114a*

Dressing in accordance with one's means
961. The son of Buneis once called on Rabbi. "Make way for one who is worth a hundred *manehs*," exclaimed Rabbi as he saw him approach. Soon after, another visitor arrived, and Rabbi said, "Here comes someone worth two hundred *manehs.*"

R. Ishmael [who was present] challenged him, saying, "Rabbi, the father of the first arrival owns a thousand ships at sea and a thousand towns ashore!" To this Rabbi replied, "When you see his father, tell him not to send his son here next time with such poor clothing."

Erubin, 85b

"When in Rome do as the Romans do"
962. A man should not depart from customary practice. When Moses ascended above [to receive the Ten Commandments] he did not eat. [2] And when the ministering angels descended to earth [to visit Abraham] they partook of food. [3] *Baba Metzia, 86b*

On securing another's attention
963. (Lev. 1:1) *And the Lord called unto Moses, and spoke unto him.* Why was it necessary to call first, and then speak? The Torah here teaches us proper conduct; that one should not impart anything to

---

[1] The priests are instructed to don special garments at Temple functions.

[2] (Exod. 34:28) *And he was there with the Lord forty days and forty nights; he did neither eat bread nor drink water.*

[3] (Gen. 18:8) *And he stood by them under the tree, and they did eat.* Angels do not engage in eating but mortals do.

another before telling him that he wishes to speak to him. This is in accord with the dictum of R. Hanina who declared that one should not convey a message to another before telling him that he wishes to speak to him. *Yoma, 4b*

Announcing one's intent before acting

964. The Holy One said unto Moses, "I have a good gift in My treasury; its name is the Sabbath. This I wish to bestow upon Israel. Go and inform them." "From this it may be inferred," said Rabban Simeon b. Gamaliel, "that if one so much as gives a piece of bread to a child, one ought first to inform the child's mother." [See also item 970.] *Sabbath, 10b*

Treating public premises with respect

965. One should not remove stones from his own premises to public ground. It once happened that someone did so, and a pious man who was walking by at the time said to him, "Why do you remove stones from premises that do not belong to you onto your own premises?" But the man only laughed at him.

Some time later the man was compelled to sell his land, and while walking on the street in front of his former property he stumbled over the very stones he had previously piled there. He then said, "How right that pious man was when he said to me, 'Why are you removing stones from premises not [permanently] belonging to you, onto your own premises [i.e., the only premises which will always be available to you]?' " *Baba Kamma, 50b*

D. GOVERNMENT

"The devious machinations of government"

966. Raba b. Mehasia said in the name of R. Hama b. Guria, who spoke in the name of Rab, "If all the seas were ink and all the reeds were pens, if the expanse of the heavens were made of parchment and if all men were scribes, it would still not be possible to write about all of the devious machinations of government."

What is the Biblical passage [supporting this]? R. Mesharshia cited: (Prov. 25:3) *As the height of the heavens and the depth of the earth, so is the heart* [reasoning] *of kings unsearchable.* Sabbath, *11a*

Power destroys its possessors

967. R. Johanan said, "Woe unto those who hold great authority, for it buries those who possess it. There is not a prophet who did not outlive four kings; as Scripture states: (Isa. 1:1) *The vision of Isaiah, the son of Amoz, which he saw concerning Judah and Jerusalem in the days of Uziah, Jotham, Ahaz and Hezekiah, kings of Judah.*"

Pesahim, 87b

But law and authority are essential

968. (Hab. 1:14) *And Thou makest man as the fish of the sea, as creeping things, that have no ruler over them.* Just as the larger fish in the sea swallow the smaller, so also is it with men. If not for the fear of government, the stronger would swallow the weaker. We are indeed taught in a Mishnah that the Vice High Priest R. Hanina said, "Pray for the welfare of the government; were it not for the fear of its authority men would swallow each other alive."[1] [See also item 973. For a different interpretation of this verse, see item 419.]

Abodah Zarah, 4a

Ultimate responsibility must rest in one man

969. R. Johanan said that Moses told Joshua: (Deut. 31:7) *Be strong and of good courage; for thou* [Joshua] *shalt go with this people,* etc. [Moses places Joshua on an equal footing with the people.] However, the Holy One had earlier said to Moses: (Deut. 3:28) *But charge Joshua, and encourage him, and strengthen him; for he shall go before* [not *with*] *this people, and he* [alone] *shall cause them to inherit the land.* This was [God's way] to show that there must be one responsible leader.

Sanhedrin, 8a

Leaders must be approved by the people

970. We must not appoint a leader over the community without first consulting the people; for Scripture states: (Exod. 35:30) *See, the Lord hath called by name Bezalel* [the master artisan who built the Ark of the Covenant], *the son of Uri.* The Holy One asked Moses, "Is Bezalel acceptable to you?" And Moses replied, "Sovereign of the Universe! If he is acceptable to You, how much more so to me!" Then

---

[1] Hanina's statement is especially noteworthy in view of the oppressive governmental decrees of the Romans against the Jews in his day. It is of interest that a prayer for the welfare of the government is included in Jewish public worship to this day.

God said to him, "Nonetheless, go and tell the people." [See also item 964.]

Moses went and asked the people of Israel, "Is Bezalel acceptable to you?" And they replied, "If he is acceptable to the Holy One and to you, how much more so to us!" *Berachoth, 55a*

Laws too must be acceptable to the people

971. Our teachers accepted the view of R. Simeon b. Gamaliel and R. Eleazar b. Zadok, who declared that no decree should be imposed upon the people unless the majority of the community is able to comply with it. [See item 651 and fns.] *Horayoth, 3b*

The people must also respect the government

972. Even the superintendent of wells is appointed by Heaven.

Baba Bathra, 91b

973. He who rebels against the royal authority is guilty of an offense deserving of death. [See also item 968.] *Sanhedrin, 49a*

E. PEACE

"A time to speak, and a time to keep silent"

974. Ilai said in the name of R. Eleazar b. Simeon, "Just as it is required that a man reproach another when the reproach is likely to be heeded, so is it meritorious for a man not to say anything which will not be heeded [for this would only create enmity between them]." [See also item 84.] *Yebamoth, 65b*

Modifying a report in the interest of peace

975. Ilai said in the name of R. Eleazar b. Simeon, "It is permitted for a man to modify a report [without lying] in the interest of peace." R. Nathan [went even further and] said, "It is a duty to do so."

Yebamoth, 65b

Converting an enemy into a friend

976. Scripture states: (Prov. 25:21) *If thine enemy be hungry, give him bread to eat; and if he be thirsty, give him water to drink;* [1] *for . . . the Lord will repay it unto thee.* [In reading this passage] do not read *y'shalem lach*

---

[1] Cf. N.T., Rom. 12:20 "Therefore, if thine enemy hunger, feed him; if he thirst, give him drink."

["will repay it unto thee"], but read instead *yashlimenu lach* ["will make him peaceful unto thee"].[1] [See also item 709.] *Sukkah, 51b*

Why the Torah honors system was devised

977. (Mishnah) The following was ordained in order to foster peace among the people of Israel: that a Priest should be [given the honor of being] called to the Torah first; following him there should be a Levite, then an Israelite.[2] *Gittin, 59a*

Promoting peace between Jews and non-Jews

978. It is proper to help the Gentile poor as well as the poor of Israel. It is proper to visit the Gentile sick as well as the sick of Israel. It is proper to bury the bodies of Gentiles as well as the bodies of Israelites. These acts are proper because they promote peace.

Gittin, 61a

One must constantly pray for peace

979. Rabbah b. R. Shila said, "One ought to pray for peace even to the last clod of earth thrown over his grave." *Berachoth, 8a*

F. PROPHECY

The passing of the prophets

980. With the death of the last prophets—Haggai, Zechariah and Malachi—the prophetic spirit was withdrawn from Israel. But the leaders who followed often acted under divine inspiration. [The uniqueness of the prophets is upheld without denigrating the sages who followed.] *Yoma, 9b*

Men of wisdom have almost prophetic powers

981. R. Abdimi of the city of Haifa said, "Since the destruction of the Temple, prophecy has been taken from the prophets but been given to the wise." Is it then impossible for a wise man to be a prophet? He meant to say that although there are no longer prophets [in the Biblical sense of the term], prophetic power is not withheld

---

[1] The root of the verb "to repay" is the same as that for "to make peace." Both carry the sense of "fulfillment." Abraham Lincoln is reputed to have said, "Am I not destroying my enemies by making them my friends?"

[2] See also item 461. The procedure is followed to this day, and families usually know if they are of priestly or Levitical descent or are classed simply as Israelites.

from men of wisdom. Ammemar added, "A wise man is to be preferred to a prophet." *Baba Bathra, 12a*

One who discerns the truth should proclaim it

982. A disciple taught in the presence of R. Hisda, "A prophet who withholds his message [being afraid to proclaim it] should receive lashes." [See also item 956.] *Sanhedrin, 89b*

"Out of the mouths of babes and sucklings"

983. R. Johanan said, "Since the destruction of the Temple, prophecy has been withheld from the prophets and has been given to fools and small children."[1] *Baba Bathra, 12b*

G. PROSELYTES

Prospective proselytes should be strongly motivated

984. When a prospective proselyte says he wants to be converted to Judaism, he should be asked, "What is your reason for desiring conversion? Are you not aware that Israel is broken under persecution? Do you not know that we are driven from place to place, beset by mourning, and subject to great affliction?"

If he then says, "I am aware of all that, but I am not as worthy as the people of Israel," he is immediately accepted. He is then instructed concerning some of the simple commandments and some of the more rigorous commandments.[2] *Yebamoth, 47a*

985. R. Helbo said, "Proselytes are [can be] as bad for Israel as a sore on the skin." [He feared a weakening of the Jewish faith, or the proselytes' possible role as informers against the Jews before government authorities.] *Kiddushin, 70b*

One should be sensitive to a proselyte's origins

986. Rab observed, "People say, 'Do not denigrate a Gentile in the presence of a proselyte, even before a proselyte of the tenth

---

[1] This may be taken to mean that only fools and children would presume to possess prophetic power, or that they actually do possess it. The unsophisticated are more likely to make embarrassing observations. Cf. the folktale made famous by Hans Christian Andersen, "The Emperor's New Clothes," in which a child announces that the emperor is naked.

[2] Many non-Jews now seek conversion to Judaism. American rabbis differ as to whether this should be made easy or difficult, but generally agree that the prospective convert must be advised of the obligations he assumes and must undertake a program of Jewish study.

generation' [i.e., one whose ancestors had been converted ten generations earlier]." [See also item 857.] *Sanhedrin, 94a*

The proselyte's family is considered fully Jewish

987. R. Isaac said, "The Lord has acted righteously with Israel in
that every family of mixed lineage is considered pure [i.e., completely
Jewish]." [See also item 601 and fn.] *Kiddushin, 71a*

In the time of the Messiah many will embrace Judaism

988. R. Jose said, "In the World to Come[1] many non-Jews will seek
to be converted to Judaism." But will they be freely accepted? Have
we not been taught [in Yebamoth, 24a] that no proselytes would be
accepted in the days of the Messiah [because their motives for conversion would not be pure]? In the days of David and Solomon [a time
of great Jewish power and prestige] was it not also the case that no
proselytes were accepted [since they might only want to share in that
prestige]?

[Answer:] They will be self-made proselytes,[2] who will put phylacteries on their arms and foreheads and fringes on their
garments [in compliance with Jewish observance].

Abodah Zarah, 3b

H. THE SABBATH

The Sabbath was established by God

989. R. Akiba was asked by Turnus Rufus, "Why is this day [the
Sabbath] distinguished from all other days?" R. Akiba replied, "Why
is this man [Turnus Rufus] distinguished from all other men?"[3] "Because it is the will of my master [the Emperor]," said he. And R. Akiba
answered, "So too is the Sabbath distinguished from all other days
because it is the will of the Lord of the Universe!" [The Sabbath is
ordained in the Ten Commandments as the will of God.]

Sanhedrin, 65b

---

[1] The term *Olam ha-Ba* ("World to Come") here seems to be used in a this-worldly sense. See
chapter 14 on Olam ha-Ba and the Messiah.
[2] There were several classifications of proselytes. The reference here is to *gerim* or *gerurim*
("camp-followers"). See *U.J.E.*, s.v. "Proselytes." See also item 632.
[3] Akiba is here answering a question with another question, a practice still common among Jews.
See Lillian Mermin Feinsliver, *The Taste of Yiddish* (1970; reprint, New York: A.S. Barnes,
1980), pp. 298–299.

The additional soul of the Sabbath

990. Resh Lakish said, "an additional soul is given to us on the eve of the Sabbath and taken from us at its close." *Taanith, 27b*

The special flavor of Sabbath meals

991. The Roman Emperor [Hadrian] once asked R. Joshua b. Hanania, "Why does the Sabbath meal have a special taste?" He answered, "There is a certain condiment in our possession, called the Sabbath flavor, which we put into the Sabbath meals and this gives them their special taste." "Give it to us," said the ruler to R. Joshua. And R. Joshua replied, "It only works for those who keep the Sabbath; it does not work for those who do not keep the Sabbath."

Sabbath, 119a

The Sabbath table should be carefully set

992. R. Eleazar said, "A man should always set his table properly for the Sabbath eve, even if he is not hungry and may eat no more than [a morsel] the size of an olive." *Sabbath, 119b*

The Sabbath meal should be somehow different

993. The sons of R. Papa b. Abba once asked him, "How can people like ourselves, who have meat and wine every day of the week, distinguish the Sabbath day?" R. Papa replied, "If you are accustomed to dining early, eat later [on the Sabbath]; and if you are accustomed to having your meals late, dine early." *Sabbath, 119a*

The function of the ministering angels

994. R. Jose, the son of R. Judah, said, "Two ministering angels escort every man to his home on the eve of the Sabbath. One of them is an angel of good, the other an angel of evil. When a man comes home and finds the Sabbath lights kindled, the table set, and the bed in order,[1] the good angel says, 'May the coming Sabbath be even as this one,' and the evil angel is reluctantly obliged to say, 'Amen.' But if the house is in disorder, the evil angel says, 'May the coming Sabbath be even as this one,' to which the good angel is reluctantly compelled to say, 'Amen.' "

Sabbath, 119b

---

[1] The merit of Sabbath observance was augmented by fulfilling also the commandment to (Gen. 1:22) *be fruitful and multiply.*

Conversation on the Sabbath

995. Is speaking of mundane matters [other than business, which is specifically forbidden] prohibited on the Sabbath? R. Hisda and R. Hamnuna said that we are permitted to speak of charity disbursements on the Sabbath. R. Eleazar similarly said in the name of R. Johanan, "It is permitted, on the Sabbath, to decide upon the amount of charity to be distributed among the needy." *Sabbath, 150a*

996. At the school of R. Manasseh it was taught that the betrothal of daughters may be discussed on the Sabbath, and the choice of schools and of a vocation for a child may be deliberated on the Sabbath. *Sabbath, 150a*

When open violations of the Sabbath are allowed

997. R. Jacob b. Idi said in the name of R. Johanan, "One is permitted to remove debris on the Sabbath in order to save a life or to act for the benefit of the community; and we may assemble in the synagogue on the Sabbath to conduct public business [i.e., matters of community concern]." *Sabbath, 150a*

998. R. Samuel b. Nahmani said in the name of R. Johanan, "One is even allowed to go to theaters, circuses and exchanges on the Sabbath if it is for the welfare of the community." [The principle is established that the Sabbath is made for man, not man for the Sabbath. See item 442.] *Sabbath, 150a*

Should one violate the Sabbath in battle

999. R. Judah said in the name of Rab, "If non-Jews besiege a town inhabited by Israelites on the Sabbath, we are not permitted to meet them with weapons of war." We have also a *baraitha* to the same effect: "If idolators besiege," etc.

However, these words apply only where matters of money or property are involved. If they come with the intention of taking human lives, they should be met [even on the Sabbath] with implements of war, and the Sabbath may be desecrated [to save human lives]. *Erubin, 45a*

I. SCIENCE

The four winds

1000. Four winds blow every day, and the north wind blows with them all; were it not so, the world could not exist even for a single hour. [See also item 633.] *Baba Bathra, 25a*

Rain

1001. The lightning strikes, the clouds are made to rumble, and the rain descends. [See also item 42.] *Berachoth, 59a*

The dimensions of earth and sky

1002. Raba said, "The expanse of the world is six thousand miles, and the expanse of the heavens is a thousand miles. The first [is derived] from learning; the second by logic." [An objection is here introduced that according to geographical calculations of the size of Egypt, Ethiopia, the Garden of Eden and Gehinnom, the world is much larger, and the objection is sustained.] *Pesahim, 94a*

1003. R. Nathan said, "The whole world is situated under [the space surrounding] one star. Proof thereof is the fact that if a man sees a star, whether he goes toward the east or in any other direction, the star would always appear above him. This is evidence that the whole world is situated under the space of one star." [Hence the sky must be more than one thousand miles in expanse. This further refutation of Raba's statement is also sustained.] *Pesahim, 94a*

Three categories of stars

1004. The big stars are visible even by day, small stars [only] by night and medium-sized stars are visible in the twilight.

Sabbath, 35b

Why the earth is warmer in the summer

1005. R. Nathan said, "In the summer, the sun is in the zenith of the sky; therefore the earth is warm but the springs are cool. In the winter, the sun is closer to the horizon, and the earth is cold but the springs are warm." *Pesahim, 94b*

How much time elapses between dawn and daylight?

1006. From the time of dawn to the appearance of the sun it takes as much time as it would require for a man to walk five miles. Whence do we know this? From the story of Lot; for Scripture states: (Gen. 19:15) *And as dawn arose* [i.e., at daybreak] *the angels urged Lot* [to leave Sodom] *saying, 'Arise, take thy wife,'* etc.

Scripture then states: (Gen. 19:23) *The sun rose over the earth when Lot entered Zoar.* R. Hanina said, "I have made the journey, and the distance is five miles." *Pesahim, 93b*

A possible reference to Halley's comet

1007. It once happened that R. Gamaliel[1] and R. Joshua were aboard a ship, and the former had brought along only bread to eat, while the latter brought along both bread and fine flour. R. Gamaliel then asked R. Joshua, "Were you certain that the journey would be prolonged, so that you took along fine flour in reserve?"

R. Joshua replied, "There is a star which appears once in seventy years [perhaps Halley's comet], which makes ships' captains err, and I thought it was due to appear at this time and cause us to go off course in our journey [and therefore brought along extra provision]."

Horayoth, 10a

Rabban Gamaliel's telescope

1008. R. Gamaliel had a tube [perhaps a telescope] through which he could look and perceive objects at a distance of two thousand cubits, on land as well as at sea. Whoever wanted to determine the depth of a valley could look through this tube and ascertain its depth. Also, if one wanted to determine the height of a palm tree, he could use this tube to measure [the length of] its shadow and compare this with [the length of] the shadow of a man whose height is known.

Erubin, 43b

The human fetus

1009. What is a child like in its mother's womb? It is like a book which is closed and laid aside. Its hands are upon its two temples; the two elbows upon the two knees; the two heels against the buttocks; and the head is set between the knees. The mouth is closed and the navel open. It is nourished by what the mother eats, and drinks from what she drinks; but it does not evacuate lest it kill the mother.

When it emerges into the world, what was closed [the mouth] opens, and what was open [the navel] closes. Were it not so, the child could not survive a single hour. *Niddah, 30b*

An exercise in logical reasoning

1010. The Patriarch Isaac was born at the Passover season.[2] Whence do we derive this? Scripture states: (Gen. 18:14) *At the set time* [the next festival], *I will return to thee, and Sarah will have a son.*

---

[1] Gamaliel II, on his journey to Rome in 95 C.E. See fn. in Soncino Talmud, Horayoth, p. 70.
[2] Passover generally falls in April.

[Abraham is promised a son.] What festival was it when this was said [assuming that this was said on a festival]?

If this was said on Passover, and the reference [to the next festival] was to Shabuoth [Pentecost, the Feast of Weeks], the interval is only fifty days, and it is impossible to bear a child after only fifty days of gestation.

If we assume that this was said on Shabuoth, and that the next festival referred to was Rosh Hashanah [New Year's Day], then the interval is again too short for bearing a child. Even if we assume that this was said on the festival of Sukkoth [the Festival of Booths], and reference was made to the coming Passover, there is also an objection, for that interval is only six months.

However, we are taught in a *baraitha* [by way of rejoinder] that the particular year involved was a leap year [which has thirteen months]. Thus the period of gestation was actually a period of seven months. And in this connection Mar Zutra said that while a child born after a nine-month gestation is not born before the nine months are completed, a seven months' infant can be born before the seventh month is completed. [Thus the prediction could only have been made on Sukkoth, and Isaac must have been born at the close of the Passover festival, before the end of a seven-month period of gestation.][1]

Rosh Hashanah, 11a

---

[1] Such Talmudic logic has been the subject of much Jewish folk-humor. One popular tale concerns a scholar traveling home on a train who notices that the ticket of another Jewish passenger is for the same community. Being familiar with all the town's Jewish families and their various pursuits, he speculates on whom the traveler will be visiting, where he has come from, his occupation and even his name. Step by step he arrives at logical answers. When he addresses the passenger by name, the latter asks how he knew his identity, and the scholar answers, "It was obvious."

BOOKS OF THE TALMUD*

1. Order Zeraim ("Seeds"), Agricultural Laws

Berachoth	Shebiith**	Hallah**
Peah**	Terumoth**	Orlah**
Demai**	Maaseroth**	Bikkurim**
Kilayim**	Maaser Sheni**	

2. Order Moed ("Appointed Times"), Festivals and Fasts

Sabbath	Yoma	Taanith
Erubin	Sukkah	Megillah
Pesahim	Betzah	Moed Katan
Shekalim	Rosh Hashanah	Hagigah

3. Order Nashim ("Women"), Marriage and Divorce

Yebamoth	Nazir	Kiddushin
Kethuboth	Sotah	
Nedarim	Gittin	

4. Order Nezikin ("Damages"), Civil and Criminal Law

Baba Kamma	Makkoth	Aboth**
Baba Metzia	Shebuoth	Horayoth
Baba Bathra	Eduyoth**	
Sanhedrin	Abodah Zarah	

5. Order Kodashim ("Holy Things"), Temple Service

Zebahim	Arachin	Tamid
Menahoth	Temurah	Middoth**
Hullin	Kerithoth	Kinnim**
Bechoroth	Meilah	

---

* The order of the Tractates is that of the Romm edition of the Talmud (Vilna, 1919).
** Tractates thus designated have no Gemara, only Mishnah.

6. Order Toharoth ("Purity"), Ritual Purity and Impurity

Kelim**	Toharoth**	Zabim**
Ohaloth**	Mikvaoth**	Tebul Yom**
Negaim**	Niddah	Yadayim**
Parah**	Machshirin**	Uktzin**

RABBINIC CHRONOLOGY

THE TALMUD provides no dates for the rabbis quoted, whether for the period of the Mishnah or for that of the Gemara, and we cannot always be certain of the time in which they lived. Some lived in Palestine, others in Babylonia. Still others moved at some time in their lives from one place to the other. Moreover, two different rabbis, living in the two different countries or in different centuries, sometimes bore similar names. Over a thousand rabbis are mentioned by name in the Talmud. The following chronology is a list of the principal rabbis, adapted from the Index Volume of the *Universal Jewish Encyclopedia,* Outline 31: The Talmud. For a sketch of the lives and teachings of these men, see *The Jewish Spiritual Heroes* by Gershom Bader.

1. The Earliest Teachers

Simon the Just	Judah ben Tabbai
Antigonos of Socho	Simeon ben Shetah
Jose ben Joezer of Zeredah	Shemaiah
Jose ben Johanan of Jerusalem	Abtalion
Joshua ben Perahiah	Hillel I
Nittai (Mattai) of Arbela	Shammai

2. Tannaim: Period of the Mishnah

FIRST GENERATION

Akabiah ben Mahalalel	Bathyra (family)
Gamaliel I	Eleazar ben Zadok* 1
Simeon ben Gamaliel I	Jonathan ben Uzziel
Johanan ben Zakkai	

---

* Names marked with asterisk indicate that the families produced long lines of rabbis. It is uncertain whether there were two or three bearing the same name, and at times unclear which is being quoted. Numerals indicate the possible order of succession.

SECOND GENERATION

Gamaliel II
Eliezer ben Hyrcanus
Joshua ben Hananiah
Eleazar ben Azariah
Eleazar ben Arach
Nahum of Gamzu (Gimzo)

Zadok
Eliezer ben Jacob* 1
Hanina ben Dosa
Dosa ben Harchinas
Eleazar of Modin
Halafta

THIRD GENERATION

Tarfon
Ishmael ben Elisha
Akiba ben Joseph
Hananiah ben Teradion (Hanina)
Johanan ben Nuri
Jose Hagelili

Elisha ben Abuyah
Judah ben Baba
Ben Zoma
Ben Azzai (Simeon)
Eleazar ben Zadok* 2
Eliezer ben Jehudah

FOURTH GENERATION

Meir
Judah ben Ilai
Jose ben Halafta
Simeon ben Johai
Eleazar ben Shammua
Johanan Hasandelar
Simeon ben Gamaliel II

Phineas ben Jair
Eleazar Hisma
Eliezer ben Jacob* 2
Jonathan
Josiah
Nehemiah

FIFTH GENERATION

Judah HaNasi
Nathan the Babylonian
Eleazar ben Simeon

Simeon ben Eleazar
Bar Kappara
Eleazar ben Zadok* 3

SIXTH GENERATION

Banaah
Hiyya bar Abba* 1

Abba Aricha (Rab)

UNCERTAIN PERIOD

Ben Bag Bag
Ben He He

Eleazar Hakappar

3. Ammoraim: Period of the Gemara

FIRST PALESTINIAN GENERATION

Hanina bar Hama

Judah Nesiah* 1

Jannai   Joshua ben Levi
Hoshaiah Rabbah   Kahana* 1

FIRST BABYLONIAN GENERATION

Mar Samuel   Abba Aricha (Rab)

SECOND PALESTINIAN GENERATION

Johanan bar Nappaha   Isaac ben Eleazar
Simeon ben Lakish   Simlai

SECOND BABYLONIAN GENERATION

Huna   Kahana* 2
Judah bar Ezekiel

THIRD PALESTINIAN GENERATION

Isaac Nappaha   Assi
Eleazar ben Pedath   Judah Nesiah* 2
Abbahu   Hiyya bar Abba* 2
Ammi   Levi

THIRD BABYLONIAN GENERATION

Hamnuna   Rabbah bar Hana
Shesheth   Rabbah bar Nahmani
Rabbah bar Huna   Amram Hasida

FOURTH PALESTINIAN GENERATION

Dimi

FOURTH BABYLONIAN GENERATION

Abaye   Nahman bar Isaac
Raba

FIFTH PALESTINIAN GENERATION

Berachiah   Hillel II
Tanhuma bar Abba

FIFTH BABYLONIAN GENERATION

Kahana* 3

SIXTH BABYLONIAN GENERATION

Amemar of Nehardea   Mar Zutra
Ashi   Rabina

RECOMMENDED READING

Books about the Talmud

Adler, Morris. *World of the Talmud.* 2d ed. New York: Schocken, 1963.

Cohen, Abraham. *Everyman's Talmud.* 1932. Reprint. New York: Schocken, 1975.

Corre, Alan. *Understanding the Talmud.* New York: Ktav, 1971.

Darmesteter, Arsene. *The Talmud.* 1889. Translation from the French. Philadelphia: Jewish Publication Society, n.d.

Deutsch, Emanuel. *The Talmud.* 1874. Reprint. Philadelphia: Jewish Publication Society, n.d.

Dimitrovsky, H. Z. *Exploring the Talmud.* New York: Ktav, 1974.

Goldin, Judah. *The Living Talmud.* 1958. Reprint. New York: New American Library, n.d.

Mielziner, Moses. *Introduction to the Talmud.* 5th ed. New York: Bloch, 1968.

Neusner, Jacob. *Invitation to the Talmud.* New York: Harper & Row, 1974.

Strack, Hermann. *Introduction to the Talmud and Midrash.* New York: Atheneum, 1969.

Trattner, Ernest. *Understanding the Talmud.* New York: Thomas Nelson, 1955.

Untermann, Isaac. *The Talmud: an Analytical Guide to its History and Teachings.* New York: Bloch, 1979.

Waxman, Meyer. *A History of Jewish Literature.* Vol. 1. New York: Bloch, 1930, pp. 60–84 and 119–135.

Translations and Anthologies

Danby, Herbert, trans. *The Mishnah: Translated from the Hebrew with Introduction and Brief Explanatory Notes.* London: Oxford University Press, 1933.

Epstein, I., ed. *The Soncino Talmud: the Babylonian Talmud Translated into English.* 18 vols. London: Soncino Press, 1936–52.

Goldin, Judah. *Avot: the Fathers.* New York: New American Library, 1957. Translation and commentary.

Habib, Jacob ibn, comp. *En Jacob: Well of Jacob.* 1515. Revised and translated by Samuel H. Glick as *En Jacob: Legends of the Talmud.* 5 vols. New York: Rosenberg Press, 1916–22. Hebrew and English.

Herford, R. Travers, ed. *Ethics of the Talmud: Sayings of the Fathers.* New York: Schocken, 1962.

Montefiore, C. G., and Loewe, H., comps. *A Rabbinic Anthology.* 1963. Reprint. New York: Schocken, 1977.

Newman, Louis I., and Spitz, Samuel, comps. *The Talmudic Anthology.* New York: Behrman, 1945.

Special Studies

Bader, Gershom. *The Jewish Spiritual Heroes.* 3 vols. New York: Pardes, 1940.

Feldman, W. H. *Rabbinical Mathematics and Astronomy.* New York: Hermon, 1937.

Herford, R. Travers. *Christianity in the Talmud and Midrash.* 1903. Reprint. New York: Ktav.

————. *The Pharisees.* New York: Macmillan, 1924.

————. *Talmud and Apocrypha.* 1929. Reprint. New York: Ktav.

Kadushin, Max. *The Rabbinic Mind.* 3d ed. New York: Bloch, 1972.

————. *Worship and Ethics: a Study in Rabbinic Judaism.* New York: Bloch, 1975.

Katz, Mordecai. *Protection of the Weak in the Talmud.* New York: AMS Press, 1925.

Neusner, Jacob. *From Politics to Piety: the Emergence of Pharisaic Judaism.* Englewood Cliffs, N.J.: Prentice-Hall, 1973.

————. *Understanding Rabbinic Judaism.* New York: Ktav, 1974.

Preuss, Julius. *Biblical and Talmudic Medicine.* Translated by Fred Rosner. New York: Hebrew Publishing Co., 1971.

Silberg, Moshe. *Talmudic Law and the Modern State.* New York: United Synagogue of America, 1973.

Snowman, J. *A Short History of Talmudic Medicine.* New York: Hermon, 1935.

Reference Works

Goldschmidt, Lazarus. *Subject Concordance to the Babylonian Talmud.* New York: Humanities Press, 1959.

Jastrow, Marcus, comp. *Dictionary of the Talmud.* New York: Shapiro, Vallentine & Co., 1926.

Landman, Isaac, ed. *Universal Jewish Encyclopedia.* 10 vols. New York: Universal Jewish Encyclopedia, 1939.

Roth, Cecil, ed. *Encyclopedia Judaica.* 16 vols.; supplements. New York: Macmillan; Jerusalem: Keter, 1971.

Singer, I., ed. *Jewish Encyclopedia.* 12 vols. New York: Funk & Wagnalls, 1901.

INDEX